BUSINESS DRIVEN PROJECT PORTFOLIO MANAGEMENT

Conquering the Top 10 Risks that Threaten Success

MARK PRICE PERRY

Copyright ©2011 by Mark Price Perry

ISBN-13: 978-1-60427-053-2

Printed and bound in the U.S.A. Printed on acid-free paper
10 9 8 7 6 5 4 3 2 1

Library of Congress Cataloging-in-Publication Data

Perry, Mark Price, 1959–
Business driven project portfolio management : conquering the top 10 risks
that threaten success / by Mark Price Perry.
   p. cm.
Includes bibliographical references and index.
ISBN 978-1-60427-053-2 (hbk. : alk. paper)
1. Project management—Finance. 2. Portfolio management. I. Title.
HD69.P75P473 2011
658.4'04—dc22

          2011002857

Phone: (954) 727-9333
Fax: (561) 892-0700
Web: www.jrosspub.com

Contents

Foreword

In the mid-1980s as a software entrepreneur, I learned much about investment and risk in product development and project management. In the years since, I've learned much more, some of it from others, some of it the hard way. But as I've written and advised on project portfolio management (PPM), I've come to put equal emphasis, not just on how much there is to learn, but how much many must unlearn.

Lots of successful organizations' good practices have been observed and documented. Theoretical standards abound. But in practice, the flexibility and dynamism that capable managers need to apply these practices and standards is missing. Worse, most must unlearn their static, inflexible approaches—and their narrow, single-project views—if they are to provide best value from their project investments.

The book that you hold in your hands won't by itself provide the experience and judgment to enable you to use PPM practices flexibly and dynamically—but it can help. When focusing on key risks, which is worse, to have no portfolio investment strategy or a flawed strategy? This book highlights the fact that *commitment*, not procedural adherence, drives PPM success. A key risk is that the prime commitment of project managers, resource managers, sponsors, stakeholders, and executives is always to their projects' or programs' success, not to better PPM performance overall. Without commitment to each other in the PPM process, even the best portfolio of project investments will stumble in execution, for lack of teamwork.

So, this book invites you to make that collaborative commitment: yes, to understand state of the PPM art, but further, to invite stakeholders throughout your enterprise—and indeed, your virtual enterprise—to join in making every project investment pay off.

Matt Light, VP, Gartner Inc.
Former Quality Manager and Executive Editor,
Select Information and American Videotex Systems

Acknowledgments

Over the years, so many folks that I have met and worked with have provided me with such inspiration, insights and ideas, as well as tempered guidance, that I can think of no words to adequately express my gratitude. While I have had a few memorable encounters with extraordinary and accomplished individuals, including business leaders, politicians, sports figures, and celebrities, it has always been the everyday trials and tribulations with business associates, friends, and family that have made the most significant and lasting impact on my life. For this I am truly grateful and can only hope that I have reciprocated in some small way.

I am tremendously thankful and would like to especially acknowledge the providers of project portfolio management thought, market, and product leadership who contributed showcase pieces and participated in the development of this book. Their insights offer answers to the challenges and pressing questions faced by today's businesses seeking to implement and improve on project portfolio management capabilities and outcomes. In order of appearance, this list of distinguished people includes:

- Doc Dochtermann of Microsoft and Gary Conley of Cisco
- Lori Ellsworth of Compuware and Jane Holden of Canada Health Infoway
- Keith Carlson of Innotas
- David Boghossian of PowerSteering Software
- Terry Doerscher of Planview and Nayan Patel and Lenore Caudle of Baylor Healthcare System
- Gil Makleff of UMT
- Mike Ward of Outperform, UK Ltd
- Bruce Randall of Hewlett-Packard
- Jeff Durbin and Julian Brackley of Planview International
- Ty Kiisel of AtTask

Additionally, I would like to acknowledge the analysts and research professionals at the Gartner Group, with special thanks to Matt Light, Michael Hanford, and Dan Stang, who have provided years of project portfolio management insights, analysis, and commentary and whose PPM & IT Governance events provide an unparalleled venue for information and idea exchange.

It would be remiss of me not to acknowledge the tireless efforts and contributions from both the Project Management Institute (PMI®) and the Office of Government Commerce (OGC) of the United Kingdom Office of the Her Majesty's Treasury that come to us in the form of knowledge areas and standards for project portfolio management. These foundational contributions enable a spirited and constructive dialog about project portfolio management and how best to meet the project related needs that businesses of all shapes and sizes face.

I would like to also acknowledge Drew Gierman, my publisher at J. Ross Publishing, for the editorial advice provided, not to mention the continual help and support that he has given me in the management, coordination, and timely delivery of this multi-year effort.

And to my loving wife, who has witnessed a growing list of undone honey-dos, weeds that have overtaken our yard and garden, and the adding of ten pounds to my already too big waist line, all on account of this book effort I maintain. I appreciate your pointed words of encouragement and colorful expressions of patience with it all.

About the Author

Mark Price Perry
Founder, BOT International

In 1999, Mr. Perry founded BOT International, a boutique firm that specializes in PMO setup. As the head of operations he manages product marketing, services, and support for Processes On Demand (POD), a productized offering for PMO content assets.

Perry has been with BOT International since its inception and has implemented *Processes On Demand* in more than one hundred PMOs in North America, Asia Pacific, Europe, and Latin America. Largely as a result of years of experience in PMO setup work with companies and organizations and with talented project management practitioners of all disciplines, he is a servant-leader and subject matter expert in the practical application of project portfolio management (PPM) applications, collaboration platforms, and PMO content assets.

In 2009, Perry authored the best-selling PMO book, *Business Driven PMO Setup—Practical Insights, Techniques, and Case Examples for Ensuring Success*, published by J. Ross Publishing. Additionally, he is the host of the "The PMO Podcast," the leading podcast for PMOs of all shapes and sizes with over 200 PMO podcast episodes to date. Perry is also the author of the Gantthead blog,

"PMO Setup T3—Tips, Tools, and Techniques," as well as the BOT International PMO "Tips of the Week," a column that has provided PMO and project management tips for nearly a decade.

In addition to formal project managers and members of the PMO, Perry has helped tens of thousands of *informal* and *accidental* project managers apply the knowledge and techniques of the PMI Project Management Body of Knowledge (*PMBOK® Guide*).

Prior to BOT International, Perry had a 17-year career with IBM, including positions as the IBM AS/400 Division telecommunications industry manager based in New York, the IBM Asia Pacific AS/400 channels manager based in Tokyo, and the IBM Asia Pacific AS/400 general manager for Southeast Asia and South Asia based in Singapore. Following IBM, he was the vice president and managing director of Singapore-based Saville Systems Asia Pacific, a leading provider of billing and customer care solutions, and vice president of Hong Kong-based Entrust Greater China, a leading provider of identity management and digital security solutions.

Perry is from the United States and attended the American College in Paris in 1978–1979 and graduated Beta Gamma Sigma from Virginia Tech in 1981. He speaks English and is conversant in Japanese, German, French, and Spanish.

Seminars by the author on project portfolio management using this book, as well as other training and consulting programs on various PPM and PMO topics are available by contacting BOT International via the internet at www .botinternational.com or toll-free at 1-877-239-3430.

Contributors

Showcase # 1: Microsoft
"Doc" Dochtermann, PMP, CISSP, MCITP, CISSP, Project, Portfolio
  Management Specialist, Microsoft
Gary Conley, BSME, PE, MBA, Manager Advanced Services, Cisco

Showcase #2: Compuware
Lori Ellsworth, Vice President, ChangePoint Division, Compuware
Jane Holden, Executive Director, Investment Programs Management, Canada
  Health Infoway

Showcase #3: Innotas
Keith Carlson, President and CEO, Innotas

Showcase #4: Power Steering
David Boghossian, Founder, PowerSteering Software

Showcase #5: Planview
Terry Doerscher, Vice President, Chief Process Architect, Planview
Nayan Patel and Lenore Caudle, Portfolio Management, Baylor Healthcare
  System

Showcase #6: UMT
Gil Makleff, Founding Partner and CEO, UMT

Showcase #7: Outperform, UK Ltd
Mike Ward, Operations Director, Outperform, UK Ltd

Showcase #8: Hewlett-Packard
Bruce Randall, Director of Product Marketing, Project and Portfolio
  Management, HP Software & Solutions

Showcase # 9: Planview International
Jeff Durbin, Senior Vice President, Planview International
Julian Brackley, General Manager, Planview Northern Europe

Showcase #10: AtTask
Ty Kiisel, Manager of Social Outreach, AtTask

Preface

Project portfolio management (PPM) is a term that is used to describe methods for analyzing and collectively managing groups of projects based on numerous factors and considerations. The fundamental objective of PPM is to determine the best projects to undertake in support of the goals, objectives, and strategies of the organization. At first glance, project portfolio management as a concept appears intuitive, innocuous, and easy to do. And that is the problem. It's not.

There are many contributing factors that make project portfolio management as a business practice difficult to pull off for even the best of executive teams. From the start, it is not beneficial to suggest that the management of a portfolio of projects is similar to the management of a financial portfolio. Yet, we hear this time after time within the project management community. Projects are not like stocks and bonds and the project portfolio management decision-making process and people required to participate in it are nothing at all like those who comprise financial portfolio management. Next, we turn to standards. One would think that standards for project portfolio management would be of help, and they are in terms of laying a foundation of knowledge that helps to define the *what* of what project portfolio management is. But standards do not provide, nor are they intended to, the *how* of how to actually go about doing it. So the idea that PPM is easy and that there are standards for it just doesn't carry water.

Fortunately, there are a number of excellent books on project portfolio management that any organization seeking to implement PPM would be well advised to read. Some of my favorites include *Advanced Project Portfolio Management and the PMO* by Kendall and Rollins, *The Program Management Office* by Letavec, *Project Portfolio Management* by Levine, and *Taming Change with Portfolio Management* by Durbin and Doerscher. However, as good as these books and others are, there is a lack of material about project portfolio management that specifically addresses why it is so hard to do, what the top risks that threaten PPM success are, and how those risks can be conquered.

This book seeks to fill that void in the current literature by offering insights, techniques, and examples to ensure a successful and business-driven project portfolio management organization. It boldly challenges some of the traditional project management thinking and institutions. It introduces and positions in a PPM context some of the leading thinking about management systems and the emergence of complex adaptive systems as an alternative to plan-driven scientific management that lies at the heart of the project management community vs. agile community hostilities. And in addition to a presentation of the top ten risks that threaten PPM success, this book features the thought, market, and product leadership of the leading providers of project portfolio management solutions by way of end of chapter "Showcase" pieces.

Business Driven Project Portfolio Management was written by and with over a dozen contributing authors from the PPM provider community; veteran executives who are responsible for the successful marketing, sales, implementation, support, and customer satisfaction with PPM products and services. The ten chapters of this book and PPM provider showcase pieces present the risks that every organization implementing project portfolio management will face and the practical tips, techniques, and approaches for overcoming those risks.

Business Driven Project Portfolio Management—Conquering the Top 10 Risks that Threaten PPM Success offers executives, managers, and all those involved in project portfolio management the information that they must know to secure a mandate for and successfully implement project portfolio management. In a few hours reading you will gain insights from the author's and contributors' decades of PPM related experience. For those seeking to commence project portfolio management, this book will enable you to immediately address the risks that threaten success, ensure an effective and healthy dialog in your organization, and spare you countless PPM execution difficulties and organizational frustrations.

Introduction

Last year I was invited to give a keynote address titled "Business Driven PMO Setup" based on my book by the same name at the Camp IT project portfolio management conference in Chicago, Illinois. This particular event was held at the Donald E. Stephens Convention Center and was extremely well attended, having nearly three hundred IT and project management executives in attendance and all of the leading project portfolio management solutions providers manning their booths at the back of the meeting hall. As part of kicking off the conference and introducing me to the audience, the President of Camp IT and Conference Organizer, Dan Horwich, first asked those in attendance to state whatever it was that they had hoped to get out of the meeting. And as Dan proceeded to the white board, slowly just one hand was raised and a gentleman said, "I want to know how you can get executive support for all of this stuff."

With that response, a number of chuckles followed as did a dozen more raised hands. Dan busily wrote down the comments that followed. An older gentleman stated, "I would like to know who needs to be involved and who doesn't need to be involved in PPM." Next, a lady offered, "I would like to know how to make decisions based upon data that you just know is not right." This elicited more laughter and raised hands and a young man chimed in, "I want to know how to educate my boss" which was followed by a lady who quipped, "I want to know how to get my boss to sit still and listen for fifteen minutes." And this was followed by a gentleman who asked, "How do you justify doing PPM and how do you assess the lost opportunity of not doing PPM."

After about fifteen minutes, Horwich had completely covered the white board with a list of expectations that the attendees had for the meeting and he was committed to ensuring each and every one of the expectations were met over the course of his conference. Horwich, a conference organizer extraordinaire, had also engaged and enlivened the audience and in essence had teed up the day for the rest of us presenting.

What was particularly interesting to me about the list on the white board was that there was not one instance of someone wanting to know about project portfolio management in terms of processes or tools, which is all too often the common refrain. Which process standard for project portfolio management is the best, PMI or OGC? Which of the many PPM vendor offerings is the best? Which implementation approach, installed software or software-as-a-service, is the best? How much does it cost to purchase and implement a PPM solution? No, these attendees weren't here to discuss processes, PPM tool features and functions, deployment alternatives, or the costs involved. All of that, they already knew. What they came to find out was how to actually do it and in particular how to effectively manage all of the issues that, in their environment, an organizational change of this kind entails.

Another interesting observation for me came while visiting the booths of the PPM providers. While there was the nonstop flow of demonstrations, questions and answers, and handing out of brochures, the serious discussions between the providers of PPM solutions and the conference attendees were not about product features and functions, but rather business and people related issues such as sponsorship, buy-in, overcoming resistances, management of change, timeframes, decision-making approaches, measurement systems, benefit realization techniques, compensation, titles, roles and responsibilities, etc. As we were wrapping up one such conversation before the start of the next presentation, the conference attendee participating in the discussion jokingly asked the PPM provider, "Do you have a brochure that summarizes everything we just talked about?"

For several days after this conference, I found myself thinking about that very question that, after a year of further thought, research, and assistance and participation from a number of leading PPM providers became this book, *Business Driven Project Portfolio Management—Conquering the Top 10 Risks that Threaten Success*. The purpose of this book is not intended to be a detailed description of what project portfolio management is or why an organization should do it, though some of that is provided. Rather, this book seeks to shed light on both the risks that make project portfolio management so hard for even the best and most well intentioned leadership teams to do and the responses, techniques, and approaches that can be employed to overcome those risks and realize the value proposition of project portfolio management. And in doing so, the book also seeks to provide, by way of end of chapter showcase pieces, additional thought leadership and advice about how to conquer these risks from those most committed to understanding and solving the challenges of project portfolio management; the leading providers of PPM solutions.

If your organization is just starting project portfolio management and investing in people, process, and tools, you can use this book to proactively call attention to the business and management issues (risks) that must be addressed to achieve success. And if project portfolio management is already underway in your organization, you can use this book to spot check and address areas of execution difficulty as well as proactively plan for ongoing improvement and the sustaining of value.

While many within the traditional project management domain continue to cling to the outdated view that project portfolio management is an easy concept to grasp and is executed much like managing a financial portfolio, nothing could be further from the truth. At its very heart, project portfolio management inherently fuses traditional plan-driven scientific management approaches with contemporary complex adaptive systems thinking and agile behaviors. For most organizations and leadership teams, this is far more likely to be a difficult journey than it is to be a walk in the park. In support of your unique adventure in the realm of project portfolio management, I hope this book proves to be of assistance and provides practical insights and ideas worthy of your consideration.

Mark Price Perry
Orlando, Florida

At J. Ross Publishing we are committed to providing today's professional with practical, hands-on tools that enhance the learning experience and give readers an opportunity to apply what they have learned. That is why we offer free ancillary materials available for download on this book and all participating Web Added Value™ publications. These online resources may include interactive versions of material that appears in the book or supplemental templates, worksheets, models, plans, case studies, proposals, spreadsheets and assessment tools, among other things. Whenever you see the WAV™ symbol in any of our publications, it means bonus materials accompany the book and are available from the Web Added Value Download Resource Center at www.jrosspub.com.

Downloads available for *Business Driven Project Portfolio Management: Conquering the Top 10 Risks that Threaten Success* consist of PPM-related episodes of The PMO Podcast™, an executive overview presentation of the book's content, solutions to end-of-chapter questions, and 100 practical tips for implementing PPM within your organization.

1

PPM Risk #1: Shared Vision, Mission, Goals, and Objectives

For many, seeking to better align the project investments with the needs of the business, the cartoon in Illustration 1.1 paints an all too familiar picture. No sooner is the word out that the executive team is considering ways to improve upon things than a runaway freight train leaves the station fully loaded with opinions and ideas. Nearly always, the cart is put in front of the horse, and lost in the debate is any understanding of the vision, mission, goals, and objectives for which any discussion of organizational change must be a predicate. Project portfolio management (PPM) is not immune to this premise. To the contrary, one could easily argue that due to the collaborative, analytical, and dynamically changing nature of PPM, any attempt to do it without reasoned and tempered business planning will assuredly be met with failure.

Take the case of a rapidly growing midsize enterprise seeking to better align project investments with corporate strategy and to do all of the work that such an aspiration entails. Without giving a great deal of thought to the shared vision, mission, goals, and objectives required to drive such a change, the company hastily hired a project management office (PMO) manager who immediately turned his attention to people, processes, and tools. After the first year, the PMO had been staffed, a project management methodology aligned to the leading standard for project management had been developed, and a PPM application had been deployed. Additionally, nearly everyone in the organization, from the executive team to the agile developers, was unsatisfied with the progress of the PMO and unhappy with its manager; each person had his or her own varied reasons.

Illustration 1.1   PPM comics—putting the cart before the horse

In hindsight, the problem was clear to everyone involved. The PMO manager and the leadership team did not take the time to establish the vision, mission, goals, and objectives for the change envisioned. The first-year goals of the PMO manager, which were approved by management, were to staff the PMO, develop a single project management methodology to be used by everyone, implement a PPM application, and develop a project management-training program. These things were accomplished. But these things are not goals. They are not objectives. They are not even strategies. At best, these are component needs of a strategy of some kind. Although the efforts of the PMO manager were herculean, the end results achieved were not. The organization fell victim to the number one PPM risk: commencing activities without first establishing a shared vision, mission, goals, and objectives.

People, process, tools—how many times have we heard these three words? We hear them in presentations at PPM conferences. We hear them from the PPM consulting firms. We hear them from PPM training companies. And yes, we hear these words from well-intended PMO managers all too eager to get things going.

What could be wrong with wanting to staff the organization (people) rapidly, wanting to develop a world-class methodology (process), and wanting to implement the latest and greatest PPM application (tools)? If driven by the needs of the business, nothing is wrong with these desires. But if driven by any other reason or set of convictions or simply at the wrong time, a better question to ask might be, "What could possibly be right with wanting these things?" People, process, tools—these three words have been overused, introduced prematurely, and have caused more problems for PMOs and organizations seeking to manage their project portfolio than any other three words in the English language.

Project Portfolio Management Is Not Easy

Why is it that so many organizations jump right into PPM without the requisite business planning? And by business planning, I don't mean a project charter document developed and carried out by the organization responsible for managing the project portfolio. Rather, I mean a business plan to introduce organizational change as validated by reasoned and tempered goals, measurable objectives, cross-functional measurements, expectations, and consequences. Could it be that the concept of PPM is easy to grasp? Some people seem to think so, but nothing could be further from the truth.

There are many who claim that the concept of PPM is an easy concept to grasp, and they compare management of a project portfolio to the management of a financial portfolio. According to IBM's Ashok Reddy (2004, p. 1), "In essence, PPM allows you to manage a portfolio of projects much as you would manage a portfolio of diverse investments, such as stocks, bonds, real estate, and so forth." Commenting to the same effect is Computerworld's Melissa Solomon (2002, p. 1), "As its name implies, PPM groups projects so they can be managed as a portfolio, much as an investor would manage his stocks, bonds and mutual funds." Also making this comparison are PMO gurus Kendall and Rollins (2003, p. 208), "Just as a stock portfolio manager looks for ways to improve the return on investment, so does a project portfolio manager."

This comparison, for some people, seems to work. But for others, including me, this comparison is hard to envision, and it generates more questions than answers. Perhaps in trying to understand the concept of PPM, I am being too analytical, but let's take this comparison of it to the management of a financial portfolio. Three assumptions are quite problematic: (1) how the portfolio manager works, (2) how the customers of the portfolio manager work, and (3) the nature of the portfolio investments.

First, do financial portfolio managers and project portfolio managers work the same way or even remotely similar to each other? I happen to know a financial portfolio manager, Hunter Cade, an expert in financial services and wealth management. He is my cousin's husband, and he helps enlarge and preserve the wealth of many clients, including the parents of his wife, my uncle and aunt, and a retired Mississippi State University department head and loving wife. With over four decades of experience, Mr. Cade is a highly trusted and highly skilled advisor equipped with tools, information, and deep, deep domain knowledge. When he offers advice, it is wise to take heed of it. In fact, such advice is usually received with a certain amount of appreciation and even thankfulness. Does this sound similar to the environment of a project portfolio manager? When a project portfolio manager brings to the attention of the customer, the steering committee, a non-performing asset, a project, and a recommendation to make changes to the portfolio, is that advice taken in a similar fashion? Or has an invitation to a debate, and possibly an organizational turf battle, just been informally given?

Next, do customers of the financial portfolio manager and customers of the project portfolio manager work or behave the same way? When the customer of the financial portfolio manager is told that one of the assets is not performing and should be dropped from the portfolio, does the customer take that advice or engage in an impassioned defense of the nonperforming asset? Most customers are all too happy and eager to drop the nonperforming financial asset. Now, is this the same kind of behavior that customers of the project portfolio manager exhibit? When told of a nonperforming asset (a project) are they eager to kill the project? Or is it more likely that one or more folks step forward to defend the merits of their project or to perhaps offer a transformation recommendation of the project to protect it. At the least, there will be folks who want to fully understand the science and rationale of why their project is a candidate for termination. These PPM behaviors and interactions are all valid and, in fact, desired and necessary. Advanced transparent economic democracy within the confines of a business organization—that doesn't sound like the management of a financial portfolio, nor does it sound easy to do.

Finally, is the nature of the portfolio investments the same? That is, can financial investments and project investments really be viewed similarly? A few years ago, Gantthead, the online community for IT project managers, was seeking the answer to that very question and thought it would be a good idea to ask an expert. They boldly and enthusiastically invited Dr. Harry Markowitz, credited as one of the creators of portfolio management theory, to an interview. In the 1950s, Markowitz introduced the concept that a portfolio of diverse investments will reduce risk and provide a higher return than individual investments. His work, known as Modern Portfolio Theory (MPT), changed the way investments were viewed and earned him the Nobel Prize in economics. When Dr. Harry Markowitz was asked in a Gantthead interview with Paul Harder (2002, p. 1) about the application of financial portfolio management to corporate project management, Dr. Markowitz did offer that the notion of treating project investments like financial investments was attractive, but he expressed caution and concern over the idea. "All I know is that in the typical investment situation one can finely subdivide one's funds among many fairly liquid assets. The same cannot be said of portfolios of projects."

In summary, if the leading expert in MPT can't quite grasp the concept of managing a portfolio of projects much as you would manage a portfolio of diverse investments, then perhaps the concept of PPM is not that easy to grasp after all. But what do the project management and PPM experts have to say? Is the concept really as simple as doing the right projects and doing projects right?

Harvey Levine (2005, p. 11) makes it sound rather easy, "Project portfolio management is not a highly scientific, theorem-oriented concept. It is just plain common sense. It is easy to implement and practical to employ." Of course, Mr. Levine is an expert in PPM and his book, *Project Portfolio Management—A Practical Guide to Selecting Projects, Managing Portfolios, and Maximizing Benefits* is a must read and one of my favorites. Although Mr. Levine comments on the need to keep PPM practical, this doesn't quite suggest the level of difficultly that it really entails. What may seem easy to Mr. Levine and all those who are invited to speak at the various PPM conferences, events, and venues, may be a bit more difficult for the rest of us.

Ironically, it is the PPM providers who have tremendous experience, practical insights, and wisdom to lend to this topic, but regrettably, they are far too often called vendors and treated as such. That is, they are invited and welcomed to sponsor and fund an event such as a conference, professional development day, or local chapter meeting within the project management community, but heaven forbid, let's not let them actually speak to the attendees. This vendor mindset may be suitable for the relationship one might have with a soda-dispensing machine, but in the context of the project management community, such a mindset is difficult to understand. But let's get back to what other PPM experts within the project management community have to say about the concept.

In Levine's PPM book, contributors Cohen and Englund (2005, p. 185) warn, "Establishing formal PPM provides a framework within which better decisions can be made and results in numerous related benefits to the organization. Nevertheless, it inevitably involves implementing significant changes that can be met with initial resistance."

Also contributing to Levine's PPM book is K. C. Yelin (2005, p. 217) who cautions, "Stating that executives need to be aligned with our portfolio management strategy seems intuitively obvious. But taking that from an intellectual statement to a behavior can be a challenge."

Commenting on the challenges of portfolio management within the federal government in Levine's book, the Federal CIO Council Best Practices Committee (2005, p. 235) offers, "Determining what to invest in, how much to invest, and then taking action to maximize the value on our return on investment tends to be a bit more difficult."

Providing a stronger warning is Vaughan Merlyn (2009, p. 1), "If PfM (project portfolio management) is not firing on all cylinders, the business won't see the value, the costs of IT and business value delivered through IT will not be impacted over more than the very short term, and PfM won't achieve a critical mass of benefit . . . and will fail."

And in his article, "Redefining Portfolio Management: It's All a Matter of Perspective," leading PMO expert Mark Mullaly (2009, p. 1) advises, "While the concepts of strategy, portfolio and project are often discussed (frequently in the same sentence), the relationship of strategy to project and of portfolio to either concept seems to play out differently in reality than it does on paper."

Mullaly further explains that projects do happen, portfolios do get defined, and strategy is formulated. However, these things do not necessarily occur together—or in the sequence that PPM theory says it should.

Perhaps most adamant is Anand Sanwal (2008, p. 1) who, in his article "2008 Resolutions for IT Portfolio Management & Project Portfolio Management Vendors & Consultants," begs, "Stop saying things like 'Manage your corporate portfolio like a portfolio of stocks'—This oversimplified comment is dangerous in addition to being meaningless." Anand's plea is particularly noteworthy since he is a recognized expert in PPM, serves as the VP of American Express, heading the corporate portfolio management for the company, and has written and given presentations on PPM and innovation at the Gartner Group and other leading conferences.

With such advice, perspectives, and cautions from leaders in the PPM field such as these, can anyone defend the often cited claim that its concept is easy to grasp and easy to implement? There are those who suggest that a concept that is easy to grasp and easy to implement is a good concept; a concept that is hard to grasp and hard to implement is a bad concept; and a concept that is easy to grasp and hard to implement is an *interesting* concept—interesting being a Confucian euphemism for full of worries, obstacles, and dangers. Hence, the ancient Chinese saying known as a curse, "May you live in interesting times!"

PPM is not easy, and the notion that it is an easy concept to grasp is dead wrong. It's not. For most organizations, the concept of PPM is probably best described and positioned as an interesting concept, one that offers tremendous opportunities, but it is not without its perils.

Shared Vision, Mission, Goals, and Objectives

The first of these perils—Risk #1—that organizations encounter when seeking to engage in PPM is the attention, or lack thereof, given to the establishment of a shared vision, mission, goals, and objectives for PPM. That this is done poorly is problematic but understandable. That this is not done at all is mystifying, and many would suggest unacceptable.

Inspiring a Shared Vision

Shared vision is the required organizational bedrock of change. It is the bridge between the current state of things and the desired state. The idea and driving force behind shared vision is that it is the common goal of individuals in an organization or a system that leads to the achievement and fulfillment of the vision. But it is not enough to have a vision or create a vision statement; the vision must be inspired in the hearts and minds of all those involved in its attainment.

Examples of vision are not difficult to find. Perhaps there is no better example of inspiring a shared vision than President Kennedy's speech given to challenge the United States to land a man on the moon during the 1960s. Or perhaps we can cite the "I Have a Dream" speech delivered by Martin Luther King on August 28, 1963. Another magnificent vision is that of Lee Kuan Yew's who strategized to transform Singapore, a tiny, multicultural hodge-podge of people who possessed none of the traditional elements of national power, into a vibrant, high growth, economic powerhouse. Sheikh Mohammed bin Rashid al-Maktoum's vision for Dubai transfigured a piece of desert into a shining city complete with health services, universities, sports centers, modern urban communities, free trade zones, palm-shaped, man-made islands, and the world's tallest building. Could these achievements have been realized without an inspired vision? Many would argue that they could not.

The value of a shared vision is not just for political leaders running for office or those managing a country. Vision can be of tremendous value to a business and even an organization within a business. In *Value Innovation Portfolio Management*, Mello, Mackey, Lasser, and Tait (2006, p. 71) cite Jack Welch, former chairman and CEO of GE, "Good business leaders create a vision, articulate the vision, passionately own the vision, and relentlessly drive it to completion."

Wherever you find complexities, competing interests, resistance to change, and a need to effectively work as a team to achieve that which is expected and tendencies to do just the opposite, you will find the need for a shared vision. And, perhaps, no activity describes those conditions better than that of PPM. But, as playfully shown in Illustration 1.2, one of the challenges of inspiring a shared vision is to ensure that the vision is actually shared. Asking three executives of the same leadership team to comment upon the nuances of PPM and explain how it should be carried out in their company can be much like asking three blind men to describe an elephant. Depending on their vantage point, it would not be surprising to find more differences than similarities in their views on PPM—what it is and how to do it.

One technique for establishing a vision as espoused by the QuickMBA (2007, p. 1) is to categorize the vision into one of four types: (1) the target, (2) the common enemy, (3) the role model, and (4) the internal transformation. This technique helps to develop and explain the vision, and is critical to inspiring a shared view of it.

The target vision is concerned with achieving a quantitative or qualitative goal such as a business target. Such business targets could be shareholder value measured by market capitalization, an industry leader measured by annual revenues, or the most trusted business measured qualitatively through industry and customer surveys.

The common enemy vision is focused on overtaking a specific enemy. Such battles where one company sets its sights on another are commonplace—General

Illustration 1.2   A not-so-shared vision of PPM

Motors vs. Toyota, MSNBC vs. FOX News, Microsoft vs. Google, and Hewlett-Packard vs. IBM.

The role model vision is engaged in attempting to become like another firm, typically in a different market or industry. For example, a business that sells yarn online (such as the online yarn store NuMei found at www.numei.com) might want to become the amazon.com of the knitting industry.

The internal transformation vision is interested in discovering ways to change activities, how they are managed, and how outcomes are achieved. Examples of internal transformation vision would be Jack Welch's vision for each of the General Electric businesses to become number one or two in the markets they serve, or to exit. Walmart's recent transformational vision from "Saving Money" to "Living Better" is evidenced by new products and services to address challenges that its customers face, including rising energy prices and elevated out-of-pocket healthcare costs. Other examples include a company that is seeking to change its internal operations to become the low-cost producer, to have the shortest cycle time for new product development, or to change the distribution of products from a direct sale to a channels-based business model.

For most organizations seeking to engage in PPM, the internal transformation vision is likely to fit the needs of the organization best. For many of these organizations, the current state of PPM may exist in a variety of forms and levels of maturity from ad hoc best efforts to some degree of adoption and adherence to a given PPM model. If an organization recognizes the need for change and wants to inspire a shared vision, while getting everyone involved and on the same page, a few questions must be answered first, or significant risks and execution difficulties are sure to follow. Three of the questions that need to be answered about the PPM are (1) what is the vision, (2) what does it include, and (3) does it change with time? Many organizations struggle in answering these questions. Let's discuss the first question as an example.

What Is the Vision of Project Portfolio Management?

It is helpful to have a model of PPM to draw from when we seek to answer this question. *The Standard for Portfolio Management*, published by the Project Management Institute (PMI®) offers us that model. According to PMI (2008, p. 3), "The primary purpose of *The Standard for Portfolio Management* is to describe generally recognized good practices associated with portfolio management."

There are many pros and cons to this publication. Stephen Rietiker comments on PMI's portfolio management standard (2007, p. 3), "However, from our point of view the standard's processes are incomplete. And since we also needed more hands-on processes stating not only the tasks at hand but also the roles and responsibilities involved in each process step, we still had to design our own processes." In his article, Rietiker summarizes his experiences with the standard and what he believes to be its pros and cons. Also commenting on PMI's portfolio management standard is SearchCIO's Associate Editor Rachel Lebeaux (2009, p. 1) who quotes Michael Hanford of the Gartner Group, "Their [PMI] portfolio management standard shows a solid understanding of a complex discipline, but I'd say it disappoints with an uneven level of explanations." Hanford also adds, "I think their PMBOK has become a bit of a boat anchor. They're trying to align with it, and it's stretching things out of shape."

However, the greatest problem for many organizations seeking to use the portfolio management standard as a reference point to get started with PPM isn't so much the level of detail of the processes and explanations, but rather the visual illustrations of the organizational context of portfolio management. To many, especially enterprise executives, these illustrations of the standard take on the look of the blueprint of a home where the garage is actually larger than the house. As shown in Figure 1.1, the PMI depiction of portfolio management graphically suggests, to most who view it, that the *management of operations* and the *management by projects* are similar in scale and size to the organization. This can be a nonstarter when corralling the leadership team to a consensus on what PPM is and can be for the organization.

A picture is worth a thousand words. Thus, it is quite important that the words that can be expected to be evoked by the picture are as accurate as possible and, ideally, the ones desired. To a typical business or organization, is management by projects really the same scale and size as management of

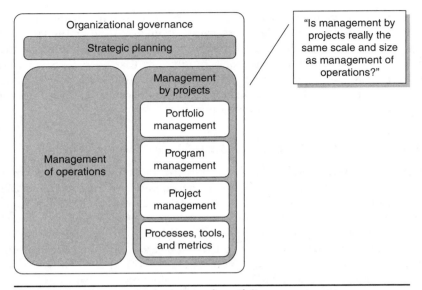

Figure 1.1   The myopic depiction of portfolio management

operations? And what do we mean by management of operations? Is it the operations of a business or is it the operations of the information technology (IT) organization?

Recently, I had the opportunity to attend a presentation on PPM. A slide similar to Figure 1.3 was shown. When asked by one of the attendees if the management of operations block was referring to IT operations or business operations, the presenter answered that it was referring to IT operations. The attendee who had asked the question disagreed with the answer and stated that the management of operations, as described in the PMI standard, was referring to business operations, not just IT operations.

The Standard for Portfolio Management, (PMI 2008, p. 11) describes operations as, ". . . a term used to describe the day-to-day organizational activities. The organization's operations may include production, manufacturing, finance, marketing, legal, information services, and administrative services to name just a few." So the attendee was correct. Some of the attendees in the presentation agreed that in this particular illustration of the PMI standard, *operations* referred to business operations; others did not. However, all agreed that if management by operations was intended to represent business operations, then the illustration was simply out of proportion and not helpful in establishing an intuitive shared vision.

For example, let's take a large Fortune 1000 firm such as IBM with $95B in revenues and 400,000 employees. Would half of the employees, or budget, or whatever business measurement one would use for purposes of making a size and scale comparison belong to the management by projects side like the PMI standard illustration depicts? Of course not. How about the Intel Corporation with revenues of $35B and 80,000 employees? Do 40,000 employees at Intel belong on the management by projects side? Not likely. Maybe Intuit? With their $3B in revenues and 8000 employees, would half of these employees belong on the management by projects side? Don't think so. Let's take a medium-size firm with $200M in revenues and 1500 employees. Would half of the employees belong on the management by projects side? I doubt it. How about a small business with $50M in revenue and 300 employees? Would half of these folks belong on the management by projects side? That would be hard to imagine.

Perhaps a much better organizational context and business-driven depiction to PPM is provided by Figure 1.2. In this illustration, it is clear that *management of operations* and *management by projects* are not the same size and scale.

In this depiction, there is no possible way to confuse whether or not management of operations is intended to refer to business operations or IT operations. Also, the size and scale as indicated by the shaded boxes is far more accurate for most businesses and far less offensive to operational executives who may be concerned over strategies, efforts, and thinking that a management by projects function would be of equal weight and importance to operations irrespective of whatever measure is implied or inferred. Just as a blueprint of a

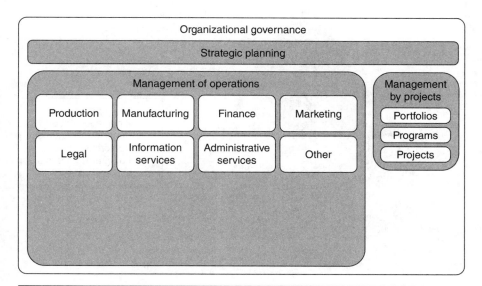

Figure 1.2   A business-driven depiction of portfolio management

home would look odd if the garage was bigger than the house, so too the blue-print for PPM can look odd if not presented in a proportional manner.

Another visual illustration within *The Standard for Portfolio Management* that is also problematic is shown on page 9 of the PMI standard. Figure 1.3 is a representation and critique of this illustration.

As already mentioned, the PMI depiction of portfolio management graphically suggests, to most who view it, that *management of operations* and *management by projects* are similar in scale and size to the organization. This is not only incorrect but incorrect by a large order of magnitude. Some may appreciate the simplicity of the model, others may not. At the end of the day, it is just not accurate or helpful for establishing a shared vision, especially for those outside of the project management fold not to mention those who may be concerned, rightly or wrongly, that the PMO folks are seeking to build their own organizational fiefdom.

More problematic, however, is the representation of vision, mission, organizational strategy and objectives as shown in the top three layers of the illustration. Strategic planning is an important activity and it is applied within businesses and organizations both formally and informally and at a wide variety of levels from the executive offices down to the field business units. It would be a mistake to suggest that strategic planning is limited to just the C-level executives,

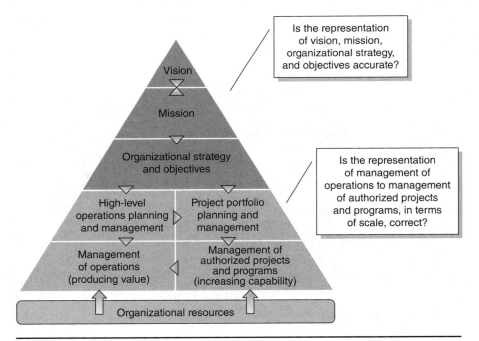

Figure 1.3   A critique of the PMI organizational context of portfolio management

but it would be a bigger mistake to get the basics of strategic planning wrong or out of order, and that is precisely what the top three layers of the illustration of PMI standard representing the organizational context of PPM does. It suggests a relationship and progression of vision to mission to organizational strategy and objectives. The order of the layers and words suggests that strategy takes place after mission and that the goal component is missing altogether; this is not quite right. As shown in Figure 1.4, it is helpful for all involved in the process to show these high-level components of strategic planning and in the correct order.

According to corporate strategy expert John L. Thompson (2001, p. 8), "Strategic management is a process which needs to be understood more than it is a discipline which can be taught." Thompson explains that strategic management is a process that enables organizations to determine their purpose (vision and mission), determine goals and specific levels of measurable objectives to be attained, and to decide on actions (strategy) for achieving these objectives in an appropriate timeframe. Even in the context of building a project management center of excellence, project management expert Dennis Boyles (2002, p. 170) advises that management team members need to work together as a team to discuss project management issues and support efforts to achieve the vision, mission, goals, and objectives of the PMCoE. What Thompson, Boyles, and many others recognize is that it is quite important to get the overall blueprint of strategic planning right. And, the realm of PPM is no exception.

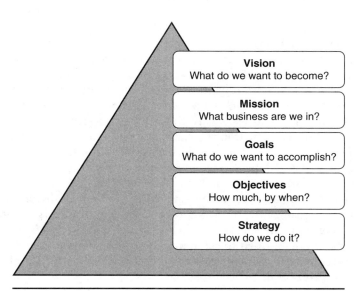

Figure 1.4 The high-level components of strategic planning

What Does Project Portfolio Management Include?

There are many definitions of PPM. Project management expert Michael Greer (2009, p. 1) writes, "Project Portfolio Management (PPM) is a management process designed to help an organization acquire and view information about all of its projects, then sort and prioritize each project according to certain criteria, such as strategic value, impact on resources, cost, and so on." As defined by the Association for Project Management, "Portfolio management is the selection and management of all of an organisation's projects, programmes and related business-as-usual activities taking into account resource constraints." Also providing an opinion of what PPM includes are Pennypacker and Retna (2009, p. 17), "From the perspective of the enterprise, all projects are in the one enterprise portfolio."

In these three definitions and all the many others, there is one word that is very troubling and that is the word ALL. Are all projects of the enterprise really represented in the portfolio? Is the project of an executive to conduct strategic competitive analysis between their firm and a leading competitor likely to be found in the portfolio? Would a project to manage the annual customer conference carried out by the marketing group be found in the portfolio? Would a project to conduct a customer satisfaction survey find its way into the portfolio? Would the confidential project of the CEO and selected members of the leadership team to evaluate a potential acquisition or offer to be acquired be found in the portfolio?

For most organizations, the answer to these questions would be, "Probably not." Yet in just about any book you read or conference you attend on PPM, there is an unwavering mindset that PPM is about having all of your projects represented in a single system capable of prioritizing projects by mathematically derived values, optimizing portfolio alternatives against constraints, performing what-if analysis to test assumptions, modeling of the efficient frontier, and providing drill-downs and graphical representations to support understanding of the portfolio components. To those outside the project management community and especially the business executives being asked to support a PPM initiative within the company, this ALL projects way of thinking may lead to an incorrect understanding of PPM from the very start.

At the 2009 PMI Global Congress in Orlando, Florida, I had the opportunity to attend a presentation on PPM. This particular speaker, like so many others, advocated that PPM was the managed process of aligning all of the projects of the organization to the strategic objectives of the organization. Not wanting to confront the speaker publicly, I waited until after his presentation and after the room emptied to ask him my question, which was, "Are you really suggesting that portfolio management is concerned with ALL of the projects of the organization?"

He replied, "Of course portfolio management is concerned with all of the projects of the organization. What would be the point of it if all projects were not subject to governance? That would defeat the purpose of doing it in the first place."

I then asked about all of those ubiquitous projects that are carried out in every nook and cranny of just about any business such as sales, marketing, human resources, finance, legal, customer support, engineering, administrative services, etc. Before I could finish, the presenter interjected, "You mean all of those informal projects carried out by informal project managers?" And he continued on, "Those aren't real projects, and the people who manage them aren't real project managers. So they don't count. In fact, those projects should really be called task work, not projects. It weakens the profession when informal projects and informal project managers are lumped in with real project management."

Had this been the first time I had heard such a perspective within the *formal* project management community, I would have been dumbfounded. But regrettably, this was not first time. I have heard this kind of perspective so often that I have come to expect it, especially in formal project management venues. These people tend to think that portfolio management is an activity that is concerned with identifying every single project of the entire organization and then applying some kind of management process to attempt to align the resulting bucket of projects to the needs of the business when, in fact, it is the other way around. Portfolio management drives projects. And as defined by PMI (2008, p. 6) in *The Standard for Portfolio Management*, "Portfolio management is the coordinated management of portfolio components to achieve specific organizational objectives."

If it helps, perhaps we should say that formal portfolio management drives formal projects and that all formal projects are subject to the governance of the portfolio management process. Or we can agree that only formal projects are real projects and that all of those informal projects are really something else. Personally, I would rather not advocate calling some projects formal and others informal or something else and the same goes for project managers. So what does PPM include? It includes those projects that are part of a particular organization's portfolio management governance process. But, it does not include ALL projects of the organization.

Does Project Portfolio Management Change with Time?

In establishing and maintaining the vision for an organization's PPM, it is helpful to ask whether or not PPM changes with time. For most organizations, the answer is yes and there are numerous PPM models to help guide this change in terms of defined levels of maturity. Also helpful to consider, as shown in Figure 1.5, is a business-driven view of PPM in terms of levels of business capability.

For many organizations, there is a natural, business-driven progression of PPM capabilities. Often, organizations start with demand management. While the intent is to get to an advanced level of PPM, the initial efforts are likely to be best described as multi-project management. Even at this level, there are significant benefits to be realized such as identification of multiple projects, overlapping efforts, and sometimes even missing or competing initiatives.

Next, attention is turned to supply or resource management where resources can be allocated according to priority helping to resolve conflicts in work assignments among several projects. With a good foundation of demand management and supply management established, the organization can further advance its capabilities to create strategic portfolios linking project investments to business strategies and thus engaging in PPM as a discipline.

With sufficient tools, the organization can identify and analyze multiple portfolios and model the efficient frontier that shows an organization the extent to which higher levels of investment create more value by funding more or different projects. As an organization's PPM discipline advances, benefits realization is performed to measure the actual product of the project benefits. This may take months or even years to do and is necessary to ensure the integrity of the PPM process and to ensure that the organization is doing the right projects. The combination of viewing PPM by both the maturity model view

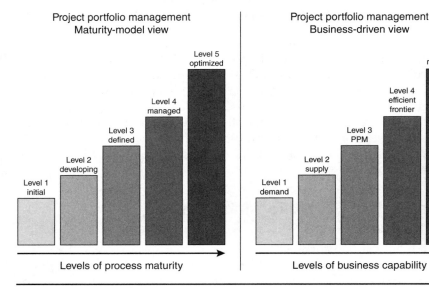

Figure 1.5 Views of PPM

and the business-driven view can be helpful to an organization for understanding how PPM changes with time.

Mission, Goals, and Objectives

Just as not having a shared vision for the organization that is responsible for performing PPM represents a tremendous risk, so too does not having a clear mission, unambiguous goals, and measurable objectives. Surprisingly, it is quite ironic that even though PPM organizations spend much of their time and effort understanding the mission, goals, and objectives of the company, few PPM organizations take the time to put in place their own mission, goals, and objectives.

Mission answers the question, "What business are we in?" In the context of making a decision and commitment to PPM, it is important for the organization to continually ask and assess this question. Stressing the importance of mission, goals and objectives for PPM are Rad and Levin (2006, p. 58), "It is necessary to determine the goals for PPM in the organization and the scope of its coverage." Few organizations can magically arrive at a workable, not to mention sophisticated, level of PPM just because they wish it. As shown previously in Figure 1.5, there are different levels of PPM capability. There are many foundational prerequisites that must first be in place to achieve these levels of PPM capabilities, so it is critical that a mission for PPM is defined and relevant for the organization. A clear mission that sets a clear tone and direction is what keeps the business on course. Even the malapropism prone baseball great, Yogi Berra, understands the value of a clear direction as evidenced in one of his many inspiring and amusing quotes (Kotzman 2004), "You've got to be careful if you don't know where you are going 'cause you might not get there."

A clear mission for the PPM organization sets the stage for the development of unambiguous goals and measurable objectives from which sensible strategies can be developed. Without mission, goals, and objectives in place, three likely outcomes will be evidenced soon.

First, there will be many people who participate with the PPM organization or are affected by the PPM process who will not have a clear understanding or appreciation of the purpose of the PPM organization. As organizational change is often threatening and met with resistance, the lack of a clear mission, unambiguous goals, and measurable objectives for the PPM organization will result in a wide variety of perceptions about the PPM organization and PPM in general. Without doubt, these perceptions will be negative and only get in the way of adoption.

Second, without mission, goals, and objectives in place, it is very likely that the strategies that are contemplated and developed, though well intended, will not be effective. Strategies that are not driven by specific goals and measurable objectives are almost always problematic. Such strategies will lack a proper context as well as an ability to determine whether or not they have been successful. After the initial introduction of the strategy and the hype that goes along with it, as execution of the strategy commences enthusiasm for it, as measured by interest and budget availability, soon wanes.

And third, without mission, goals, and objectives in place, even if the strategy is successful, there would be no ability, other than gut feeling, to account for the success of it. Regrettably, this happens far too often. A PPM organization is established likely consisting of dedicated resources, shared resources, and committee participants of some kind. Among this backdrop and collection of people, there are a number of views of what the PPM organization could do and be. Without any real business planning in terms of developing its vision, mission, goals, and objectives, the PPM organization goes to work on people, process, and tools. Over the first period of time, whatever that period of time may be, the PPM organization truly accomplishes something. But, what is that something? And, what is the likelihood of that something that was accomplished actually being what was expected to be accomplished by all involved? And, were the perceived accomplishments achieved sufficient to deem the PPM organization a success and worthwhile endeavor or is the value of PPM, relative to all of the effort to actually do it, called into question? At the end of the day, what would be the grade given to the PPM organization and, for that matter, the manager of the PPM organization?

Perhaps no better example of the need to establish mission, goals, and objectives for the PPM performing organization is illustrated in Figure 1.6.

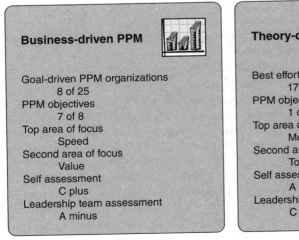
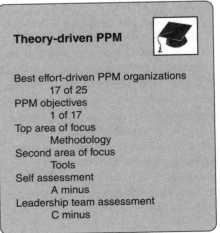

Business-driven PPM

Goal-driven PPM organizations
8 of 25
PPM objectives
7 of 8
Top area of focus
Speed
Second area of focus
Value
Self assessment
C plus
Leadership team assessment
A minus

Theory-driven PPM

Best effort-driven PPM organizations
17 of 25
PPM objectives
1 of 17
Top area of focus
Methodology
Second area of focus
Tools
Self assessment
A minus
Leadership team assessment
C minus

Figure 1.6　Business-driven vs. theory-driven PPM survey

As a student and aspiring servant-leader in the PPM domain, I continually solicit advice from experts and engage in research, polling, surveys, and questionnaires to better understand the approaches, skills, and techniques that lead to success and that produce good PPM, PMO, and product of the project outcomes. In 2009, one of many such efforts involved surveying twenty-five PPM organizations to gain insights for the purposes of developing more detailed research. In this high-level survey, the objective was to gather information for the purposes of making an inference about the correlations, if any, between goals of the PPM organization, focus of the PPM organization, and value of the PPM organization. Toward that aim, a questionnaire was prepared consisting of six simple questions:

1. Does the PPM organization have goals to be achieved in place?
2. Does the PPM organization have measurable objectives (how much, by when) in place?
3. What is the top focus of the PPM organization?
4. What is the second area of focus of the PPM organization?
5. What grade (A through F) would the PPM organization give itself?
6. What grade (A through F) would the leadership team give the PPM organization?

The results of this simple survey are illuminating. First, it was quite surprising that only eight of the twenty-five PPM organizations had goals to be achieved for themselves, as a business unit organization within the company, in place. The other seventeen of the twenty-five did not have any goals in place. Of the eight PPM organizations that did have goals, all but one also had measureable objectives. Of the seventeen organizations that did not have goals, there was one organization that had a set of objectives, two to be precise: (1) install a PPM tool and (2) develop a PPM process.

Next, the simple questionnaire revealed differences in focus between those PPM organizations that have goals in place and those that do not. The PPM organizations with goals in place had speed as their top area of focus and value as their second area of focus. This was quite surprising as one would think that the top area of focus of a PPM organization would be the alignment of project portfolio to the needs of the business. In subsequent phone interviews with these survey participants it was clarified that *doing the right projects* was a given, a PPM mandate, and most important to all involved in the PPM process was *speed* which meant streamlining the process, shortening the cycle time, and ensuring that the decision-making process does not take too long. The PPM organizations that did not have goals in place had *methodology* as their top area of focus and *tools* as their second area of focus. This was actually not surprising as organizations that are not highly driven by goals and measurable objectives are often found myopically focusing on tools and standards usually because of rushing into *getting things done* rather than taking the requisite time needed to first determine what should be done.

The last two questions of the survey, the assessment questions, revealed the million-dollar insight that all organizations, not just PPM organizations, would be well served to reflect upon. The PPM organizations that were business-driven, meaning they had goals in place, gave themselves a rather mediocre level of assessment, a C plus. They clearly did not view themselves as honor role candidates. However, their leadership did offer an assessment of A minus. This difference between the business-driven PPM organization self-assessment and the leadership team assessment was an interesting insight and twist, but even more interesting was the assessment of the PPM organizations that did not have goals in place and the assessment of their leadership team. The PPM organizations that were theory-driven, meaning that they did not have goals in place, gave themselves a glowing assessment worthy of the honor role, an A minus. However, the leadership teams of these theory-driven PPM organizations were far less impressed with results achieved as evidenced by the C minus grade that they handed out.

The overall inference that can be drawn from this high level and simple survey is that organizations driven by the needs of the business are likely to be goal-oriented, focused on areas that help to achieve specific objectives, and are more likely to be appreciated by those whom the organization exists to serve. And conversely, organizations that are not driven by the needs of the business are likely to be theory-oriented and best effort-driven and though they may believe in their soul that their achievements are exemplary, those whom the organization exists to serve may feel quite differently.

Summary

There are many risks that organizations seeking to engage in PPM will face. Though often overlooked or taken for granted, the first of these risks have to do with how well the organization performing PPM has established its own vision, mission, goals, and objectives. There is no better way to snatch defeat from the jaws of victory than to rush into PPM without first establishing a shared vision, clear mission, unambiguous goals, and measurable objectives. Nonetheless, time after time, this is exactly what takes place. Also problematic are the various depictions and views of what PPM is. A picture is always worth a thousand words. However, a picture can easily also be misleading and thus actually harmful in establishing a shared vision that is badly needed to get all involved off to a good start. The mere fact that the illustrations in *The Standard for Portfolio Management* published by PMI, as discussed earlier, are somewhat out of proportion relative to both the business realities between management of operations and management of projects and the order and relationships between vision, mission, goals, objectives, and strategy suggest that it is quite easy to get things wrong and to quickly get off track.

All of this leads to an important point and conclusion. PPM is not easy. It is certainly not a one-shoe-fits-all-sizes proposition, and those that commence PPM with a mindset that it is much like managing a financial portfolio of stocks and bonds are likely to be in for a rude awakening. For most organizations, the foundation and key to successful PPM starts, not with a hasty discussion and rush into people, process and tools, but with a deliberately thought out and established shared vision, mission, goals and objectives for the organization performing PPM.

Questions

1. What is the premise of the Modern Portfolio Theory?
2. Who is attributed with the creation of Modern Portfolio Theory?
3. What are the pros and cons of comparing the management of a project portfolio to the management of a financial portfolio?
4. What is the value of vision to an organization?
5. What are the four categories of vision?
6. What is the purpose of the PMI publication, *The Standard for Portfolio Management*?
7. In what ways are the PMI depictions of portfolio management in *The Standard for Portfolio Management* helpful and in what ways are the depictions inaccurate and potentially unhelpful?
8. What are the relationships between vision, mission, goals, and objectives?
9. What are the benefits to the PPM organization of being driven by mission, goals, and objectives?
10. What risks are PPM organizations that are driven by best efforts, as opposed to goals and measurable objectives, likely to encounter?

References

Association for Project Management. 2009. "Definitions." http://www.apm .org.uk/Definitions.asp.

Boyles, Dennis. 2002. *Building Project Management Centers of Excellence.* New York, NY: AMACOM.

Greer, Michael. 2009. "What's Project Portfolio Management (PPM) & Why Should Project Managers Care About It?" http://michaelgreer.biz/?p=147.

Harder, Paul. 2002. "A Conversation with Dr. Harry Markowitz." http://www .gantthead.com/content/articles/119883.cfm.

Kendall, Gerald, and Steven Rollins. 2003. *Advanced Project Portfolio Management and the PMO*. Fort Lauderdale, FL: J. Ross Publishing.

Kotzman, Mandy. 2004. "Inspiring/Fun Quotes." http://www.creativepursuits .net.

Lebeaux, Rachel. 2009. "Revised project and portfolio management standards get critical review." http://searchcio.techtarget.com/news/article/ 0,289142,sid182_gci1353693,00.html.

Levine, Harvey A. 2005. *Project Portfolio Management—A Practical Guide to Selecting Projects, Managing Portfolios, and Maximizing Benefits*. San Francisco, CA: Josey-Bass.

Mello, Sheila, Wayne Mackey, Ronald Lasser, and Richard Tait. 2006. *Value Innovation Portfolio Management*. Fort Lauderdale, FL: J. Ross Publishing.

Merlyn, Vaughan. 2009. "Common Mistakes in IT Portfolio Management." http://www.pmhut.com/common-mistakes-in-it-portfolio-management.

Mullaly, Mark. 2009. "Redefining Portfolio Management: It's All a Matter of Perspective." http://www.gantthead.com/content/articles/249244.cfm.

Pennypacker, James, and San Retna. 2009. "Project Portfolio Management—A View from the Trenches." Wiley and PMI.

PMI. 2008. *The Standard for Portfolio Management*. Newton Square, PA: Project Management Institute.

QuickMBA. 2007. "The Business Vision and Company Mission Statement." http://www.quickmba.com/strategy/vision/.

Rad, Parviz, and Ginger Levin. 2006. *Project Portfolio Management Tools & Techniques*. NY, New York: IIL Publishing.

Reddy, Ashok. 2004. "Project Portfolio Management (PPM): Aligning business and IT." http://www.ibm.com/developerworks/rational/library/4779.html.

Rietiker, Stephen. 2007. "In Search of Project Portfolio Management Processes." http://www.key-9.com.

Sanwal, Anand. 2008. "2008 Resolutions for IT Portfolio Management & Project Portfolio Management Vendors & Consultants." http://www.corpo rateportfoliomanagement.org.

Solomon, Melissa. 2002. "QuickStudy: Project Portfolio Management." http:// www.computerworld.com/s/article/69129/Project_Portfolio_Management.

Thompson, John. 2001. *Understanding Corporate Strategy*. Florence, KY: Thomson Learning.

Showcase #1: Microsoft

First Things First!
The Significance of Mission, Vision, Goals

"Doc" Dochtermann, Project Portfolio Management Specialist, Microsoft
Gary Conley, Manager, Advanced Services, Cisco

Linking Mission, Vision, and Goals of the Enterprise to the Work of the Organization

There are a tremendous number of books, articles, white papers, and these days BLOGS and Wikis, on the subject of Portfolio Project Management (PPM). Throughout this vast (dis)array of literature however, the fundamental question *"If Project Portfolio Management is the Answer . . . then what is the Question?"*[1] rarely (if ever) gets asked. This is a critical question that needs to be answered before PPM can deliver true *business value* to the enterprise. The first key step in linking the shared mission, vision, and goals of the enterprise is to ensure that the goal-set of the enterprise is clearly defined and embraced by everyone in the organization and that outcomes can be measured in terms of *business value* to the enterprise.

The next critical step, linking the enterprise's work to its strategy, is to ensure that we are also *prioritizing* our investments and resources in those areas that can really add value to the *business* of the organization. This unfortunately, is not necessarily how things work in corporate America today.

Execute Your Strategy? . . . A Novel Idea

In a recent study, 658 CEOs from multinational companies (with revenues greater than $5B) were asked to prioritize their most pressing management challenges. *Consistent execution of strategy by top management ranked as first priority!* According to a joint study by Renaissance Solutions, CFO magazine, and Business Intelligence however, the following critical factors were cited for failing to execute the strategy across the organization:

◆ *Awareness:* 95 percent of the typical workforce does not understand the strategy

---

[1]Mark Morgan, Microsoft 2010 PPM Forum, San Francisco

- *Financial resources:* 60 percent of organizations do not link budgets to strategy
- *Governance:* 44 percent of board directors cannot identify the key drivers of value in the companies they govern
- *Executive agenda:* 85 percent of executive teams spend less than one hour per month discussing strategy
- *Incentives:* 70 percent of organizations do not link middle management incentives to strategy
- *People:* 55 percent of human resources organizations either interpret strategy or deal only with operational priorities

Clearly, what we have here is a huge disconnect between the executives and their number one priority (i.e., to consistently execute corporate strategy) and the performance of the workers across the enterprise (i.e., who, although they are busy, perhaps are not focused on the priorities of the business).

Performance consultants indicate, "The need and desire to improve performance is clear. . . the key reason why most companies around the world care about performance management is because they want to better execute their strategy."[2]

Here's Another Nice Mess You've Gotten Me Into[3]

So, perhaps we don't have a *resource management* issue? What we just might have here is a *work management* issue! In a large number of IT organizations, 60 to 70 percent of the time is spent on *keep-the-lights-on* activities, leaving little time left over for high-priority business initiatives. It is fair to say that most organizations actually are struggling with the sheer volume of work they have and are very often unable to articulate the relationship between the investments in IT, relative to the value it brings to the business.

Bottom line, the performance of our corporations is being severely impacted because our work management practices are so poorly being managed. The 90s approach of selecting best of breed methods and tools has largely failed, primarily due to the inability to integrate the large variety of disparate information sources into an overall common operating picture. Spreadsheet and PowerPoint® reporting has become the de-facto industry standard for management and executive operating/reporting, where key decisions are being made on incomplete, inconsistent, inaccurate (even doctored) information! Sound familiar?

So, why are there so many spreadsheets and PowerPoint® reports being used to manage the work of our multi-billion dollar corporations? The proliferation

---

[2]Bruno Aziza, Joey Fitts, Drive Business Performance, ISBN 978-0-470-25955-9, Wiley
[3]Laurel and Hardy, Another Fine Mess, http://www.patfullerton.com/lh/movies/finemess.html

of millions of spreadsheets, reports, and other disparate and disconnected information sources has come about for a number of reasons; a typical one being the necessity to solve a specific point solution without regard (or time) for how it all fits into the bigger picture. Another reason is the severe shortage of skills and experience in the workplace and "our collective failure to educate ourselves on PPM and understand how we should adopt it in our organizations."[4]

Formula for Disaster

Organizations vary in complexity and maturity. It seems that with the larger organizations, not only are there more spreadsheets in use attempting to consolidate all of the management and executive reporting, but there are also larger varieties of work and resource management methods, processes, and tools, introducing further complexity into the enterprise, and often resulting in the "fool with a tool is still a fool" syndrome. Now, imagine what happens with the increase of multiple human resources, ERP, CRM, and other business information systems, accelerated through corporate merger and acquisition, added to this Rube Goldberg[5] like infrastructure!

At some point in time, corporations deem that it is time to initiate a PPM effort, either within a specific department (e.g., IT) or at a higher level within the enterprise, perhaps even consolidating several project or program management offices (PMOs) into a single common entity. According to a key source of project management experts[6] these reengineering initiatives will typically only succeed when one of the following conditions is true:

◆ People perceive that the pain caused by current business performance is greater than their perception of the pain caused by the change.
◆ The organization carefully and aggressively manages the change.

Unfortunately these efforts are *not* always successful, for a number of reasons, leaving the executives with the distinct impression that they either chose the wrong vendor solution (most often) or went about implementing the solution incorrectly and blame themselves for poorly managing the amount of organizational change required (much less likely). Reasons for failed PPM implementations typically include:

◆ There is a lack of a senior (and influential) executive sponsor
◆ The implementation of the PPM process becomes the project.

---

[4]Baby Steps, Craig Curran-Morton http://www.gantthead.com/article.cfm?ID=256731& authenticated=1
[5]Rube Goldberg, Wikipedia, the free encyclopedia http://en.wikipedia.org/wiki/Rube_Goldberg
[6]Microsoft Project Server 2010 for Project Managers, Gary L Chefetz, Dale Howard, & Tony Zink, http://www.MSProjectExperts.com

- ◆ We need PPM immediately to help out with a multi-billion dollar project that is currently failing.
- ◆ This is the third PPM tool we have tried, must be the software (AGAIN)!
- ◆ Boiling the ocean (we have 50,000 employees and we need to understand where they spend their time).
- ◆ Let's do it ourselves (how hard can it be?).

Perhaps some of these reasons sound familiar (almost humorous) to you?

Now that we have examined the problem, let's explore some potential strategies for implementing PPM successfully.

Strategies for Successful Implementation

While culture, strategy, goals, vision, and purpose are all the elements that are key to a successful project portfolio deployment and adoption, they are seldom uniformly accepted, shared, or applied in organizations, particularly in large organizations. It is not uncommon to find within the same organization enthusiastic support, apathy, and outright opposition. Differences are to be expected, even in organizations with high levels of alignment, as the very concepts of PPM are not uniformly accepted.

While there are obvious issues with fragmentation in the company DNA, it does not mean you cannot be successful with establishing, governing and fully establishing a PPM culture. Note I stated culture, and not system, tool, or process, but *culture*. Because basically, that is what you are doing when you implement PPM—you are changing *culture*. The whole point of PPM is to establish a culture that allows a process that systematically aligns those differences to into a cohesive aligned (and prioritized) portfolio that yields better results of investment of company resources.

What it also means is that your strategy for implementation needs to be mindful of these differences. It means that you will likely need to sell up and down the organization. In itself, this should be expected. Project portfolio processes and methods typically impact the *entire* project organizational hierarchy. Since it does impact the *entire* organization, it is important in your selling and training efforts that you illustrate WIIFM (What's In It For Me?) attributes. Systems and processes that clearly provide tangible value in day-to-day activities of employees tend to be accepted easier and become part of the organization's standard operating procedure on "how things are done."

Organizational fragmentation also means finding and grouping likeminded individuals with a shared vision. Sharing successes and best practices reinforces goals and objectives, and provides a means to capture and bring light to those less enlightened or frankly just too busy in their day job to spend much time figuring out alternative approaches. It is important for those with the heaviest workloads to gain acceptance, as they typically carry heavy influence among their peers.

Adoption will also likely be more fragmented and/or take longer than you would initially expect. It does mean perseverance will be key to the long-term success of your PPM endeavor. Successes and achievements will need to be recognized along the way—building on success, leveraging others experiences, and making successes visible. Experience has shown that seeds planted months (if not years) ago do not germinate immediately; they typically require a period of time where an early adopter shares, shows, and discusses their success, until enough likeminded individuals adopt the idea to move the concept forward. Once this "Tipping Point"[7] occurs, things may move forward at great speed as followers jump on board, then slow down or even stop for a time, then move again in a great burst of momentum, as perspectives, concepts, or understanding come together with enough people to reach yet another level in maturity.

Organizational differences can impact the ability to carry out a successful PPM deployment, but in many ways, they are simply part of the adoption and maturity process. A Center for Business Practices surveyed senior practitioners with knowledge of their organizations PPM practices and their organizations' business results. The report[8] concludes, "Over 90% of organizations are at Level 1 or 2 in PPM maturity and none are at Level 4 or 5."

So, the typical organization is at Level 1 and 2 in their understanding and use of PPM. Almost by definition, it is highly unlikely that you can expect to get rapid adoption uniformly across an organization. Most organizations have developed their PPM process in-house (87 percent) and only 13.2 percent of organizations have implemented a PPM software tool. These facts also underscore the low level of maturity in these organizations.

Working through differences, making agreements, and developing sound practices, is what the adoption process is and how culture is changed. PPM is a vision; it is the direction that you want to go to change your company DNA[9].

User Adoption—The Importance of WIIFM

Enterprise project management systems are interesting tools. In project-oriented organization there has to be something for everyone—strategic value for senior management, execution metrics and dashboard reporting for mid management, and detailed planning and execution for the program and project teams—by providing collaboration through plans and workspaces. Systems or

---

[7]The Tipping Point, Malcolm Gladwell, http://www.gladwell.com/tippingpoint/index.html
[8]Project Portfolio Management Maturity, Center for Business Practices http://www.pmsolutions.com/uploads/pdfs/ppm_maturity_summary.pdf
[9]Executing Your Strategy, How to Break It Down & Get It Done, Mark Morgan, Dr. Raymond E. Levitt, and William A. Malek, http://executingyourstrategy.com/book/index.php?option=com_content&task=view&id=24&Itemid=40

processes that leave the feeling of *feeding the machine*, run the risk of dying from lack of commitment at lower levels of the organization.

Clearly, without user adoption at the project level, those higher-level reports can't be created, and your project portfolio is not as rich or effective in managing the overall enterprise portfolio. To get the true portfolio value, you will need fairly broad adoption at the project team level. This means particular emphasis at the team level and identification of early adopters.

Early adopters do so for different reasons; some want to be the first on board, some see a better way of doing things, and others have been told to do so by their management. Some adopt because they are techies and others simply from curiosity, or because they want to list it on their resume.

There will be teams and individuals who jump full force into the system, running faster than you can follow. Others will ignore, drag their feet, outright resist. There will be those who go along and do the minimum. These behaviors are not unique to the project level but will be observed up and down the organizational structure; everyone after all is a human being.

Questions that get asked often include: Do I put every project into the system? Do I apply the same rigor to large scale program as I do to a three-week project? The recommendation is to track those projects that are important to your organization and apply the appropriate rigor to the appropriate level of investment. It is quite possible to set up different criteria for different levels of project efforts and yet have all projects in an overall portfolio. Smaller, well-defined projects should not require the same level of review and analysis that large-scale programs require. Defining the level of rigor required for various sizes of projects and programs, will not only help in adoption, but will keep you from wasting valuable project team and management time on efforts that provide little return.

Architecture—What Tool for What?

One of the biggest challenges in companies today is the increasing proliferation of tools with increasing levels of overlapping functionality. With the advent of converged IP networks, along with increasing lower cost for network connectivity and data storage, there has been an explosion of collaboration applications, all attempting to allow teams to work better together. It's not uncommon to find instant messaging tools that allow at least some level of document repository and security workspaces along with real-time communication. These tools have added considerably to a team's ability to collaborate in both real and non-synchronized time.

Yet because of this increasing level of capability, it is not often clear to users how yet another tool fits into the toolbox, and even more importantly, what is the architecture that incorporates these tools into an understandable framework.

Individuals need to understand the objectives and goals established for the enterprise project management (EPM) environment, what you expect to accomplish, and how other tools fit into the big picture—as no tool does it all. Illustrating how the tool meets project team needs, as well as the extended team of management, finance and support teams, creates that framework of the bigger picture and allows them to plug into their mental thought processes.

Just as all projects are not necessarily appropriate for an EPM system, a given tool is not appropriate for all projects. Even within an EPM system, it is important to recognize that the level of processes, practices, and governance should vary with the scale of project/program. Applying the same rigor to a short two-month project as you would to a multi-million big-bet effort really does not make sense. Adjusting thresholds in overall governance to the appropriate level will go a long way in attaining adoption and results out of the EPM deployment.

EPM environments are not casual undertakings and need to be deployed within a framework that is encompassing of processes and architecture, to be successful. Architecture enables processes through tools and it is often beneficial to map architecture to PMO processes and tools. In the absence of any internally developed process framework the PMI process groups as shown in Figure 1.7 can provide a good starting point to do this.

This process framework provides a basis to outline activities that are common to most PMO operations and functions. It is important to note that the PMI process groups are not phases but processes that can span across the entire lifecycle of a the project. This means even in small organizations there is a need for information continunity. Your PMO architecture needs to address this need! As shown in Figure 1.8, this is illustrated in the area of program/project communication.

Once process and tool mapping is done, it is also important to map it to the PMO architecture.

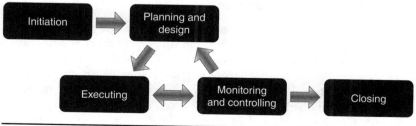

Figure 1.7   PMI process groups

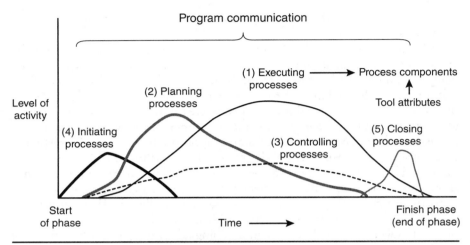

Figure 1.8   Program communication

Another good starting point would be to use a PMO architecture outlined in Figure 1.9. Specific examples are shown to illustrate the mapping process.

It is common that this process is iterated several times and periodically as elements of tools, systems, and organizations change with business needs. While the above PMI process groups address project and program management, they do not address the topic of portfolio management. However all companies manage a portfolio in some form. In the event that portfolio management is within the charter of the PMO and objectives and goals are defined, the PMO architecture, processes, and tool mapping process is similar even though the skill and methodology are quite different. Mapping tools that enable or enhance processes within process groups and aligning it to an architecture helps clarify direction, creates a sustainable vision, reduces redundancy, and enhances adoptions and standards.

Viral vs. Top-down Adoption

There are two key ways for adoption to occur: (1) *viral*, which is spread by word of mouth, and (2) *top-down*. Adoption is a combination of both, thus, it is most effective when achieved by factors that drive both approaches. Find the pieces that most people readily accept as value-added. What are those pieces, or hot buttons? There is no need to take on everything (boil the ocean, so to speak), and I would highly recommend that you don't! Just like any other major cultural change, incremental adoption will help to move your organization.

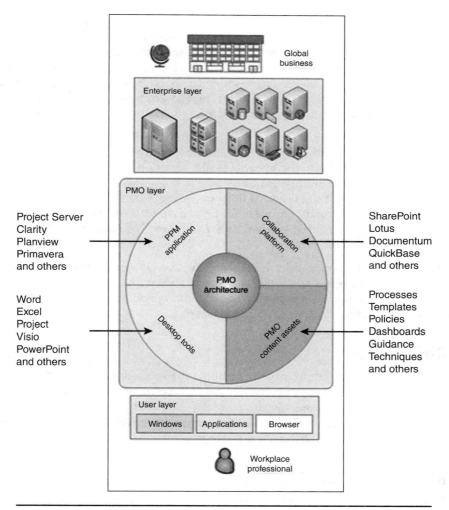

Project Server
Clarity
Planview
Primavera
and others

Word
Excel
Project
Visio
PowerPoint
and others

SharePoint
Lotus
Documentum
QuickBase
and others

Processes
Templates
Policies
Dashboards
Guidance
Techniques
and others

Figure 1.9   PMO architecture (Source: *Business Driven PMO Setup*, Perry)

Summary

You should now understand the critical importance of doing first things first! There are two critical considerations that you must take into account when establishing your PMO plan:

1. Linking mission, vision, and goals of the enterprise to the work of the organization is an extremely critical step for successful project portfolio deployment and adoption.

2. Recognizing that establishing and governing a PPM capability is not just a system, tool, or process—it's all about changing the culture that allows a process that systematically aligns those differences of an enterprise into a cohesive aligned portfolio. This is THE top risk that will threaten PPM success, so it is time to take the blinders off, understand the key factors, and put plans in place to mitigate their damaging effects (if allowed to go untreated):

   ◇ Most organizations are very immature in PPM concepts
   ◇ It's not just about the tool, method, or process
   ◇ It's all about the approach and adoption in alignment with the priorities of the business
   ◇ If it is not top down or bottom up; it is both
   ◇ Align around a common framework to set a foundation for success
   ◇ Make sure that you not only *Do Things Right* but that you *Do the Right Things*

In the words of Thomas Edison, *"Being busy does not always mean real work. The object of all work is production or accomplishment and to either of these ends there must be forethought, system, planning, intelligence, and honest purpose, as well as perspiration. Seeming to do is not doing."*

References

A Guide to the Project Management Body of Knowledge (*PMBOK® Guide*) —4th ed., http://www.pmi.org/Resources/Pages/members/Library-of-PMI-Global-Standards-projects.aspx
Implementing Project Portfolio Management, Part 6: Achieving Best Practice http://www.prioritysystem.com/reasons6.html

Recommended Reading

Strategic Project Portfolio Management: Enabling a Productive Organization, Simon Moore, Wiley, 2009.
Executing Your Strategy: How to Break It Down and Get It Done, Mark Morgan, Raymond Levitt, William Malek, Harvard Business School Press, 2008.
Business Driven PMO Setup: Practical Insights, Techniques and Case Examples for Ensuring Success, Mark Price Perry, J. Ross Publishing, 2009.

2

PPM Risk #2:
Executive Level Support

For most organizations seeking to introduce change of any kind, and especially project portfolio management (PPM), executive level support is not optional; it is critical and should be viewed as mandatory. Yet, it is hardly a surprise to hear of a company or an organization that, without a full understanding and commitment by the leadership team for the change envisioned, went ahead with some kind of skunkworks effort under the pretense that, if successful, the informal and non-supported effort would be revisited for potential approval, executive level support, and adoption. As the cartoon in Illustration 2.1 suggests, this is a déjà vu proposition, the outcome of which we know all too well.

My first, most memorable, and frustrating experience with attempting a change without executive level support occurred years ago as a newly hired executive in a high growth security software company. The CEO of the company hired me for a number of reasons, one of which was to bring strategic planning to the company. Though the company had enjoyed tremendous success as measured by the development of competitive products, market acceptance, year over year revenue growth, and acquisition of investors, the CEO was concerned that the firm lacked the needed planning rigor and measurement systems to both manage the growth of the company and to ensure that investments we received from our venture capital firm and lead investment partners would truly help the company achieve higher levels of success. Hence, one of my duties was to facilitate the change required to better align the internal investment opportunities, that the leadership team referred to as projects and initiatives, to the strategic objectives of the company.

Illustration 2.1   PPM comics—déjà vu all over again!

One would think that this endeavor would be met with all kinds of support, ideas, and participation by my leadership team colleagues. To the contrary, none of my peers had any interest in changing the current system. For one, the current system had served them well. For another, most of my leadership team colleagues had come from big companies where they had toiled for years, as I had at IBM, and the last thing that they wanted to do was to bring big, frustrating, company bureaucracy to their new, more agile and enjoyable world. There was some merit to these concerns and premise that the speed, innovation, and agility of the company might be compromised, but there was also merit to the CEO's belief that the company would simply get outcompeted if it relied solely on talented people, best efforts, and to some degree luck as a management system.

As two men on a mission, the CEO and I tried but could not convince the leadership team about the merits of aligning our project initiatives as portfolio investments aligned to the strategic objectives of the company by way of formal planning and ongoing review. Sure, everyone understood the concept and even agreed, in theory, that it would be a good idea to manage the business that way, with more discipline, rigor, and transparency. New product development; internal infrastructure; deployment of sales, marketing, and customer service applications; international expansion; OEM; and business development initiatives were opportunities we faced that lent themselves well to strategic alignment and portfolio management in theory. But in practice, none of the leadership team members wanted to do it. And, as a small software firm with a number of the key executives holding equity positions in the company as well as having amenable relationships and direct access with the board of directors and lead investors, the CEO was not in a position to single-handedly edict policy without at least a quorum of support.

As a compromise position, the CEO offered that we would continue business as usual and that he and I would go about aligning and managing the portfolio on our own. We would give it a try, do all of the work, and review the results of this new approach, nowadays referred to as PPM, with the team as we went with the idea that once we got started and finished all of the heavy lifting, the others would join in. To no surprise, this approach failed miserably and after six months of effort, which was a long time for a small, high-growth software firm, we gave up on it.

Not long after that frustrating experience, I happened across the famous quote on change given in 1532 in the work, *The Prince*, by Nicolo di Bernardo dei Machiavelli (McKinney 2009, p. 1), "There is nothing more difficult to take in hand, more perilous to conduct, or more uncertain in its success, than to take the lead in the introduction of a new order of things." Machiavelli continues, "For the reformer has enemies in all those who profit by the old order, and only lukewarm defenders in all those who would profit by the new order."

What I learned years ago from this experience was that to ensure success and to avoid failure, not to mention avoiding a big waste of time, change such as PPM requires executive level support, not just the CEO or a well intended executive spearheading the initiative, but all of the principle executives on the team. Hence, in this context, executive level support should not be viewed in the singular as in one executive, the CEO. Rather, it should be viewed in the plural, as in the entire senior management team.

Starting at the Top with Senior Management

There are a number of reasons why effective PPM requires starting at the top with senior management. As shown in Figure 2.1, senior management buy-in is required to build consensus, motivate members to participate effectively, and to ensure adherence to the requisite processes, tasks, and activities that must be carried out to select, manage, and realize the benefits of the project portfolio, to resolve conflicts along the way, and to reinforce behaviors and end results achieved with recognition and rewards. Without senior management participation, PPM doesn't work, and the organization is likely to end up with, or return to, a squeaky-wheel-gets-the-grease mindset for all those involved.

Although it may sound easy to do, it is actually quite difficult to start at the top, and the difficulties span in two directions: the scope of the work that needs to be done in getting executive team buy-in and the time that it takes. For most organizations, getting executive buy-in, as an activity, can't be forced or rushed, though often this is exactly what happens. Starting at the top with senior management is really all about anticipating in advance that it is far more likely that the leadership team will not be on the same page in terms of understanding, enthusiasm, and support for the change and far less likely that the leadership team would be on hand and available, anxiously waiting, and eager

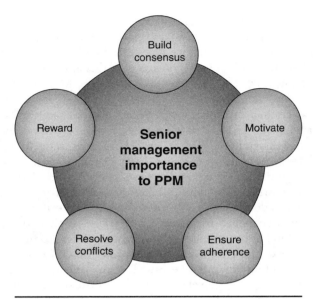

Figure 2.1   Senior management importance to PPM

to take on yet more organizational change and work amidst all of their existing and mission critical priorities.

Another difficulty to consider is the heterogeneous nature and alpha-tendencies of the senior management team. It would be hard enough to get fifteen homogeneous folks, such as experienced practitioners in PPM, to come together as a team and to quickly develop, agree to, and execute a strategy for PPM. Can you imagine how difficult this would be to do with fifteen senior management team members each with their own areas of responsibility within the organization, skill sets, and years of experience? As PPM guru and PMI® Fellow, Harvey Levine (2005, p. 57), notes, "My experience has been that the design and implementation of PPM capability has often been derailed for the simple reason that the two groups (project-oriented people and business-oriented people) do not speak the same language (as well as having a different focus)."

PPM also brings to the senior management team a process, set of roles, and required behaviors that may seem foreign at first and tedious soon after. The required behaviors needed to effectively do PPM as a senior management team must be rooted in open and honest dialog as well as idea and information sharing. Many senior executives are experts in managing their career and quite willing to engage in politics and number games. Such behaviors though often needed to advance through the organization by way of lobbying for the interests of one's business unit, negotiating higher levels of resources and lower levels of performance targets, and using personal powers of persuasion to overcome an inadequate business case, are all counter-productive when it comes to PPM. Offering a warning is Johanna Rothman (2009, p. 81), "Project portfolio decisions are difficult enough when everyone collaborates. They are next to impossible if someone plays zero-sum games." Just one member of the leadership team, not on board, can wreak havoc on the process and outcome.

One of my worst experiences and most bitter memories as a young executive and member of the senior management team was a workforce reduction program that we had to administer. I was one of sixteen business unit executives who each had to reduce our staffs by 10 percent, a non-negotiable and mandatory target set by headquarters. As we each had about one hundred employees in our business units, we each had to identify ten employees to dismiss. To avoid negatively impacting employee morale, which was already poor, we met as a leadership team in the evening, well after normal working hours, to review our planned cutbacks with our executive vice president.

All but one of us did the gut wrenching work, followed the process, and came to the meeting with the names of fine employees who had to be let go. One of us, a crafty senior executive with a great deal of informal power, did not. In the days leading up to the meeting, unbeknownst to any of the rest of us, he continually met with the executive vice president to lobby his case and his belief that none of his employees could be let go and that the workforce reduction target was just too high. The executive vice president urged him to do his best and also let it slip out that the overall target was uplifted just in case the business unit executives could not meet their targets.

During the all-hands-on-deck review meeting with our executive vice president, each of us business unit executives reviewed our workforce reduction candidates. There was marked and significant compassion and questioning as we each presented and interacted with one another in this difficult task. One by one, each of the fifteen of us had done what was asked and now it was the turn of our peer, most senior among us, and last to go. When our senior colleague announced that he had no names to provide and that he could not identify a single candidate for workforce reduction, the meeting erupted into a furor. Our executive vice president, at this point, had enough workforce reduction candidates and ended the meeting stating that the rest of the workforce reduction process would be offline and in one-on-one meetings as needed. Shortly thereafter, the candidates for workforce reduction were finalized. As the real target was lower than our individual targets, our executive vice president was able to allow all of the fifteen of us that did identify our candidates to save one person each and to allow our colleague, the very senior business unit executive and peer among us, to not have to let a single person go.

From an overall business perspective, there were people who were let go who should not have been and there were people who should have been let go who weren't. From the perspective of the senior management team, we never worked effectively as a team, nor even tried to. This is the result that not having executive level support, engaging in politics, and playing zero-sum games can quickly have on a leadership team.

Focusing on Business Goals from the Start

Effectively adopting PPM as a leadership team discipline, skill set, and core competence requires a focus on the goals of the business from the start. For some organizations, this will be a top-down business focus where PPM, as an organizational activity, drives project opportunities. For example, according to Chris Potts (2010, p. 1), an expert in the field of IT strategy, "The fundamental principle of portfolio management is that you first choose the goals for your portfolio and then select the investments that will achieve them." The greater the focus on the goals of the business, the greater the chance that the PPM efforts of the organization will answer the question, "Are we really doing the right projects?" Many PPM purists are strong advocates who believe PPM is not simply another technique of project management or next step in the maturity of a project management office (PMO), rather it is a giant leap forward, from a best practice perspective, on a scale of importance equal to Henry Gantt's development of the graphic schedule for the planning and controlling of work commonly referred to today as the Gantt chart. As shown in Figure 2.2, projects are the outcome of the portfolio management process.

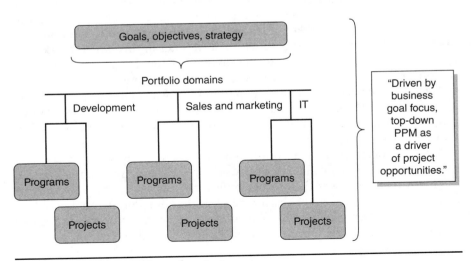

Figure 2.2   PPM as a driver of projects

And for other organizations, focus on the business goals, with respect to PPM, is a bottom-up business focus where an organization's management of their projects evolves into something more and, over time, takes on the appearance and reality of PPM.

In his article, "Using Project Portfolio Management to Demonstrate IT Value," Scott Berinato (2001, p. 1) describes how Schlumberger's Jane Walton, an IT analyst for the IT Services Company, started PPM within her organization somewhat by accident. It began as an effort by project manager peers to collect the projects that they were working on and to amass all of them in a single spreadsheet. When the comprehensive list of projects made its way to Walton, she instantly recognized it for the opportunity it presented. A cursory analysis revealed that two thirds of the more that one hundred projects had significant overlaps and 10 percent of the projects were virtually identical, that is, they were trying to accomplish the same thing.

It didn't take long for Walton and her team to envision that the list of projects in the spreadsheet would be very interesting to see in a database where the projects could be defined and analyzed in terms of benefits, risks, priorities, and alignment to the goals and objectives of the business. Initially, Walton's wild enthusiasm was met by management with blank stares not too different than the stares you get from a herd of deer looking into the headlights of an oncoming eighteen wheeler at the midnight hour. However, once the activity, analysis, and management team discussions started, those stares quickly passed, and Walton soon enjoyed a new title, portfolio manager. In this case, as shown in Figure 2.3,

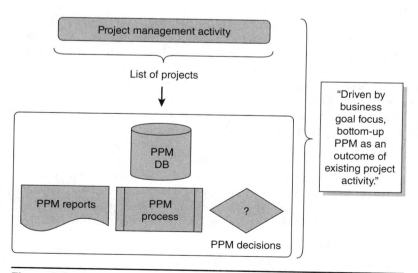

Figure 2.3   Projects as a driver of PPM

the new portfolio management efforts and practices of the organization were the outcome of the existing project management related activity.

In both cases, top-down and bottom-up PPM, the ensuing PPM was a result of first having a focus on business goals, then taking part in some kind of management team collaborative activity, supported by better information and aimed at answering the question, "Are we doing the right projects?"

Establishing the Project Portfolio Management Executive Playbook

In addition to starting at the top with executive buy-in and focusing on business goals from the start, another key characteristic of success for many organizations getting started with PPM is the establishment, use, and ongoing improvement of the PPM executive playbook. What is that? The PPM executive playbook is the common sense, suitable for leadership team use, condensed version of the overall process and policy framework for PPM.

The PPM executive playbook is what brings the team together. Much like the way a playbook helps the coach of a sports team to ensure that everyone on the field playing the game knows what they must do in order for plays to succeed and games to be won, the PPM executive playbook does the exact same thing. It helps the leadership team come together to effectively select and manage the project portfolio of the company. Important to note, the PPM executive playbook is not the set of detailed processes and metrics for PPM. Those details are indeed important and, in fact, are contained in a stand-alone chapter (see Chapter 5).

Recently, the matter of PPM executive playbooks was subject to one of our research exercises. We surveyed and questioned twenty-five companies about their PPM environment for the purposes of making an inference about good, better, and best approaches (best practices) for ensuring the success of PPM. All of the organizations surveyed had PPM best practices in place. In fact, many of these organizations had detailed PPM processes aligned to accepted standards along with supporting policies and guidance, so the presence of a documented best practice was not the issue. However, as shown in Figure 2.4, only six of twenty-five, a mere 25 percent, had a PPM executive playbook in place.

Again, the PPM executive playbook is the condensed version of the best practices that serve to ensure all involved are aware of, and participate in, the process as required. The PPM executive playbook provides a high level and intuitive view into the work process and answers such questions as:

◆ What are the goals of the PPM process?
◆ What is the scope of the PPM process?
◆ Who is involved in the PPM process?

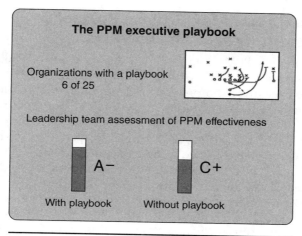

Figure 2.4 The PPM executive playbook

- What are the roles and responsibilities of each participant?
- Who makes decisions in the PPM process?
- What is the overall calendar timeline for PPM within the organization?
- What key leadership team PPM activities are performed and when are they performed (yearly, quarterly, monthly, weekly, and on demand)?
- What key metrics drive the PPM process?

Ideally, the PPM executive playbook provides the answers to all of these questions in no more than a few overview illustrations and accompanying pages of text. The detailed PPM best practices do this as well, of course, but do all of the leadership team members actually take the time to read through all of the PPM methodology detail? For many organizations, the answer is, "no."

In addition to the findings of how many organizations have or do not have a PPM executive playbook is the interesting and insightful comparison of the assessment of the leadership team of PPM effectiveness. Those organizations that provided their leadership team with a playbook for PPM enjoyed a much higher level of assessment than those that didn't. The collaborative nature of PPM makes it complicated and not easy to do even when all involved are giving it their best effort. It is virtually impossible to do if just a few members of the team are not participating whether out of lack of understanding, inability to make the time for it, or perhaps, due to conscientious objection and individual mischief. The PPM executive playbook helps to address all of these potential difficulties. It institutionalizes the mandate for PPM by providing a time and motion context that all involved can easily understand.

Reserved Powers for Project Portfolio Management Executive Discretion

While it is true that PPM requires a high degree of process adherence, also required are reserved powers for key members of the leadership team and especially the executive who presides over the organization. This seemingly poses a contradiction and a concern to many PPM professionals seeking to ensure that the PPM process is followed and given a chance to succeed. As Simon Moore (2010, p. 5) espouses, "A simple transparent process is important because, in order to collect a large number of strong proposals, idea submission must be encouraged by building faith in the proposal system. Without it, there will be a reluctance to submit proposals in the first place." If too many decisions are made, with respect to selecting new and managing existing project opportunities, outside the boundaries of the PPM process, then there can be the appearance of a squeaky wheel gets the grease approach to making decisions and running the business. This can quickly compromise the PPM efforts of an organization and faith by all involved that often requires continual reinforcement through transparency in the decision-making process. Nonetheless, businesses are not managed as democracies. There are times when the executive team will need reserved powers to make decisions outside of the agreed to PPM process.

Two common situations, where deviation from the PPM process and reserved powers for PPM executive discretion, are when certain information and activities must be strictly confidential and when the needs of few, or even one, outweigh the needs of many. In terms of confidential information, initiatives, and even projects, it is not uncommon to have secrets within an organization that are only revealed on a need to know basis. Such secrets could be the acquisition of a company, the sale of a business unit, the withdrawal of a product, or the plans to enter or exit a new market. Such secrets may not be ready for release, yet there may be important implications to the management of the project portfolio.

Take the case of a CEO and board of directors who are in the extremely confidential, early stages of planning the acquisition of the company by an industry leader. There will no doubt be a number of specific priorities and projects in support of readying the firm for acquisition discussions and ensuring an optimal valuation of the firm by the various parties involved such as investment bankers, industry experts, and others on both sides of the negotiations. As part of the PPM process and leadership team activities, there might be a number of projects that appear more attractive than the projects related to readying the firm for acquisition. The CEO, and whoever else might be privy to the confidential initiative, may not be in a position to make public the true facts and strategic priorities of the company with respect to the acquisition plans.

There is no surer way to distract the operations of a business than to leak highly confidential secrets. As made famous by the War Advertising Council during WWII and adopted even today in leading businesses around the world, "Loose lips sink ships!" Hence, the PPM process and those involved need to understand and not only tolerate, but permit, executive discretion and reserved powers for decision making that may on the outside appear to contradict a transparent PPM process.

Likewise, sometimes the needs of few, or even one, can outweigh the needs of many. For example, there can be a strategic imperative to support entry into a new market, industry, or line of business. Though not competitive in terms of ROI, certain projects are required and need to be selected to support the new mandate. In theory, such situations could be addressed by revisiting the values and weightings that drive strategic priorities. To a large extent, this is precisely the way most leading PPM applications work. They enable you to model various portfolios with respect to different criteria and the ease of use and sophistication of the tools enable multiple and iterative forms of what-if analysis. At the strategic planning level, these capabilities are a must and the modeling and analysis that they make possible produces optimized portfolios. In practice, however, if the various ranking system elements are changed merely to support a certain desired decision, it can appear as if some members of the team are playing *the answer is* game. That is, the variables and factors that go into the analysis are tweaked until the resulting answer is what was desired in the first place.

Like the example of confidential initiatives, PPM executive discretion and reserved powers for decision making need to be permitted. As noted by Australian project management expert and PPM thought leader, Neville Turbit (2010, p. 1), "It (PPM) is a way of helping business prioritise within a pragmatic framework." A PPM framework can be tremendously valuable to businesses, and also provides the leadership team with certain levels of flexibility for selecting and managing the project portfolio, but it does not run on autopilot.

Summary

Executive level support is required for PPM to have any chance to succeed. In obtaining executive level support, there are those who advocate giving PPM a go, informally so to speak, and to let results achieved be the proof of it's success or failure. Sometimes this does work, but often this approach can be frustrating and lead to lackluster results and abandonment of PPM altogether. Though it can be difficult and also take more time, it can be a wise option to postpone efforts to commence PPM until all the members of the executive team understand it and truly support it.

In achieving executive level support, there are a number of factors to consider and techniques to use such as starting at the top with senior management, focusing on business goals from the start, establishing the PPM executive playbook, and providing for reserved powers for PPM executive discretion. Also important to consider when seeking executive level support is the composition of the executive team. Most executive teams faced with the proposition of supporting PPM are not homogeneous individuals with years of experience in formal project management and an appreciation for the benefits that PPM can bring to an organization. You can, and should, expect to find skepticism, resistances, and concerns, not to mention differences in opinions, for how to go about it all.

To some, the difficulties of achieving executive level support can seem insurmountable. To others, such difficulties can seem to be a Catch-22; executives are not inclined to support PPM because they don't think it will work, but if PPM is attempted without executive support, it won't work. This is why any organization seeking to engage in PPM should consider executive level support a key requirement for success and, if not truly in place, a top risk that will threaten its success.

Questions

1. Why is executive level support important to the success of PPM?
2. How can senior management impact organizational commitment to PPM?
3. What are the benefits of commencing PPM prior to obtaining full executive understanding and support?
4. What are the risks of commencing PPM prior to obtaining full executive understanding and support?
5. In commencing PPM, what is the benefit of focusing on business goals from the start?
6. In what way can PPM be a driver of the projects of an organization?
7. In what way can project management activity be a driver of PPM to an organization?
8. What is a PPM executive playbook?
9. How is a PPM executive playbook different from the detailed PPM processes of an organization?
10. What are reserved powers for PPM executive discretion and in what kinds of situations are they needed?

References

Berinato, Scott. 2001. "Using Project Portfolio Management to Demonstrate IT Value." http://www.cio.com.

Levine, Harvey A. 2005. *Project Portfolio Management—A Practical Guide to Selecting Projects, Managing Portfolios, and Maximizing Benefits.* San Francisco, CA: Josey-Bass.

McKinney. Michael. 2009. "Quotes on Change." http://www.leadershipnow .com/changequotes.html.

Moore, Simon. 2010. *Strategic Portfolio Management: Enabling a Productive Organization.* Hoboken, NJ: John Wiley & Sons.

Potts, Chris. 2010. "Using Portfolio Management to Meet Company Goals." http://www.cio.com.au/articles/.

Rothman, Johanna. 2009. *Manage Your Project Portfolio.* Raleigh, NC: The Pragmatic Bookshelf.

Turbit, Neville. 2010. "Project Portfolio Management (PPM)." http://www .projectperfect.com.au.

Showcase #2: Compuware

A Recipe for Securing and Retaining Executive Support

Lori Ellsworth, Vice President, ChangePoint Division

Compuware and Obtaining Executive Level Support

Our premise is that executive understanding and support is critical to the success of PPM to create an environment of success and user acceptance. Let's begin by talking about the risks associated with failing to gain that executive support. Nearly every day, organizations move forward and invest critical resources in PPM projects that have not received executive blessing and result in failure. With this in mind, we offer up a couple of scenarios we've seen play out in our many years of implementing our PPM solution in large enterprises:

Scenario 1—The Heroic Effort

In this scenario, a PPM initiative is moved forward driven by the heroic efforts of a single person—a true believer if you will—but that individual lacks executive support. At some point in the project's lifecycle, our hero moves on from the role or the organization, and the PPM project fails. In this situation, the lack of executive support and understanding of the project undermined the project's ultimate success. Faced with the loss of its champion and with a corresponding lack of executive support, the PPM investment is called into question and sits undefended. The organization is unwilling to backfill with the necessary resources to ensure the project's continuation and long-term success. Time and money have been wasted, and PPM earns a bad name.

Scenario 2—Misalignment

In this scenario, the executive has one set of priorities and goals for the PPM initiative, and the working team has yet another (and entirely different) set of goals. This misalignment at the highest level essentially dooms a PPM initiative's success from the very outset. In this situation, the working team could fully complete the PPM project as defined by them, only to experience executive disappointment and disillusionment with the final outcome. This scenario is the project management equivalent of delivering on time and on budget, while forgetting to properly define the customer's requirements—the end result is still failure. The executive's business goals remain unmet, and the project is deemed a failure and waste of effort and budget dollars.

With these common pitfalls in mind, let's turn our attention to setting out a recipe for gaining and retaining executive support for your PPM initiative. And *initiative* is the right word—rarely will an organization be successful if PPM is perceived as a single, finite project. We'll discuss the process of winning approval early in the game, offer advice on constructing a rock solid business case, and propose some strategies for keeping your executives engaged throughout the initiative. Finally, we will outline some best practices derived from our experiences in the industry for ensuring long-term success of your PPM initiative. It is easier, better, and less risky to invest in maintaining executive support along the way rather than to try and win it back once lost.

Before the Game Begins

Based on our industry experience, the process of earning executive support should begin long before an organization turns its attention to which methodology or which tool. Keeping in mind our misalignment pitfall outlined above, a PPM initiative leader must first begin by understanding and confirming the executives' goals and priorities, and ask the vital question, "does a PPM discipline and tool solve a compelling business problem?"

Your investigation should begin with a clear understanding of corporate strategy. What are the corporate goals and objectives for this year? The next two to four years? What business problem(s) are your potential executive sponsors looking to solve? Which challenge has the highest priority? What barriers do they foresee that may limit achievement? If the objectives and highest level priorities of the business are not well understood, there is no context within which to justify investment in PPM. If this information does not exist in written business plans, then one-on-one interaction is in order.

The second step in preparing to obtain executive approval is to get into the mind of the executive. This requires that you start by identifying all the executives who are impacted by the business challenges you are looking to solve. Understand their world view, the contribution of their respective departments to the corporate strategies mentioned above, and the related business objectives. This may be a harder investigative task as personal beliefs and biases held by individual management team members and an executive's individual work experience may not be something found in a written business plan. It may require some investigative sleuthing with information gained through personal interviews, hallway conversations, or other informal means. This work is an important investment because it will allow you to position the value of what you intend to deliver through the executive's eyes, which means your business case will resonate clearly.

With this information in hand, you can now build a plan to gain the support of your executive sponsors. You understand the key stakeholders who make up executive approval. You have validated corporate and individual goals, and you have identified the highest priority pain points in the business. But before you move ahead, make sure you understand the decision-making process—who sees the business case, how frequently are investments of this magnitude considered, and so on.

This investigative process is equally applicable to an individual who is assigned by the organization to head up an in-progress PPM initiative. In this case, it is critical that, as someone inheriting a PPM initiative, you go back to first principles and perform the appropriate due diligence and risk assessment. This process begins by gaining a clear understanding of the origins of the project. If your executive has identified the PPM project as a funded initiative and assigned it to you, theoretically you can assume support. But beware—plunging in without a full understanding of the project history and origins could be deadly to the company and to your career. In accepting this responsibility, you need to understand how the PPM initiative originated, who has and has not been involved in the discussions, and what other attempts might have taken place to solve this problem. And finally, ask the question, "Is PPM the right solution to the problem?" Validation of the logic behind the decision, particularly if it is someone else's decision, is critical to ensuring your success.

Gaining Support for Sign Off

You have done your homework and verified that this initiative is critical to successful achievement of goals that are aligned with the business. You have established a premise around the business benefits to multiple stakeholders, and you understand the budgeting and sign-off process. With this preliminary legwork done, you now must begin an intensive selling job to win support and sign off on your PPM initiative. In this section, we will cover some of the elements of a business case a PPM champion should consider when bringing forward a PPM initiative to your executive team. First, focus on making the connection between this project and the business's strategic goals and objectives. But be realistic—the more direct the relationship, the easier it will be for the entire executive team to understand. Apply the learning you have acquired early in the game to match the benefits of PPM to business needs.

Respect that your business case is not the only one under consideration and that there are many good ways to invest. Even if the benefits to the business seem obvious to you, it cannot simply be assumed that your PPM project is a given. You have to display the same business discipline in developing your PPM business case that you are asking the organization to adopt. Just as one uses a PPM solution to weigh the pros and cons of various IT investments, your executive team is also faced with investment tradeoffs. Like in any sales process, you must face the competition and convince your executive by selling your PPM initiative based on value versus an alternative.

You also must ensure the entire chain of command sees value in the business case. To do this, you need to tap into the understanding of the players you gained as part of the preparation we discussed above. Otherwise, you risk a situation where you successfully sell your boss on PPM, only to later find out the entire initiative is shot down by an executive with a competing agenda. Executive consensus on a PPM investment is vitally important. Keep in mind the primary role of a PPM solution is to drive and enable collaboration across the business.

To achieve consensus agreement, you must move beyond top-level business goals to address the specific needs and challenges of individual members of the executive team in your business case. Use the *what's in it for me?* factor. Imagine, if you will, a scenario where you can produce information from the PPM solution that answers an unmet need (to date) of your CFO or CIO. By showcasing in real terms tangible deliverables from the PPM solution, expressed in highly individualized terms, you can paint, for each executive, what business will be like in the new world. One of our customers, the CIO of a United States-based health services company, successfully sold his management team on a PPM initiative by building a personal business case for each of his executive counterparts. He used his knowledge of their specific business issues to tailor information—available only from the PPM solution—to provide focused answers tailored to each individual's concerns. If you can give your finance executive information via a PPM report or dashboard that they've longed to receive but have never been able to obtain, you'll quickly convince them of the value of a PPM system.

As depicted in the application screenshot shown in Figure 2.5, add a visual component in the form of a dashboard to your PPM business case. Executives like exception reports, graphs, and charts. Use the information gathering you performed early in the game to work with your vendors to provide executives with mock ups of reports and dashboards displaying information specific to their challenges. As the saying goes *a picture is worth a thousand words*.

Quantifying your project's expected financial benefits in terms of potential revenue gains, market share gains, or cost reduction should be standard operating procedure for any business case going forward to an executive team or board of directors. Make sure you address this to the extent that the result is quantifiable. But I would also encourage PPM champions to extend this process to define the ongoing process for measurement of success. By defining key performance metrics and associated targets, and by securing executive agreement on these KPIs, you lay the groundwork for future measurement of project return on investment. Many organizations do a good job of building a tangible and attractive case but fail to revisit these numbers later in the process

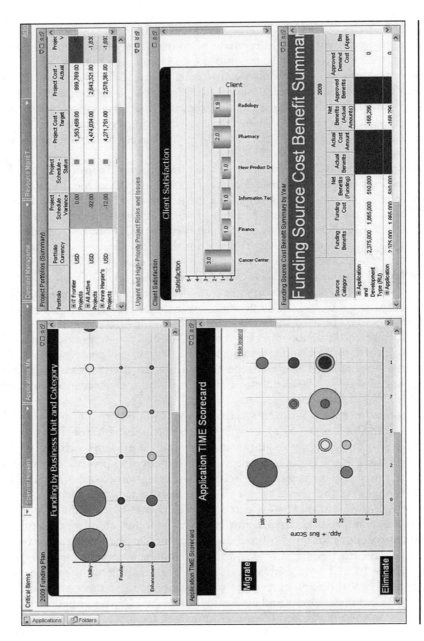

Figure 2.5   PPM executive dashboards

to determine ROI. We'll talk a little later in this chapter about the critical role measurement plays in sustaining executive support over the long-term.

Remember to address the status quo in your PPM business case. A little fear factor never hurts, especially if the consequences of inertia or non-action are significant to the business. You can accomplish this task by leading your executives through an analysis of what if scenarios: what won't be achieved; what can't be achieved; and what will happen if existing problems continue to get worse. Then point to the potential for resolution of these concerns through a PPM initiative.

Paint a complete and realistic picture for your executives. Your business case should consist of more than budget for the software. Executives must understand and buy off on the effort to support the accompanying process and culture changes required for PPM success, and they must have a full understanding of the resource commitment needed (internal and external) for project success. It is critical to gain support for the right scope. Every surprise uncovered later is an opportunity to your executive to revisit the funding of this initiative.

Finally, remind your executives of their ongoing role in ensuring the success of the PPM initiative and set out a schedule to achieve that success. Set expectations to keep executive champions engaged after the contract to purchase is signed and help them realize that they will be ongoing participants and beneficiaries of the PPM project. This early expectation setting will lay the groundwork for ongoing project communications. PPM solutions are often jeopardized by huge scope increases as the organization begins to recognize ways the technology can be applied to solve problems. Executives should understand and agree to a project scope prior to beginning so that you do not run the risk of trying to tackle too many problems too quickly. Their understanding of the project and its scope can help you focus the organization later in the implementation.

Game On

The vendor is chosen, the contract is signed, your resources are in place, and your PPM project is underway. At this point, executive support has never been more critical. Your role as a project champion now transitions from salesperson to communicator. This section discusses your transition to the communications role and outlines some strategies for ensuring ongoing executive commitment.

Meet regularly with your executive champions to keep them apprised of the project's progress, adherence to the established timeline, and to showcase early project successes. We strongly urge PPM project leaders within our customer accounts to use this opportunity to validate that there is continued alignment between the project and the goals and objectives of the business. In organizations large and small, change is frequent and often rapid. Your PPM project may need to adapt as these changes occur. Perish the thought that the business retracts its funding or support for your initiative without your knowledge. Your executive champion should be well informed and so vested in the project that he/she speaks informally on your behalf at the executive level and cannot fathom an abandonment of the initiative. Even in a worst case scenario, where the project champion leaves the business, a highly invested executive will personally ensure that the project is sufficiently staffed to ensure successful completion.

As a next step, get them hooked on automation. In your business case, you made sure to understand each executive's business problems. Now, in the implementation phase, you have an opportunity to build a reliance on the information a PPM tool can provide. This can be achieved through the provision of certain reports or the creation of dashboards tailored to the information needs of key executives.

If your executive is well informed, in tune with the project's successes, and getting early value from the solution, you have an ideal opportunity to transform your executive champion into a spokesperson for your cause to the rest of the organization. Perhaps their support will help enlist other reluctant executives to the cause, or convert a lagging business unit to adopt PPM. Top-down enthusiasm and leadership will also help spread the word about the benefits and value of PPM to the broader organization. This in turn can help facilitate accelerated user adoption and/or overcome any lingering resistance to change.

Finally, throughout the project, communicate with your executive in terms they understand and appreciate. Just sending your executive sponsor your quarterly project status report is not likely to achieve the desired result. Meetings should be short. Messaging must be crisp and highly visual—preferably expressed through tangible metrics and financial results.

Building Value

The project's moving along, and you're demonstrating to your executive that you are solving the primary business challenges that precipitated the investment in PPM. You are doing your thing, communicating and showcasing short-term results. But is that enough to retain executive commitment over the long term?

One thing to keep in mind is that PPM solutions have an incredibly broad scope. The technology is typically very flexible, and your existing investment can be leveraged to solve any number of additional business challenges. Your organization may initially have sought to invest in PPM to solve a PPM issue, but the solution can be easily extended to solve an application portfolio management or demand management challenge or to improve a product development process. Keeping extension of value in mind and remaining in lockstep with your vendor to determine the application of their technology to new and different business problems can be a key factor in demonstrating long-term PPM value to your executive. You have it within your control to drive an internal roadmap, such as shown in Figure 2.6, for your broader PPM discipline and system footprint. It's critical that as the PPM champion you are always keeping an eye open for the next opportunity to demonstrate new levels of value.

What happens when you lose executive support? It certainly is a real possibility given the fluid nature of business today. A change in command, merger/acquisition, or some other fundamental business change may affect your level of executive support. It is possible to regain lost executive support, but it is a hard battle. We have all seen organizations that have purchased and partially implemented large systems such as PPM tools, expending significant capital amounts, gaining some level of a user base only to lose all momentum and executive support due to poor communication, lack of measurement of success or some other internal failure. Lack of executive understanding of the value of your project may result in you and your team heading back to square one—into a new vendor selection process and PPM implementation.

To wrap up on a positive and optimistic note, you have the potential within your organization to initiate, and see through to completion, a highly successful PPM initiative. The most successful organizations we've seen in our practice have accomplished this goal with a three to five year PPM roadmap that clearly sets out for the executive the project's goals and objectives and the deliverables to be accomplished by organization. This roadmap also highlights potential areas to be addressed in the future. One of our most successful customers, an international pharmaceutical, offers up an excellent example

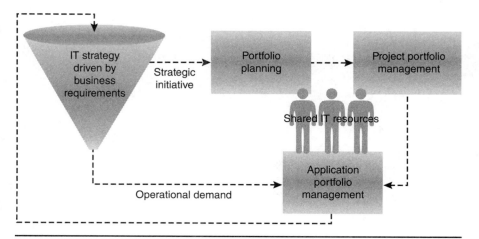

Figure 2.6   PPM roadmap

of this project management discipline. In their roadmap, they set out a key focus area for PPM each year in the context of a three-year plan that reminds them of where they are heading next. The plan contemplates automation, but also methodology, training, culture change etc. Such a plan can survive even a change in executive sponsorship, as it is already planned out and in the works to some degree, and the longer term visibility it provides to the organization keeps everyone on plan and reduces the risk of project atrophy.

Summary

The recipe for winning and retaining executive support for your PPM is as follows: perform your homework in advance, appeal to and tailor your business case to the needs of the business and the individual, and as the project progresses communicate, communicate, communicate. If you stop and think about the approach defined in this chapter, you are, in essence, leading your organization's journey into the PPM discipline. Know that the goal is not simply to successfully guide your executive and organization through a PPM implementation. By adhering to PPM principles in managing and ensuring your project's success, you will have gathered a base for PPM best practices that can, in turn, be leveraged across the organization and within many other projects for years to come.

Obtaining Executive Level Support

*Jane Holden, C. A., Executive Director, Investment
Programs Management, Canada Health Infoway*

Every company thinks itself unique, but, in the case of Canada Health Infoway (Infoway), that's actually true. Infoway is an independent, not-for-profit corporation funded by the government of Canada. There are fourteen members of the corporation, each being the Deputy Minister of Health from one of the ten provinces, three territories, and the federal government. Our mission is to foster and accelerate the implementation and use of pan-Canadian electronic health record (EHR) systems, bringing our largely paper-based health care system into the twenty-first century. Electronic health records will increase patient safety, reduce costs, and increase access to health care services. To achieve all of this, Infoway is currently responsible for a $1.6 billion portfolio of hundreds of information technology (IT) projects across ten strategic investment programs, in collaboration with thirteen provinces/territories and thousands of individual stakeholders spanning the country. Infoway's role is that of a *strategic investor* in those projects, monitoring and providing advice but not actually executing the projects.

To deal effectively with such a large and complex mandate, Infoway has developed a variety of project portfolio management (PPM) tools and techniques and embedded them into its daily way of doing business. The most recent step in our PPM chronicle has been the two-year journey to acquire and implement an enterprise-wide, top-calibre PPM system (our choice was Changepoint by Compuware Corporation). One of the most challenging aspects of that journey was convincing senior executives that we needed such a system, which would represent one of the largest internal technology projects in Infoway's history. This is the story of how we obtained that executive level support.

In many ways, working at Infoway is a dream for a project management type like me. Our core business is projects, so belief in the importance of project management discipline and rigor is built into our corporate DNA, across the organization and right up to the executive level. One of my mandates on joining the organization six and a half years ago was to implement a project management office (PMO). In contrast to my peers at other companies, I didn't have to struggle to convince senior management that we needed a PMO; several of them had spent decades as project executives and had long ago realized the value of PMOs. With senior management's support, we have been able to establish a top-notch PMO with solid processes that, among other benefits, have helped us successfully withstand the many external audits we are subject to as a publicly funded corporation.

Like many organizations, we began our PMO using just what was available to us: Excel and other desktop productivity tools—simple, cheap, and flexible when you're developing and refining your processes. Within a couple of years, we had really pushed the boundaries of what these tools were intended to do and had received accolades from inside and outside the organization on what we'd been able to accomplish with such rudimentary tools. But, over time, we became increasingly aware that our PPM effectiveness was at risk because of the inherent limitations of these tools:

◆ Information lived in hundreds of Excel workbooks and Access databases, so cross-portfolio transparency was difficult to achieve and not sustainable.

◆ There was no up-to-date, single source of truth on individual projects, programs or the portfolio. The numerous stakeholders had different sub-sets of the information, to varying degrees of currency.

◆ There was duplication of effort across the many information silos.

◆ There were data integrity risks due to the manual nature of the tools and processes.

◆ There was inability to scale with future changes to the business—a likely prospect in a pioneering field such as health information systems.

For these and many other reasons, it was clear to me that Infoway needed an enterprise-wide integrated PPM system. But the scale of such an undertaking (in terms of scope, cost, and human change management) would be unprecedented within Infoway, so I knew senior management was likely to be sceptical. We had invested more than $1.5 billion in our external investment projects but had always run our internal operations as economically as possible, to maximize the capital available for the investment projects.

I first approached my own boss, the senior vice-president, whose many responsibilities include accountability to our board of directors for Infoway's investment projects. He immediately recognized the need for a PPM system and agreed to serve as executive sponsor of the initiative. However, he cautioned me that some of his peers, notwithstanding their extensive backgrounds as project executives, might initially be unconvinced that Infoway should embark on such a major change. And, as we all know, without solid, pervasive executive-level support, any major project is doomed to fail.

In building a case to enlist senior management's support, I thought about some of the key guiding principles and priorities that underlie how Infoway conducts its business. These principles and priorities have been established, formally or informally as the case may be, by our senior executives and have been fundamental to Infoway's success to date. It seemed logical to me that executives would be more likely to support the acquisition and implementation of a PPM system if I could demonstrate how the system would support Infoway's principles and priorities. Some examples are:

◆ A clear-cut mission
◆ Published, measurable annual corporate objectives
◆ Focus on risk management
◆ A high-performing organization
◆ National EHR thought leadership
◆ Responsible stewardship of public funds

The balance of this chapter describes the messaging provided to senior executives on how a PPM system would strengthen Infoway's ability to achieve the above-noted principles and priorities. The result: executive approval to acquire and implement a PPM system, which has now been rolled out across the entire organization and is achieving measurable benefits.

◆ *A clear-cut mission*—virtually everyone who works at Infoway was drawn there by belief in the organization's mission: nothing less than the transformation of the universal health care system, which is one of the cornerstones of Canadian life. Electronic health records will provide a single source of truth on each Canadian's health care history to his/her authorized clinicians—in short, supplying the right information, in the right place, at the right time, no matter where the physician, the patient, or the data is physically located. This vision is in sharp contrast to the way (before the PPM system) Infoway's investment project data was managed in hundreds of Excel spreadsheets and some Access databases, all of which made it extremely difficult to see the big picture or have confidence in the accuracy and timeliness of the data. By providing web-based access to an enterprise-wide integrated database of project information updated in real time, a PPM system echoed the promise of an electronic health record: a single source of truth providing the right information, in the right place, at the right time.

◆ *Published, measurable annual corporate objectives*—Infoway has been entrusted with $1.6 billion in public funds and is accountable to the federal, provincial, and territorial governments as to how those funds are spent and the benefits achieved as a result. Each year, Infoway reports to those governments and to the Canadian people on its progress toward a set of published corporate objectives. As in many private-sector organizations, a portion of Infoway management compensation is based on achievement of these objectives. I identified specific ways a PPM system could increase the likelihood of achieving several of the objectives.

◆ *Focus on risk management*—Infoway's business is inherently risky for a number of reasons. First, it is pioneering in nature, with all the uncertainty that brings. Second, the mandate is enormous and complex, entailing the transformation of one of the largest sectors of the Canadian economy, one that touches every single Canadian life on a very personal level. Third, Infoway is reliant on the performance of its provincial and territorial partners who actually execute the projects in which Infoway invests. Fourth, because of the pivotal role of healthcare in Canadian society (and the vast amounts of taxpayers' funds spent on it), any major adverse event is likely to result in extensive media coverage that could undermine the public confidence essential to Infoway's success. Not surprisingly, therefore, Infoway maintains a sharp focus on risk management in all areas of the business. One of the biggest anticipated benefits of a PPM system was its ability to enhance Infoway's risk management practices. Some examples are:

◊ There was maximum executive visibility into significant risks across the entire investment project portfolio. For instance, protecting the privacy of personal data is a major concern in health information technology, so all Infoway investment projects must comply with stringent privacy requirements. Through a PPM system, executives could analyze, monitor, and manage any privacy-related risks across the hundreds of investment projects.

◊ There was better management analysis and decision making based on a single source of consolidated, aggregated up-to-date information, using a common platform accessible across the company, regardless of location.

◊ There was an enhanced ability to respond quickly to significant business changes. For example, the government of Canada recently increased Infoway's funding by almost one third, from $1.6 billion to $2.1 billion. Incorporating this major business growth into the PPM system will be relatively straightforward, but it would have been very difficult to absorb using our previous set of tools.

◊ There were robust audit trails to ensure process compliance and minimize audit risk. As noted earlier, by virtue of its publicly funded status, Infoway is subject to several external audits. Positive audit reports are important in maintaining public confidence in Infoway. PPM systems provide functionality, such as electronic workflow and document management, that help ensure processes are executed as required with all the necessary checks and balances (e.g., electronic sign offs).

◆ *A high-performing organization*—Infoway attracts very talented people and expects a lot from them. In return, employees are supported by a highly positive culture that values learning, invests in people's growth and development, and emphasizes work/life balance. Finding and retaining top talent is always a challenge in the expanding health care IT sector, thus, I knew executive management would be interested in hearing how a PPM system could help their employees further increase their performance, potentially also increasing their job satisfaction and reducing turnover. Some examples:

◇ I met with representatives from a broad cross section of Infoway business units to understand their business problems and identify how a PPM system could potentially help make their lives easier. This created demand for the system at the business unit level, which was then transmitted to the respective executives so that by the time I met with each executive individually, he had already heard from his own team members about the potential value of a PPM system to his line of business. The business unit consultation process also provided early identification of potential objections to the system or other obstacles that could then be resolved before reaching the executive level.

◇ A key aspect of the message was how, by the reduction of manual processes and the elimination of duplicate sets of data, a PPM system would enable employees to be more productive. Instead of spending significant chunks of their time grappling with spreadsheets, they would have more time to focus on the truly value-added aspects of their jobs, such as in-depth analysis and external stakeholder management.

◇ I had attended a PPM conference where I met an analyst who claimed that organizations spend 15 to 30 percent of their time gathering data and then arguing about it. While I couldn't put a time estimate on it, I knew data validation and reconciliation across Infoway departments was an issue every month and quarter end, resulting in frustration for all concerned. Implementing a PPM system meant all departments would be working from the same single set of information, so the need to validate and reconcile data across departments would disappear, thus improving interdepartmental relationships and collaboration.

◇ At the same time, because of the way most PPM systems are designed, each department could control its own piece of the system without giving up any turf.

◇ Having one centralized system would also simplify Infoway's internal IT architecture and reduce the number of applications to manage, thereby allowing the IT team to focus on other critical priorities.

◆ *National EHR thought leadership*—in addition to providing investment project capital, Infoway's role is that of a national coordinator across the thirteen provincial and territorial EHR programs. Infoway sets pan-Canadian standards and provides subject matter expertise in critical areas such as architecture, privacy, and interoperability. Consequently, management is always interested in opportunities for Infoway to demonstrate leadership to the healthcare IT sector. A PPM system and enhanced PPM practices would represent additional areas of subject matter expertise for Infoway to share with the provinces and territories, with the objective of helping them ensure successful outcomes for their healthcare IT projects.

◆ *Responsible stewardship of public funds*—as mentioned earlier, Infoway has been entrusted with $2.1 billion in public funds. Responsible stewardship of these funds is a factor in every area of Infoway's business, including internal IT infrastructure projects such as a PPM system. The proposed initiative would be the largest and most expensive inward-facing technology project in Infoway's history, and executive management would need to be convinced of a positive return on such an investment. To achieve this, we created a comprehensive formal business case document that laid out a solid justification for acquiring and implementing a PPM system. Important elements of the business case included:

◇ Independent third-party research (from sources like Gartner, Forrester, IDC, etc.) supporting the need for PPM systems in project-based organizations and the risks of not having such systems.

◇ *Realistic* acquisition and operating cost estimates, based on real information supplied by a number of PPM solution vendors. These estimates included an adequate contingency factor. The eventual project costs were well within the estimates used in the business case.

◇ Significant anticipated productivity savings—according to our calculations, if the system made Infoway employees an average of just 5 percent more productive, it would pay for itself.

◇ Cost savings in the form of existing IT applications that could be retired and planned IT acquisitions that could be avoided because the same functionality was inherent in a PPM system (e.g., electronic workflow).

◇ How the project would realize a foundational component of Infoway's Enterprise Information Strategy and reduce overall IT risk.

◇ A depiction of the broad applicability of the system, potentially into all Infoway business units if their leaders so chose, thus maximizing the return on the investment.

◇ A commitment that, even though this would be an internal project, it would be executed using the same level of project management rigour as our external investments, thus maximizing its chances of success.

As mentioned, the result was executive management's approval to proceed with the selection, acquisition, and implementation of a top-calibre PPM system. It wasn't easy, and it took a full year to go from the initial idea of a PPM system to formally getting executive buy-in. Four months later, we had selected Changepoint by Compuware; four months after that, we had our first in a series of deployments. Infoway's entire core business was migrated to the new system within one year of receiving the executive go-ahead. The implementation project itself was delivered on schedule and under budget. Today, the system has been deployed throughout the organization, where it is used (to varying degrees) by almost every employee (including the same senior executives who gave it life). After the usual initial reticence, user feedback (measured using Changepoint's own survey functionality!) is highly positive, and the expected savings described in the business case have begun to materialize. It has been a challenging, at times frustrating, yet always exhilarating journey. It couldn't have happened without executive level support. It took a year to accomplish, but in the end, it made all the difference.

3

PPM Risk #3: Functional Champion

Some projects are very easy for the leadership team to envision and support. Typically, these kinds of projects have a strong business case proposition and generate a can do, let's get started now, aura. Also present in such projects is a good and compelling answer to the question, "What's in it for me?" that all those involved in the leadership team project vetting process ask, whether out loud or quietly to themselves. These kinds of projects are no-brainers and seemingly run and conclude to a successful end as if on autopilot. For most organizations, implementing PPM will not be one of these no-brainer projects, nor will it conclude to a successful end merely running on autopilot. As the cartoon in Illustration 3.1 playfully suggests, a decision to implement PPM would be well served by the appointment of a very good, respected, and capable functional champion.

Project Champion vs. Functional Champion

Many people use the terms project champion and functional champion interchangeably. And, when speaking of the project champion, often this person is the actual sponsor of the project. In her article, "Project Sponsorship - How to Effectively Champion a Project," Lisa Koning (2008, p. 1) writes, "The Project Sponsor is more than a figurehead. It is a vital role on a Project and an effective Sponsor can be the difference between success and failure." Ms. Koning's excellent article provides insights and ideas for project sponsors on how to ensure the success of their project by actively being involved in the project—playing the roles of the project driver, the project champion, and the project leader. Ms. Koning advises that while the project manager manages the project

Illustration 3.1   PPM comics—the PPM functional champion

on a day-to-day basis, it is the sponsor of the project that has the real influence on the organization, and ultimately is the one who can make things happen.

Also commenting on the efficacy of the project champion is Australian IT veteran, Scott Withrow (2004, p. 1), who cautions, "An axiom in project management circles is, 'If you don't have a project champion, you don't have a project.' In other words, if there isn't someone in your organisation who is actively promoting, supporting, and advocating the benefits of your project, your project may be at risk." Withrow advocates that project champions provide significant assistance in the overall advocacy for the project and in removing roadblocks that the project will no doubt face. Withrow also suggests that project champions can exist at all levels within an organization and that a natural breeding ground for effective project champions is among the stakeholders who are most ardent for the project.

Another view on the project champion, in speaking of IT projects, is provided by healthcare CIO and blogger, Will Weider (2005, p. 1), who advocates the concept of a Project Champion Agreement that serves as a guide for the champion of a project. The merits of such an approach is that it takes the traditional approach to initiating a project and the preparation of a project charter to a higher level of organizational and individual commitment in the form of an agreement much like a legal agreement. And in this context, the project champion is not only vital to the project, but the champion specifically agrees to the expected benefits of the project and its successful management.

In all three of these valuable views on the project champion as advocated by Koning, Withrow, and Weider, as well as countless others, the role of project champion is important to the overall success of the project and is typically carried out by the sponsor of the project or one of the key project stakeholders. For many projects, especially those performed at lower levels within the organization or at levels where projects are commonplace, these views of the project champion are valid and appropriate. However, for projects that involve

Table 3.1 Functional champion vs. project champion

Characteristics	Functional champion	Project champion
Interest	Interest in the project by decree	Personal interest in the project
Role	Oversees the project	Cheerleads the project
Focus	Monitors the participants of the project	Monitors the progress of the project
Decision making	Does not make project decisions	Contributes to decisions about the project
Authority	Is top management	Reports back to top management

executives and members of the senior leadership team, often a different kind of champion, a functional champion, is needed. In addition to the project sponsor or enthused project stakeholder, this additional champion, the functional champion, is appointed and serves to ensure the success of the project.

As depicted in Table 3.1, the functional champion, by design, is not the project champion, nor a project sponsor, nor stakeholder of the project, for that matter. The champion, the sponsor, and the key stakeholders are already committed to the success of the project and are already acting as champions within their sphere of influence. The functional champion, on the other hand, is involved on the project by being assigned, in many cases reluctantly, to it.

Where the project champion is often viewed as the head cheerleader, the functional champion quietly oversees the project and is viewed by project team members and others as the eyes and ears of the executive management and leadership team. Hence, the role and focus of the functional champion is not so much concerned with such things as project progress against the plan, project decisions that need to be made relative to project performance (schedule and cost), and project reporting. These things are handled via the normal project management process and expected project manager and project team duties. Rather, the role and focus of the functional champion is to ensure that all involved in the project and resulting business change are truly onboard and committed to the new paradigm.

Why Is a Functional Champion Needed?

A functional champion is needed for a number of reasons. Three common reasons and drivers for the appointment of a functional champion are: when there are significant resistances to change, when there are new and unchartered business complexities, and when there are organizational interdependencies that must be seamlessly managed with a high degree of transparency.

For organizations of all shapes and sizes seeking to implement PPM solutions and to exhibit PPM best practices and capabilities, these drivers and many more are likely to be present.

There are numerous reasons why business professionals, even those who claim to be open to new ideas and approaches, resist change. At an initial level, business professionals often first think about whether or not the proposed change will work, which is soon followed by a *what's in it for me* contemplation. As shown in Figure 3.1, this results in a two by two matrix of outcomes in terms of mindsets for the change at hand, of which three out of four present significant challenges to successful PPM.

Not too long ago I had the opportunity to work with the executive team of a middle-market company seeking to improve the manner in which they selected and managed projects. The CEO and leadership team were committed to the concept of PPM and had been doing it informally for years. The CIO was assigned the full responsibility for the PPM strategy and although the CIO had a project management office (PMO) reporting to the Director of IT, the CIO created and staffed a small enterprise project management office

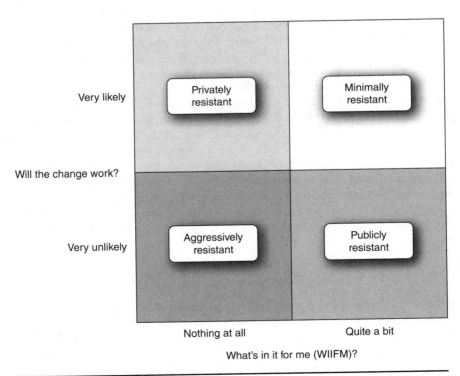

Figure 3.1   Resistance to change mindsets

(EPMO) reporting directly to him. The CIO, working with the CEO, also established a PPM executive steering committee, and the CIO made it clear to all involved that the EPMO really reported to and worked for them.

The CIO had a vision and strategy that called for the EPMO to be responsible for, and a key driver of, both the PPM processes and activities to select the correct mix of enterprise level projects and to manage those projects correctly, through delivery of the product of the project. The mantra of the EPMO was to do the right projects and to do the projects right. Guiding this vision and strategy was a five-step roadmap and detailed plan that addressed:

- ◆ Securing executive support
- ◆ Establishing a PPM governance structure
- ◆ Developing a common currency for evaluating project opportunities
- ◆ Implementing the required processes and tools
- ◆ Establishing a communications and decision-making process for the PPM executive steering committee

Though the initial start of the EPMO and management of the strategy to commence a more formalized approach to PPM was met with enthusiasm, it did not take too long for the high hopes to begin to fall.

It surprised the CIO to soon discover that just about everyone involved in, or affected by, the PPM initiative had some degree of resistance to change. Those who had the most to gain and who were the biggest proponents of PPM had some degree of minor resistance usually in the form of a lack of tolerance for information that was not perfect and a continual flow of constructive criticism that, though well intended, only served to complicate the plan of record and delay progress. And these guys were the proponents—the good guys! More significant resistance to change was found among those who had some degree of doubt about whether or not formal PPM would work as advertised and if the effort required was worth the time, expense, and bother. And of course, those who felt they had little to gain and potentially something to lose were soon discovered to be quite resistant to the change that PPM entailed. Also surprising to the CIO was the tendency that so many had to revisit the already made decision to go forward with the PPM as if that decision was re-opened and up for debate!

The CIO continued to lead the PPM initiative through the various minefields of resistance and the EPMO under his charge continued to muddle through the PPM plan and process for six quarters of performance, activity, and work with the PPM executive steering committee. The view of the EPMO team, as supported by the data, was that the organization was trying to take on far too many projects with too few resources and budget. The common view of the leadership team was that business as usual was being slowed down and that it was taking too long to get existing projects completed and new projects underway.

The truth and reality of the situation was that for the first time the leadership team was engaged in truly understanding the total demand for projects, the real capacity of the organization to take on and effectively manage projects, and the degree to which the project mix was aligned to the needs of the business. Rather than setting anyone free, this truth was frustrating for the leadership team and with no easy answers or solutions to the problems now in sight, many simply wanted to go back to the old way of doing business. Predictably, when the CIO left the company to accept an executive position at another firm, the EPMO and strategy for formal PPM was soon up for debate with most of the leadership team wanting to abandon it and return to business as usual. This is the impact and result that resistance to change can have on any new initiative; PPM is by no means immune to this or above being at some degree of risk.

When the new CIO of the company arrived and settled in, one of the first tasks at hand was to resurrect and bring to new life the initiative to formally manage the project portfolio. The CIO and CEO reviewed the overall PPM strategy and discussed the progress made to date and the key issues and obstacles still in need of being addressed. They also discussed the need to have a functional champion, a Primus Inter Pares—first among equals. This person would be one of the PPM executive steering committee members, the one best suited for the task at hand, which was to ensure that all of the members of the committee would give their full support and effort to making PPM a success, not just showing up at the meetings and paying lip service to the process.

A number of candidates for this role stood out. In fact, all of the PPM executive steering committee members had traits and characteristics that would be ideal for the assignment. In the final analysis, however, it was the Vice President of Human Resources who was the most compelling candidate. The VP of HR was a young, energetic, and highly talented executive. She was also very charismatic, endearing, and a pleasure to work with. All of the members of the executive team enjoyed working with her, and she was a role model for many others, both men and women, throughout the company. Simply put, she was a more than equal adversary to anyone not fully on board or committed to PPM. When announced as the functional champion for PPM to the rest of the leadership team, all were supportive, enthusiastic, and aware of the fact that PPM was not going away; rather, it was going to be made to work.

Over the next few months, the CIO and VP of HR led the PPM effort. While the CIO managed the EPMO and the formal strategy and plan per the agreed to governance, communications, and decision-making process, the VP of HR met from time to time with the various members of the PPM executive steering committee. Unlike the one-on-one meetings with the CIO where the peer executives could, and often did, voice concerns and give criticisms over the various PPM issues and challenges of the day and reminisce about willingness and ability, of the follower. For example, one who is able to perform a task but not willing to do so must be led differently than another who is unable to do a task but willing to give it a try. And important to note, even the same individual must be led differently with respect to different tasks for which the individual has different levels of ability and willingness.

The PPM functional champion can benefit greatly by first understanding these readiness dynamics and then exhibiting the most effective leadership style. As functional champion, leading peers can be a delicate matter. While ample opportunity exists for humility and being respectful to colleagues, there is also the opportunity and need to directly confront unhelpful mischief that can take the form of stubbornness, belligerence, and intentional or habitual resistance.

Summary

For most organizations seeking to commence a more formalized approach to PPM, it will be a given that the project to implement PPM systems, behaviors, and attitudes will not run on autopilot and will not run without some degree of fair game execution difficulties. Even in the best of environments, it will not take long for many of those involved to publicly challenge any and every detail of the PPM strategy and to privately ask the question, "What's in it for me?" Some individuals may voice a desire to go back to business as usual because of a belief that the effort, as measured by time, expense, and bother, is far greater than the benefit. Others may simply interfere with team speed by having an impatient and intolerant mindset for processes that take a bit of time and effort to get right, data that is not initially, nor may ever be, perfect, and new techniques for analysis and decision making that may or may not benefit those who have fared well under the old order.

Enter the functional champion. In addition to executive level support and a solid foundation for PPM that is rooted in a shared vision, mission, goals, and objectives, the functional champion for PPM can play a key role in facilitating and ensuring success. Though many people use the terms project champion and functional champion interchangeably, these are two different people with two different roles on the project and for the product of the project initiative. Where the project champion is primarily concerned with the performance of the project and acts as the head cheerleader for the project, the functional champion quietly oversees the project and is concerned with the behaviors, resistance to change attitudes, and softening commitments of the participants to the PPM strategy and new way of doing business.

There are many different approaches for selecting the functional champion for PPM. Ardent supporters of the PPM concept as well as PPM experts, internal or external to the organization, can be very effective at facilitating leadership team success. Often times, selecting an individual from the camp of the naysayers can prove to be an effective way of turning an unenthusiastic doubter into the leading proponent of PPM and an agent for change. In essence, the functional champion is the eyes and ears of the head executive in charge such as the CEO or COO. Regardless of the individual selected, it is important that this person is announced to the leadership team and viewed by them as the Primus Inter Pares, first among equals.

Though the functional champion for PPM will likely not have positional authority over leadership team peers, the functional champion will need to lead and will need to exhibit effective leadership. Among the many leadership techniques at the disposal of the functional champion, three time-tested techniques (nemawashi, MBWA, and situational leadership) can prove to be invaluable in building consensus, keeping abreast of progress, and ensuring support for and adherence to the overall PPM game plan. Perhaps one of the greatest values of the functional champion is that this person can interact with leadership team members in an informal yet direct and effective manner. If one of the members of the leadership team is not abiding by, or fully committed to, the new strategy, the functional champion can call that person to the carpet, so to speak, and demand a marked and immediate change in attitude and behavior. The functional champion can entertain a heated discussion, allow and even encourage passions to be vented and vetted, and after it is all over, shake hands and get back to work. And, all of this is done without formal management needing to be involved, much like the way the captain of a sports team can play a key leadership role with other teammates without every single mishap or difference of opinion having to rise to the attention of the head coach. Just as sports teams need and have a captain, so do leadership teams— and in the challenging contest of PPM, that person is the functional champion.

Questions

1. What is the role and focus of the PPM functional champion?
2. How does the role and focus of the PPM functional champion compare and contrast to the role and focus of the PPM project champion?
3. What are the three common reasons and drivers for the appointment of a functional champion?
4. What two key factors lead business professionals, who claim to be open to new ideas and approaches, to have a resistance-to-change mindset?
5. What are the pros and cons of selecting an existing and ardent supporter of PPM to be the functional champion?
6. What are the pros and cons of selecting an outside consultant and expert in PPM to be the functional champion?

champion is critical to guiding the organization through the valley of despair and plays an important role in the four steps to crossing the valley of despair.

Four Steps to Crossing the Valley of Despair

Step One: Get your sponsors lined up, particularly the functional champion

People will get on board with a PPM initiative quickly and seamlessly if they see that it's being sponsored at the right levels. Naturally, the CIO and the project champion have to be on board, but a good functional champion will have even more pull/influence in the success of the PPM initiative. The functional champion will vary based on the organization. In my experience, this person needs to have passion, savvy, smarts, power, and influence. Previously in my career I was an IT executive at a fast-growing technology company and drove the implementation of a new PPM initiative. When I first proposed this initiative a lot of people didn't understand why it was needed. The company was used to acting in a very reactive manner and generally, due to the culture, liked it that way. To ensure the success of the PPM initiative, I recruited the VP of Sales as the functional champion. The VP of Sales was a smart, aggressive, and successful woman who was very keen on the idea of a PPM system. Why was it so important to her? Because she was savvy enough to realize that the PPM system would help the organization deliver more projects on time and on budget. And these projects would help her sell more products and services. This is a classic case of "what's in it for me" (WIIFM). She willingly and enthusiastically signed up to be the functional champion. When the organization saw that she was on board, everyone else pretty much followed suit . . . including the CEO. This woman became a great champion and cheerleader for the PPM initiative, which ended up being critical to the success of the PPM initiative.

Step Two: Communicate!

When someone has to change, they are naturally going to be resistant to it unless they know why they need to change and how it benefits the overall organization. This is simply human nature. Try this simple exercise. Walk up to a friend, grab his/her arm, and start tugging on it (gently, of course). What does your friend do? They pull their arm back and say, "What the heck are you doing?" People inherently resist change when it's presented to them. Now walk up to that same person and say, "Hi, may I take your arm and lead you down to the ice cream shop, so I can buy you an ice cream sundae?" Chances are you're going to get a very different reaction primarily because you communicated your intent with your friend. Good communication can break down people's resistance to change and help overcome the valley of despair.

A good friend of mine is a project manager at a large New York-based financial services firm that has spent two years and several million dollars implementing a very large and robust PPM system. I called my friend, who is a respected and intelligent manager, and asked him about his experience. He is currently a user of the system, but is not the functional champion or project champion. In his words, "I've been told that I have to enter information about my projects into this new PPM system, but I haven't been told WHY. I don't get anything out of it personally, and I don't know how this system benefits the company. In fact, I talked to my boss (a senior executive), and he couldn't really give me a good reason why the PPM system was benefitting the company. If I knew the big picture, I'd feel a lot better about entering my project information every week." Eventually this organization cancelled its PPM initiative and wrote off several million dollars. Why? Well there are certainly many reasons, not the least of which was lack of good communication with those who are using (and supposedly benefitting from) the new system.

So what's in a good communication plan? Think of it as a marketing plan, but for the internal audience of the PPM system.

- ◆ Who are the recipients? Users, project managers, and executives, for example.
- ◆ What is the message to be communicated? That a new system/process is coming, when it's coming, how users are going to be trained and notified, and how the new system benefits the company.
- ◆ How often and with what medium are you going to communicate about the upcoming change? Town hall meetings, emails, intranet, blogs, and wikis are included.
- ◆ Who does the communication come from? This is where the functional champion plays a key role as the functional champion should be a core part of the communication process.

Step Three: Training

A PPM system affects many different people and organizations—project managers, resource managers, business analysts, IT executives, business users, functional executives. Each of these functions plays an important role in the success of the PPM initiative, and they all need to be trained.

Just as a good communication plan is needed, a good training plan is even more critical.

- ◆ What are the components of a good training plan? First of all, it's role-based. You can't do one-size-fits-all training for PPM as each role has different responsibilities when it comes to the PPM
- ◆ What medium are you going to use to train people? E-learning? Classroom? Paper-based? These are all decisions to be made.

The functional champion is an important sponsor of the training plan and should be involved in its development and review. The functional champion should also sit in on the first few training sessions to show strong support; this will help overcome resistance as the functional champion can use these training sessions to stress the importance of the PPM initiative to the users.

Step Four: Get early success with a quick win

PPM implementations can be expensive, long, and comprehensive. I've seen PPM implementations that are so long and expensive that they literally die under their own weight. By the time the system is ready to be implemented, the sponsors have moved on and people have forgotten why they're implementing PPM in the first place.

This is why I'm a big advocate of quick wins. The functional champion will be critical to deciding the best quick wins for the organization. So where are the quick wins? There are typically three categories of quick wins:

1. *Manage supply and demand*—The quick win here is to determine the current inventory of projects and people. Getting a handle on what IT is working on and who is working on what initiatives can yield significant early benefits.
2. *Putting in place a consistent prioritization and governance process*—There can be a good quick win in simply utilizing the new PPM system to enforce the prioritization/governance of projects and initiatives.
3. *Delivering a critical project using the new PPM system*—The new PPM system can certainly help in delivering an important initiative on time and on budget.

Of these three "quick win" categories, I'm a big advocate of the first one. Using the PPM system to inventory all current initiatives in IT can uncover many areas of potential value. What I typically find is that 30 to 40 percent of projects that IT is working on can be eliminated because they're duplicates, unnecessary, or unaligned with the company's business objectives. The PPM system will typically pay for itself simply in this one area, through the elimination of unnecessary work. Figure 3.5 shows a project inventory dashboard that can be generated quickly from the Innotas system, highlighting current initiatives by status and by business objective.

One of our customers is a midsized appliance distributor. Prior to the implementation of PPM, the CIO believed there were about 20 projects being worked in IT at any given time. After inventorying the projects for the PPM system, he found out they had more than 60 projects being worked in his organization. The CIO was appalled at all the "back door," duplicate, and unnecessary projects that were being worked on. In consulting with the functional champion, he was able to eliminate several of them immediately, paying for the PPM system in about a month.

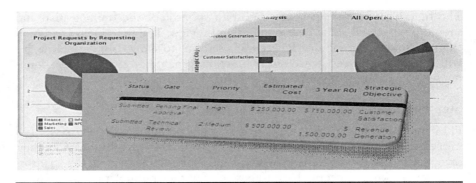

Figure 3.5   Project inventory dashboard (Innotas)

Case Study—City of Tacoma

The City of Tacoma is the third-largest city in the state of Washington, with approximately 202,700 residents. Located at the foot of Mount Rainier and along the shores of Commencement Bay, Tacoma is recognized as a livable and progressive international city. Tacoma's IT organization employs more than 100 IT professionals with an average tenure of 25 years. The IT department provides technology services for city employees, customers, vendors, and partners.

The Challenge: Business Results Through Visibility and Alignment

Bradd Busick is the executive responsible for the PMO in the City of Tacoma, and he faced significant challenges.

- ◆ Business customers were demanding more value. "They wanted visibility into projects that were in flight, delayed, cancelled, or partially abandoned. IT was tracking the business on eight different spreadsheets," says Bradd. The business saw project delivery as an area for improvement.
- ◆ With 100 people in the division, IT needed to find a way to categorize the work in terms of enhancements, growth, maintenance, and cost. This group was challenged with communicating to senior management where people were spending their time, and how work was being prioritized and aligned with the city's overall strategic objectives.
- ◆ The mandate to optimize costs in this economy drove the requirements for governance, accountability, and visibility.

To address these challenges, Bradd and his team implemented the on-demand IT governance solution from Innotas.

The Importance of the Functional Champion

Bradd recognized that the approach to the PPM implementation was quite crucial. Rather than tackling it like a normal project and "slamming in" the technology, Bradd recognized that Tacoma needed to take into account the political and cultural challenges inherent in the implementation of a PPM system. Given that, Tacoma took a "change management" approach to the PPM initiative.

The first thing Bradd and his team did was to listen to the customers. Prior to selecting the Innotas software, they conducted extensive interviews and focus groups with their customers. Their conclusion was that their customers "wanted a PPM solution . . . they just didn't realize they were asking for a PPM solution." The second thing they did was to develop requirements and select the Innotas tool. Innotas was selected because of its end-to-end IT governance capabilities, as well as its ease of use and configuration. The third thing they did was to form the leadership team to drive the PPM change program. The leadership team consisted of an executive sponsor, a project manager, and a functional champion. Bradd talks about the necessity of the functional champion, "We realized we needed to have a champion internally to drive this. We could have driven adoption through executive edict, but realized that customer edict was more powerful and would help ensure the success of the project."

The functional champion had multiple skills (a "Swiss army knife" of capabilities, according to Bradd) that were critical to the role and the success of the PPM program:

◆ She had a mix of charisma and savvy. She also knew the ins and outs of the Tacoma culture. This allowed her to communicate well with both business and IT staff.
◆ She was proactive and enthusiastic about being part of the change. This helped overcome people's concerns and resistance to change.
◆ She was an excellent communicator. Not only did she personally communicate well with others about the need for change, she knew how to identify the proper senders/recipients of messages. She was also excellent at scripting messages.

As a by-product of using a change management approach to their PPM implementation and having a charismatic functional champion, the City of Tacoma now uses this approach on all initiatives. This is an excellent example of IT being a model for how all business initiatives should operate.

Results and Benefits

Using Innotas, IT is better positioned than anyone else in the city. "With a click we can justify the workload at multiple levels," says Bradd. Innotas eliminated two ad hoc systems and numerous spreadsheets. The IT organization used to manually track projects and change requests, resulting in decreased throughput and challenges with backlog management. "Our five-year backlog is finally manageable," says Bradd. The IT organization has become more agile and nimble. The business now knows what IT is working on: growth versus sustaining versus urgent requests. Now, IT can "hot swap" to better balance the IT portfolio. As a result, IT is able to service the requests with more predictability. IT is now able to provide KPIs to senior management and power the growth and value-add of IT. "We now facilitate and enable cultural change and can implement new initiatives in a streamlined manner," says Bradd.

4

PPM Risk #4: Big Bang vs. Incremental Adoption

One of the keys to successfully implementing PPM and the processes, policies, and techniques that are sure to be entailed with the new way of doing business is to eliminate any escape routes back to the old order of things. For many members of the leadership team, it can be tempting to retreat to business as usual especially when confronted with the challenges and difficulties that are often accompanied with change of any kind. PPM is no exception. As the cartoon in Illustration 4.1 playfully suggests, if the transition to the desired state takes too long or is happening at too slow of a pace or if there is a perception that there is not enough commitment and buy-in to the strategy from all involved, there can be a desire to take draconian action to speed things up.

In the 1500s, Captain General Hernando Cortez, the infamous Spanish Conquistador, landed in Mexico to conquer the Aztec Empire, take possession of its wealth, and settle New Spain. According to legend, before launching the attack on the Aztecs, Cortez ordered his men to burn the ships to prevent his men from retreating from the fight. This brazen act was needed, Cortez felt, to get all of his men committed to his course of action, a course that was fraught with risks and perils and not fully supported.

These days, when business executives invoke the term *burning the ships*, they are referring to managing change in such a way as there is no possibility of returning to the old order and, thus, no need to debate decisions already made or find reasons to not fully support the new order. For some organizations seeking to implement PPM, the burning the ships option might be appropriate and effective, but for most organizations a well planned, incremental

Illustration 4.1   PPM comics—burning the ships

roll out offers a less disruptive and lower risk approach to rapidly transitioning from the current state to the desired state of managing the project portfolio.

A common mindset for implementing PPM that many organizations have used includes the following considerations:

◆ Don't overwhelm the organization
◆ Use a gap analysis
◆ Use a proof of concept
◆ Tolerate imperfect information
◆ Allow sufficient time to get systems in place
◆ Recognize that data integrity is not a tool issue

Collectively, these considerations enable an organization to incrementally, rapidly, and successfully roll out PPM.

Don't Overwhelm the Organization

Many PPM experts advocate a smooth, gradual roll out of PPM. Lee Merkhofer (2008, p. 3) advises, "Don't overwhelm the organization. Match the pace of change to the organization's capacity to evolve." Similarly, in his white paper, "Seven Habits of Highly Effective Portfolio Management Implementations," UMT founder and PPM pioneer Gil Makleff (2005, p. 4) offers as his second habit that those responsible for implementing PPM should not overwhelm the organization with a big-bang approach. Also advising against the rush into a big-bang approach is Microsoft's EPM expert, Simon Moore (2010, p. 97), "An initial broad and overambitious deployment can not only derail a single portfolio management system but also introduce pessimism about future systems." Moore adds, "Creating a phased and structured approach to the introduction of a system [PPM] is critical to its success." These experts, and many others, recognize that the desire to hastily and over ambitiously take on more than an organization is capable of is usually met with frustration, execution difficulties, and sometimes even failure.

On the other hand, while it is well advised to adopt an incremental approach to rolling out PPM, this too can be problematic if demonstrated results and behaviors are not achieved within an acceptable timeframe. In many cases, the effort to implement a PPM system, develop the requisite processes and best practices, and marry the business and management planning cycle to the new PPM process and calendar can take quite a bit of time to get right. Even the most patient of executive teams can become overly anxious to see marked and tangible progress as opposed to witnessing ongoing work in process and best efforts.

One approach to deal with this risk that many PPM providers and consultants recommend is to define the scope of the incremental roll out in such a way as to be able to achieve the scope in specific, measured increments of time, such as quarterly or whatever duration that is appropriate for the organization and leadership team. Much like an agile scrum sprint, though longer of course, the benefits of this approach are twofold. First, tangible results are delivered sooner rather than later. And second, the fixed iteration of time, whether quarterly, monthly, or some other duration of time, conditions the leadership team into expecting and receiving an outcome. As represented simplistically in Figure 4.1, the fixed iteration of time approach provides the leadership team with a consistent review process. This is helpful for not only delivering results more rapidly over the course of the PPM roll out, but it also fosters the established the ongoing behavior and expectation of the PPM

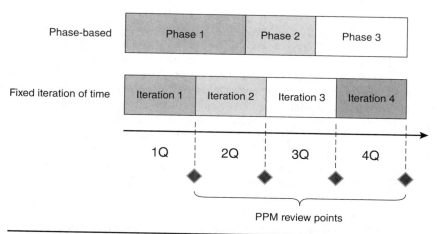

Figure 4.1   Fixed iteration of time vs. phase-based

leadership team to meet, review, and make decisions via a planned process and regular, predictable PPM calendar of events.

By way of contrast, the phased-based approach to the PPM roll out will consist of start and stop times for the end of one phase and the start of another that will likely have no consistency in duration. This will result in two options: either calling the PPM leadership team together at irregular intervals to review progress or to postpone review of such progress until the next regularly scheduled PPM leadership team meeting is to take place. For many organizations, neither of these two options is particularly attractive. Hence, by using both an incremental approach to rolling out PPM and fixed iterations of time to achieve the scope of the roll out, the PPM leadership will be able to witness and appreciate forward progress against the plan in a manner that is both timely and consistent.

Use a Gap Analysis

In a PPM context, gap analysis is a technique that helps a company to compare its actual performance in managing the project portfolio with its potential performance. Some people refer to this as a comparison of the current state to the desired state. A gap analysis seeks to answer two fundamental, yet challenging, questions: "How are we currently performing?" and "How do we want to be performing?" A gap analysis naturally flows from benchmarking and other assessments both quantitative and qualitative. Once a general expectation of performance or capability is understood, it is then possible to compare that expectation to the current level of performance. This comparison reveals the gaps and establishes the basis for understanding and addressing areas of improvement.

A gap analysis can provide an excellent foundation for establishing short- and long-term plans to move toward the desired state as well as a set of projects to close the gap in the most effective, timely, affordable, and practical manner, relative to the culture and capabilities of the organization. In guiding the effort, many experts in organizational maturity advise that prior to any kind of assessment, a first step in the process involves *knowing excellence* in terms of industry best practices. One such expert in organization maturity is John Schlichter, the CEO of OPM Experts. John was the Project Management Institute (PMI®) Program Director of that effort that produced the Organizational Project Management Maturity Model known as OPM3®. In his subject matter expert contributor piece to the book, *Business Driven PMO Setup*, Schlichter (Perry, 2009) advocates four hierarchical steps that are critical to any cultural transformation. As shown in Figure 4.2, John suggests that the leaders of an organization might not all have a clear sense, or the same view, of what a project management culture is, according to industry best practices.

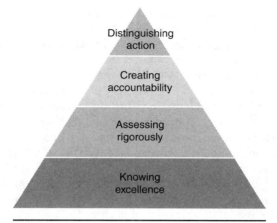

Figure 4.2   Hierarchical steps of cultural transformation

Hence, a first and foundational step is all about knowing excellence and the context of the culture of the organization.

In the second step of the hierarchy, leaders of the organization need to assess the organization methodically to determine the true current state-of-affairs according to the views of the people throughout the organization who actually do the work. This is about assessing oneself rigorously. The third step of the hierarchy is about creating accountability. The organization might not have clear ownership in place for transforming the culture; this is a key requirement to the success of any change. And the final step of the hierarchy is about distinguishing action. In this final step, the organization must create a realistic and measurable plan for transforming the culture.

Seasoned experts in organization maturity like Schlichter recognize that there is quite a bit more than meets the eye when it comes to understanding the desired future state whether based upon industry best practices, standards, management judgment, or a combination thereof and performing an assessment of the current state of capabilities and analysis of the resulting gaps. Far too often organizations are tempted to take shortcuts in the overall effort to get to the answer quickly and inexpensively. While there is some value in these kinds of efforts in terms of arriving at an inference of the current state, typically that inference needs to be taken with a grain of salt and not interpreted to be a finding of fact or even necessarily an accurate observation in terms of what would be expected from a rigorous assessment.

Two vivid examples of this come to mind. Not long ago, I had the opportunity to work with two organizations seeking to improve upon their PPM processes. Both organizations were in the beginning stages of establishing a

PPM culture and both of their PMOs were key drivers and enablers of project management and PPM processes and policies. In both companies, rather than hiring an outside expert to facilitate the process, the PMO manager informally assessed the current state and compared it to what the future desired state should be as envisioned by the PMO manager.

As shown in Figures 4.3 and 4.4, both PMO managers used PMI standards as a basis from which to assess the organization. One of the two PMO managers used the PMI Project Management Body of Knowledge known as the *PMBOK® Guide* for the purposes of performing a PPM gap analysis and the other PMO manager used the PMI Standard for Portfolio Management.

The two PMO managers self assessed the current level of PPM maturity using PMI knowledge area standards as a construct to assign numeric scores. Following the popular maturity model leveling of 1 through 5 and using publicly available maturity model descriptions of each of the five levels, the two PMO managers each designed a way to provide a numeric score for the current state, the desired state, and the perfect state. Interesting to note, both PMO managers set the desired state of PPM maturity to a level of 3. That this kind of effort produces nice charts is of no debate. But whether or not this kind of effort

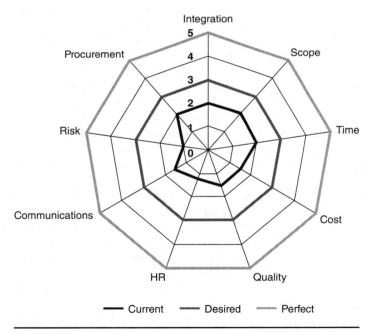

Figure 4.3 PPM gap analysis based on project management standard

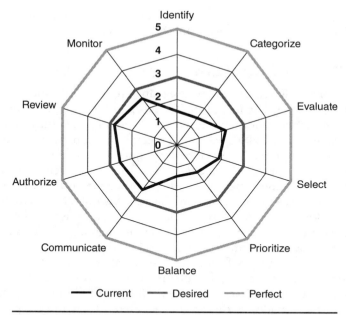

Figure 4.4 PPM gap analysis based on portfolio management standard

truly produces the kind of actionable data that can only be obtained from a rigorous assessment is debatable.

Many PPM experts advocate that an informal, high-level gap analysis is of little value to an organization, and that it is well worth the time and money to bring in an outside expert to facilitate if not lead the gap analysis. Skeptics may view this advice as an attempt to sell consulting services, but others disagree, as there is tremendous value in utilizing an outside subject matter expert whose sole focus is helping organizations with this difficult task. It is hard to argue against using an outside expert solely because of the fact that the benefits of effective PPM and the value of getting it right scales into millions of dollars. Against this backdrop, the consulting fee of an outside expert to perform a gap analysis pales in comparison. In fact, many of the leading PPM providers not only have deep expertise and years of experience in performing PPM gap analysis, but they often provide this as a no-charge service and value add as part of doing business with them.

In any event, an incremental adoption of PPM is well served by the performance of a PPM gap analysis. An informal assessment can be a good start and can help to reveal the scope and level of detail that should be undertaken in a more rigorous assessment and finding of fact. The better the gap analysis, the better the ensuing plan for a successful PPM roll out.

Use a Proof of Concept

A proof of concept is a short, and by design incomplete, realization of a method or idea to demonstrate its feasibility. The purpose of a proof of concept is to verify that the concept or theory is likely to work in a real, fully designed and deployed system. Generally speaking, there are two approaches to a proof of concept. The first approach is what many people refer to as a functional proof of concept. In this approach, the objective of the proof of concept is to demonstrate that the business use case of the proposed idea is fit for adoption and that a preponderance of the issues and objections, if not all of them, have been sufficiently addressed in order to make a go or no-go decision. The functional proof of concept can be tremendously helpful in enabling the decision-making team to further assess the merits of the proposed idea as well as to discover and confirm critical success factors and key areas of risk that must be taken into account to have a successful implementation. Additionally, the functional proof of concept can facilitate the achievement of a full buy-in by those who may not yet have made up their mind or offered their full support for the proposed new approach.

The other general approach for a proof of concept is what many people refer to as limited-scope implementation. The limited-scope implementation is usually conducted within a single department of the organization with the intent to gain support of others and to roll the solution out to the rest of the organization upon success of the proof of concept. Some organizations have success with this approach, yet, for others it can be very risky. For instance, some complex systems that involve a high degree of collaborative use and decision making cannot be effectively implemented on a departmental or partial use basis. The features of the system and the best practices that the system enable and require may not be possible to fully or even correctly use at the departmental level. Also, if the limited-scope proof of concept is being performed in order to obtain full executive support, the mere nature of the limited-scope implementation may not lead to an accurate assessment of the full value of the system when implemented as intended. Additionally, the value that is verified via the limited-scope implementation may not be sufficient to convince others to give their support for a full roll out of the system. Commenting on this risk is PPM expert Lee Merkhofer (2009, p. 1) who suggests that an initial limited-scope implementation of PPM within a single department might help the organization get started but don't expect to get very far without top-level executive support.

As shown in Figure 4.5, there is a natural proof of concept *sweet spot* with respect to the degree of perfection that organizations should be mindful of when considering conducting a PPM proof of concept.

Often, there can be a tendency to conduct a proof of concept to perfect a working trial of the system in terms of both processes and tool functionality. This is outside of the PPM proof of concept sweet spot and can be problematic as a proof of concept inherently has limitations on not just the scope of the proof of concept but also on the amount of time, expense, and resources that can be made available to it. Hence, if perfecting a working trial is required to obtain executive buy-in, this can be a sure way to fail from the start. Most organizations will have far more success in their PPM proof of concept by keeping the degree of perfection for processes and tool functionality to the appropriate level relative to the objectives set by management for the proof of concept.

Tolerate Imperfect Information

Successful PPM requires speed, patience, and toleration for information that is not perfect. For many people, these can seem to be contradictory requirements. Speed is needed to get PPM going, quickly show progress, and to continually

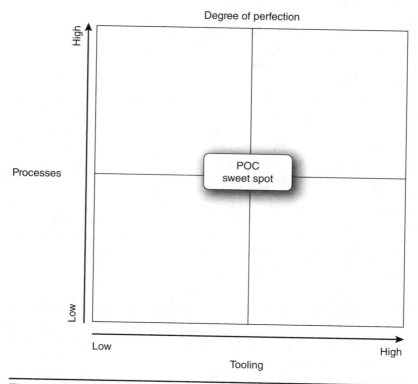

Figure 4.5   PPM proof of concept sweet spot

improve upon all aspects of the process. Patience is needed because it takes time to get PPM right. There are many foundational prerequisites that can impact success. For example, if core project management processes and capabilities are not in place, there can be a significant lack of integrity to project assumptions and data which will directly impact the ability to successfully select and manage the project portfolio. Toleration for imperfect information, in terms of the use of the PPM system, following PPM best practices, and making PPM decisions, is needed because much of the core data is not perfect to begin with. Consider the following:

- How stable is the economy?
- How predictable is market demand?
- How fixed are the business goals and objectives?
- How resilient are management plans and strategies?
- How effective are our processes?
- How effective are our people?
- How effective is our business culture?
- How aligned is the project portfolio to the needs of the business?
- How accurate are project benefit estimates?
- How accurate are project cost estimates?
- How accurate are project schedule estimates?
- How shareable are people resources?
- How effective is our ability to manage risk and uncertainty?

These are just some of the many considerations that contribute to an environment of less than perfect information. For most organizations implementing PPM, there will be a tremendous gap between perfect information and the information that is on hand. However, this should not be a cause for despair. In the face of uncertainty and imperfect information, it can be easy to give up on PPM and go back to the old way of doing business. This is always the easiest alternative, but seldom the best alternative. PPM tools and processes enable an organization to commence upon a journey that seeks, and is committed to, getting things right. Information will get better with time, as PPM capabilities evolve and mature. The initial information will be far from perfect, so there must be a mindset that can tolerate imperfect information rather than becoming paralyzed by it.

Allow Sufficient Time to Get Systems in Place

The timeline is one of the most important elements in creating a successful and achievable project plan for managing the implementation of a PPM system. Often, organizations seeking to purchase a PPM solution do not realize that they might spend one to two years waiting for it to be fully implemented.

This means that the investment in time, money, and energy that you are making right now will probably not result in the desired state of PPM capabilities not to mention achieving an ROI, for a long time. Forward thinking buyers must engage the providers of PPM solutions for real answers on what the full implementation timeframe will likely be. And, rather than trying to cut in half, compress, or reduce this timeframe to a duration that is simply not achievable, it is far more effective and meaningful to allow the full amount of time that is needed to truly experience success.

Fortunately, all of the leading PPM providers exhibit tremendous leadership in this area. Rather than sugar coat the work that must be done and the time that it will take, PPM providers traditionally provide implementation roadmaps that enable an organization to get started and show results quickly, as well as to plan and allow for sufficient time to mature the organization, develop higher levels of PPM capabilities, and to realize the outcomes achieved by exhibiting those capabilities. Additionally, all of the leading PPM providers are willing and eager to facilitate conversations with their clients who can speak about their implementation experience, results achieved, and phases and timeframes for their implementation.

Though unintended, there are numerous drivers that result in a mindset that a PPM implementation must be done quickly and that a long implementation is a bad implementation. Leading PPM experts are quick and correct to cite the fact that if the executive team does not witness noticeable results quickly, then there can be a change in heart and commitment to strategy. It is not uncommon to read or to hear in conference presentations that the PPM system must be implemented within six months and must achieve a measurable ROI sufficient to pay back the initial investment as well as to justify the ongoing commitment by the executive team and all involved in the process. There are the occasional PPM providers and new entrants to the Software as a Service (SaaS) PPM market that lead off their marketing messages with the promise of being the fastest and easiest PPM solution to implement. But just as it takes time to turn bread into toast to no discredit of the toaster, it takes time to turn the project related activities of an organization into effective PPM to no discredit of the PPM tool. Is it important to achieve success, whatever that success is deemed to be, as soon as possible? Of course it is, especially when the desire for speed is because of a business-driven need, such as responding to a market demand, out competing a competitor, or preparing for or facilitating a merger or acquisition. However, the decision to implement PPM is not a short-term tactic; it is a long-term strategic change. As such, sufficient time must be allowed to get systems in place. That timeframe should be business-driven and realistic.

Recognize that Data Integrity Is Not a Tool Issue

Perhaps one of the biggest challenges of successfully managing a project portfolio is managing data integrity. Data integrity is defined as data that has a complete or whole structure. The characteristics of data must be correct for data to be complete and have integrity. This means that such things as data definitions, dates, business use rules and context, what the data can mean and how it can relate to other data must also be complete and correct. In the context of PPM, data integrity is typically not a tool issue. PPM tools perform functions and ensure the integrity of the data within the parameters of the functionality of the tool usage. But unlike transactional data, such as daily sales revenue that is mathematically derived from known and precise inputs, the inputs to PPM data such as an estimate of product of the project benefits realization are far less known, precise, and mathematically derived. Hence, the challenges and issues with PPM data integrity are more likely to be centered upon best practices, organizational capabilities, and leadership team and individual judgment as opposed to the functionality of one vendor PPM tool compared to another.

Good data makes for good PPM; bad data makes for bad PPM. To a large extent it can be argued that if you have good PPM best practices you will have good PPM data as an outcome of those best practices. Some even suggest that the quality of PPM data is far more important than the PPM tool functionality and that if you have good PPM data you can manage a project portfolio in Microsoft Excel. Likewise, if you have poor quality of PPM data, the most elegant and rich in function PPM application will quickly be rendered to that of a very expensive spreadsheet.

For many organizations seeking to implement a PPM application and to establish and institutionalize best practices for managing the project portfolio, there can be a debate and legitimate differences of opinion on what should be focused on first: best practices for managing the project portfolio or evaluation, selection, and implementation of a PPM solution. As shown in Figure 4.6, the holy grail of PPM is having both quality data as an outcome of good best practices, and good PPM functionality as a result of implementing a quality PPM tool.

When this is achieved, PPM *magic* can happen; projects are aligned to the needs of the business, decisions are made to optimize organization and project constraints, and the portfolio management outcomes meet the requirements of the business and expectations of the leadership team. Conversely, when the quality of data is poor and the tool functionality is limited, PPM can be a painful exercise. Even under best of efforts and intentions, if the PPM data significantly lacks integrity and the PPM tool lacks any ability to facilitate leadership team review, debate, and decision making, it is likely that the enthusiasm for PPM, as a leadership team effort, will lose momentum and soon come to a halt.

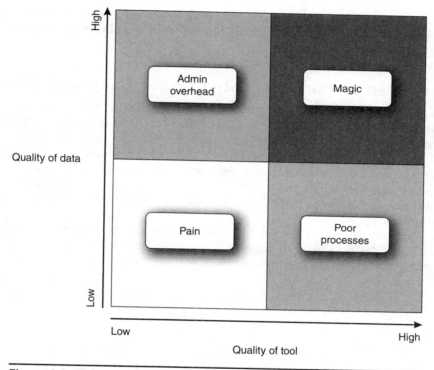

Figure 4.6   Relationship of PPM tools and data

When seeking to improve PPM from a current state of poor data and poor tools to a desired state of good data and good tools, many experts advocate focusing on processes and improving data first. Then, after usage with whatever tools that are already available (which are typically spreadsheets), attention can then be turned to reducing the administrative overhead and the evaluation and selection of the best fit PPM solution. Others advocate immediately working with PPM tool providers and consultants to in essence, partner in the journey and to start the immediate work effort of defining and improving PPM processes and best practices relative to the needs of the business and the features and capabilities of the selected PPM solution. There are merits to both approaches, and the reality is that both views enable an organization to improve the quality of data and tooling. To a great extent, the work effort to improve PPM data and tool functionality is iterative and symbiotic. A commitment to one drives the other.

PPM experts all agree and advise that there is no one right approach or universally correct answer. Some organizations are far more likely to experience PPM success by first addressing PPM best practices; others discover that only until such time as a PPM tool is put in place can capabilities be improved upon.

Be Open to the Possibility of a Big Bang Approach

When is a big bang approach for implementing PPM the right approach to take? How can an organization recover from a failed big bang approach? Do the benefits of a big bang approach outweigh the risks? In this day and age of agile project management and incremental delivery, should a big bang approach even be considered? For many organizations, the answer is, "no" and not because an incremental approach based on phases is necessarily better but because most organizations are not open to the possibility of a big bang approach.

There are many merits to incremental phased-based approaches to implementing PPM. As shown in Figure 4.7, incremental phase-based approaches can help to effectively address resistances to change that come in many forms

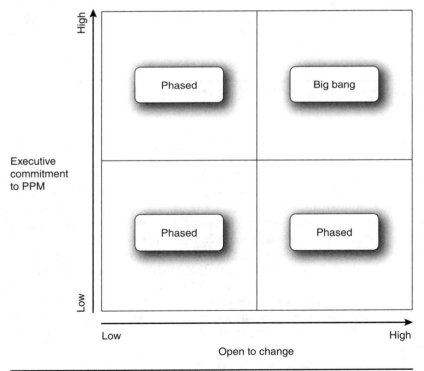

Figure 4.7   Considerations for a big bang approach

as well as levels of executive commitment that may vary among the executive team.

For many practitioners seeking to implement PPM in their organizations, the effort can take on the form of walking upon eggshells. Regrettably, practitioners have to be extra careful because so many involved in the effort can be objectionable, disagreeable, and easily offended. In such an environment, an incremental phase-based approach is all but essential to have any chance of success amid the critics, skeptics, and naysayers. But, how about the organization that has an open mind to change culture and an executive team that is committed, ready, willing, and able to implement PPM? In such an environment, is an incremental phase-based approach a better alternative than a big bang approach? Surprisingly, for PPM, the answer might very well be, "no," for two very simple reasons.

First, unlike many applications that can be rolled out on a departmental basis, adopted by users, and then adopted throughout other parts of the organization, PPM applications, in terms of portfolio management functionality, processes, and capabilities, do not lend themselves particularly well to departmental trials. Of course, some functionality, such as managing projects and resources, can be taken up within just about any department, but this is project management, not PPM. Leadership team functionality, such as using the PPM tool to debate the merits of different portfolio investments, align and optimize investment decisions to the needs of the business, monitor and control all aspects of the process, outcomes, and leadership team participation, behaviors, and capabilities seldom can be rolled out departmentally in any way similar to that of the executive team's actual use.

In fact, deploying a PPM solution at a departmental level with the intent of somehow overcoming lack of executive support might be the quickest way to fail, as PPM at a departmental level is simply not the same. This is in no way meant to discredit departmental or business unit deployments of PPM, but rather to strongly emphasize them, as IT Governance and PPM guru Steve Romero (2010, p. 1) suggests, "Many people argue that PPM is PPM is PPM. I beg to differ. PPM can manifest itself in numerous ways and it comes in many shapes and sizes." Romero goes on to explain that an optimal PPM implementation is one that addresses the business needs that initiated the necessity for PPM in the first place. Therein lies the rub; needs at the departmental level and executive level are seldom the same. Hence, a departmental deployment of PPM, for the purposes of simulating how PPM would work at the enterprise level, may be of little actual value to the executive team.

Secondly, not every business is resistant to change; some businesses have an organizational culture that is open to change. Rather than a resistance-to-change mindset and a reluctance to adopt approaches that may not yet be perfected, continuous improvement oriented organizations recognize and embrace the adoptive nature of applications and best practices. Only with adoption and use can the systems and processes be improved upon. No amount of planning and phased-based rollouts will change the fact that once the system is introduced in terms of tools and processes, the real opportunity for refinement and improvement has just begun. Hence, if the leadership team is already committed to the business value of PPM and the culture of the organization is open to change, a big bang approach enables all involved to participate in quickly planting the seeds of PPM in terms of tools, processes, and capabilities and in nurturing those seeds into fruit bearing trees. In this kind of climate, an incremental phase-based roll out, at best, would slow down the PPM initiative and, at worst, might even put it at risk.

Summary

PPM is not easy. It is hard to understand why so many people within the project management community suggest that it is. Fortunately, all of the leading providers of PPM applications and consulting services have years of experience in helping organizations face and overcome the challenges of change that PPM is sure to bring about. For many, these challenges will be best served with an incremental, phase-based roll out and adoption. This approach will seek to employ such techniques as not overwhelming the organization, use of a gap analysis and proof of concept, tolerating information that is not perfect, allowing sufficient time to get systems in place, and recognizing that data integrity is not a PPM tool issue but rather driven by best practices and demonstrated capabilities. Collectively, these techniques enable an organization to avoid risks, manage uncertainty, and address organizational and individual resistances to change. Additionally, an incremental approach that first achieves success at a departmental level can serve to facilitate leadership team buy-in and support for an enterprise roll out and adoption.

Though rarely advised, there are merits for the consideration of a big bang approach to implementing PPM capabilities. When the executive and leadership teams are firmly committed to establishing PPM tools and processes as a means to improving business effectiveness, when that commitment is not at risk, and when the organization is highly receptive to change as a means of continuous improvement and competitive vitality, a big bang implementation approach fosters a quantum shift way of rapidly transitioning from the existing current state to the desired future state.

In virtually every article or presentation on PPM implementation, the prevailing wisdom is that an incremental, phase-based roll out is far superior to a big bang approach. This wisdom is acquired and based on past experiences of having great difficulties, or even outright failure, with a big bang approach to implementing PPM and managing change. If the big bang approach had a better track record, there would be few proponents of any other strategy. Nonetheless, a big bang approach is always worth considering. Even if it does not does not prove to be the desired approach, the mere consideration of a big bang approach is sure to reveal considerations, factors, and risks that serve to justify specific reasons for, and parameters of, an incremental approach to getting started with PPM.

Questions

1. What is the origin and meaning of the business term *burn the ships?*
2. How does a fixed iteration of time implementation compare and contrast to a phased-based implementation?
3. What is the purpose of a gap analysis?
4. What are the pros and cons of informal assessments and rigorous assessments?
5. What is the purpose of a proof of concept?
6. How does a functional proof of concept compare and contrast to a limited-scope implementation?
7. In what ways does implementing PPM require toleration for information that is not perfect?
8. What characteristics of data must be correct for data to be complete and have integrity?
9. When implementing PPM, is there a universally correct approach for whether a PPM tool or a PPM process framework should first be implemented?
10. Though not typically recommended, in what kind of environment would a big bang approach for implementing PPM be advised?

References

Makleff, Gil. 2005. "Seven Habits of Highly Effective Portfolio Management Implementations." http://www.umt.com.

Merkhofer, Lee. 2008. "Choosing the Wrong Portfolio of Projects, Part 6: Achieving Best-Practice." http://www.prioritysystem.com.

Merkhofer, Lee. 2009. "Implementing Project Portfolio Management." http://www.prioritysystem.com.

Moore, Simon. 2010. *Strategic Project Portfolio Management—Enabling a Productive Organization.* Hoboken, NJ: John Wiley & Sons.

Perry, Mark Price. 2009. *Business Driven PMO Setup—Practical Insights, Techniques and Case Examples for Ensuring Success.* Fort Lauderdale, FL: J. Ross Publishing.

Romero, Steven. 2010. "Who should lead PPM?" http://community.ca.com/blogs/theitgovernanceevangelist.

Showcase #4: PowerSteering Software

PPM Rules of the Road
How a Flexible, Incremental
Approach Accelerates PMO Results

David Boghossian, Founder, PowerSteering Software

Introduction

Paula was leaving the first management review of her company's big bang PPM implementation, and she was in a foul mood. It was her responsibility, and it had been a disaster. The steering committee tried to review the portfolio of projects in real time in the executive conference room, including a list of projects, their status, current milestones, and open issues. "This is a good start" the COO offered encouragingly, "but why can't we also see the financial impact?"

"Uhm, eventually," Paula stammered hesitantly, "I'm pretty sure that we can get the vendor to build any kind of report we want." That sounded like a good answer, but clearly the internal expectation was for more reporting, more flexibility, and more self-sufficiency.

Then suddenly the system froze. "That won't happen," reassured the CIO, "once we get the full production system set up, in about six months." Paula winced. She swore the original plan was six weeks.

Back from the dead, the system was clicking through its paces pretty well. The VP of Strategy wanted to see the list of proposed projects on a matrix of ROI vs. risk. Paula had an answer for that request as well. "We'll get to that in phase 2. In phase 1 we had to start with time sheet data and detailed project tracking." She thought to herself, "*Oh yeah, this is going quite well.*"

"Wait," said the CEO, "where is Project Alpha?" Project Alpha was the most visible project across the organization. The board of directors even knew about it. Marketing, IT, R&D, operations—practically everyone in the company was involved. A huge effort, a huge budget, a huge financial impact on the company, and a huge reporting omission. It wasn't there because it was too big, and many of the teams assigned to Project Alpha were not part of the phase 1 implementation. They were projected to come online in three to six months if Paula could convince them that the new system would support their needs, unique workflow and proprietary methodology. *"Fortunately, I have an updated resume,"* thought Paula.

The effort had started over a year ago with the usual high hopes. Her boss had approached her with a simple request, "We've got to get a better handle on the projects we are doing around here." On further examination, it was clear that he was talking about two pretty basic requirements (1) do the right projects, and (2) do them right. Oh, and by the way, provide visibility and data to show that we are accomplishing those two goals. Simple, right? Apparently not!

Paula had read all the vendor literature on establishing PPM maturity, sat through countless software demos, and practically memorized every word of every analyst report. But in the real world, in her organization, in front of her executive steering committee, it wasn't nearly so black and white. Paula had made a fundamental error assuming that a big important problem required a big, complicated solution.

While PPM on the enterprise scale can be a daunting challenge, for most organizations, successful project selection and execution is a key element in strategy execution. Need to develop new products? A project. Drive down operating costs? More projects. Understand how to manage trade-offs and synergies between these efforts? A project and portfolio management system.

To get to the *all singing, all dancing* version of PPM that many vendors promise and many PMOs imagine is an immense amount of work but, based on our experience implementing PPM for hundreds of world-class companies, it need not be an all or nothing, multi-year, *bet the organization* (or, more important, *bet your career*) effort. Not if you are able to follow a few simple rules that will help you achieve a manageable, phased approach and avoid the risks covered in the previous chapter:

Rule #1: Crawl, Walk, Run

The CIO at Ingersoll Rand called it the *Crack System*. If users like it, he said, they will come back for more. He started with a central group of about fifty users managing portfolios and driving execution in a few departments. Today, two thousands users in virtually every part of the enterprise, managing IT, operational improvement, innovation, mergers, and virtually every other type of project in a single system that allows for unified reporting, trade-offs, and synergies between projects across the organization.

Ingersoll, like nearly all our clients, took a *crawl, walk, run* approach to implementing PPM. Yes, this may sound a lot like the incremental approach you just read about, and it is—with one crucial addition. We would go further and maintain that the optimal state for each organization, or even each part of each organization, is not necessarily a full gallop. In fact, some parts of your organization might be better settling into a comfortable stroll, while others need to sprint on some projects and hold to a brisk walk on others. Flexibility is the key.

Failure to build this kind of flexibility into a PPM system can be a fatal flaw that leaves most of your users unhappy—most of the time. The ability to recognize and accommodate a wide range of needs across a large organization can make the difference between broad enterprise adoption of PPM and rejection.

Crawl, walk, run can operate on several dimensions. Your company may choose to implement specific features first, before turning on others. You might start in a particularly well suited department or group. You might choose a top-down or center-out style of implementation. It is important that your system can support all variations and combinations. Because PowerSteering is a highly configurable, software-as-a-service solution, our clients deploy just the features they need for the people who need them and then expand and extend over time. Perhaps more importantly, our top-down approach of driving projects from objectives and milestones, and leaving the granularity of project-level management up to the individual group or department, allows the organization to focus on the highest-value, most critical benefits of PPM first. It affords each area a sense of independence.

Ingersoll Rand chose an extreme version of the crawl, walk, run approach. They limited the number of users, capabilities, and groups that were implemented at first and built rapidly from there. Other organizations may find that enterprise-wide visibility is the key to success and that detailed resource scheduling can wait. In any case, nearly every organization can benefit from adopting an incremental, continuous improvement oriented approach to PPM.

Rule #2: Begin with the End in Mind

The PMO manager at Boots, the largest pharmacy chain in the United Kingdom, handed us an Excel spreadsheet. "We need to automate this," she said. "It is taking us four weeks of every month to produce." A small but important start, and a few hours later we were able to understand what was essential about the report, how the data was used, where we could make some useful improvements, and configure a system to deliver it at the click of a button. We applied an incremental improvement approach to executive reporting and helped Boots create a much more robust reporting system over time, ultimately adding time tracking for contractors, resource planning capability, and data that allowed her to track service levels and value delivered by her outsourced IT partners. But starting with that single Excel spreadsheet allowed the team to drive a very specific, high-value early success.

In contrast, Paula began with a simple but very broad objective—get a better handle on projects. Given a general goal like this, it might have been a good idea to make use of the *five whys* to establish root cause. Ask the question why five times. Lean practitioners use it to diagnose quality problems, but you can use it to fully understand your objectives. Why do we need to get a handle on projects? To do the right projects. Why? To align people with strategic priorities. Why? To make better use of resources. Why? To better meet our demand. You get the picture.

After five layers of why's, you will have a much clearer picture of what you are trying to accomplish through PPM and you should be a lot *WHY-ser*! The result of this exercise also reveals how critical good projects and good PPM systems are to strategic success. At the end of the exercise, the fundamental reasons will almost always have to do with creating competitive advantage or capitalizing on some other strategic opportunity.

Unfortunately PPM teams (and sometimes providers as well) often forget what they are trying to do and begin to see their PPM system as a bundle of really cool features rather than a means to a specific end. Keeping that end in mind will vastly increase your chance of success. Start with the reporting that your senior executives use to manage the business—a balanced scorecard or other key performance metrics (KPM) and determine how PPM can contribute to this report and provide insight into what is driving results. For every KPM, there is a portfolio of projects designed to move the needle. Are we doing the right projects? Are they being executed effectively? Will the portfolio deliver the improvement of this KPM that we need and expect? PPM executives can monitor critical performance metrics using flexible dashboards like the example in Figure 4.8.

Rule #3: Focus on Capability, Not Maturity

GE Commercial Finance had a classic portfolio issue—lack of visibility—which became painfully obvious when a multi-million dollar project in France went down in flames, forcing a large write-off. The new CIO came to us in August and by September 30 all projects over $50k in value were in the system, and 200 users were using the system to report progress. On October 1, the new CIO used the system to cancel over 15 percent of the projects in his portfolio that were redundant, off-strategy, or poorly defined and doomed to failure. He redeployed personnel, saved millions of dollars, and improved the focus and productivity of his organization by focusing on two very particular capabilities—project selection and portfolio review. Unlike Paula, he wasn't updating his resume, instead he was fielding internal offers!

This kind of focus is surprisingly rare in PPM deployments. We find many organizations that are insistent on improving their *maturity* without ever asking whether level 5 (in CMMI, for example) or any other framework is always the goal, whether the costs and overhead are worth it, and whether the achievement of level 5 will translate into quantifiable business value. These

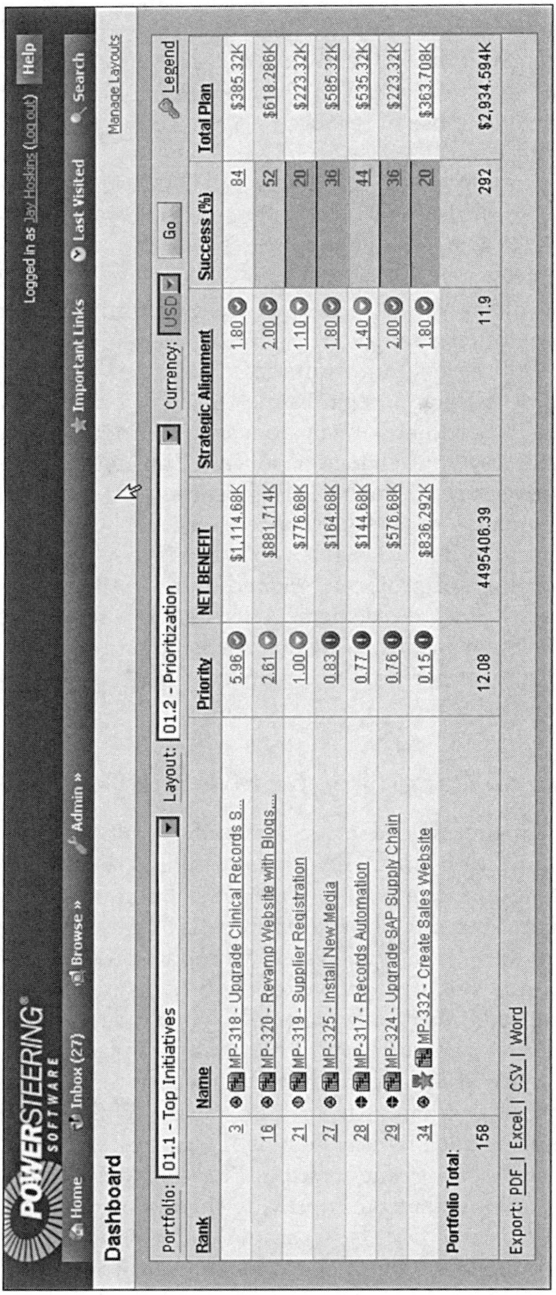

Figure 4.8 PPM executive dashboard

Table 4.1 Benefits by process and capability

	Select projects	Manage portfolio	Improve execution	Optimize resources
Crawl	18%	18%	8%	8%
Walk	11%	11%	5%	5%
Run	7%	7%	3%	3%

companies don't recognize that maturity is driven by many different processes and that improved capability is what they should be focused on to generate sustainable results.

We advise our clients to concentrate on building capability in key processes such as project selection, portfolio governance, project execution, and resource optimization—and focus that effort on the areas that are critical to the organization's success and represent the most improvement upside. We also work hard with clients to determine the right level of capability that balances the benefits with the level of effort. Our experience suggests that different processes and capability levels contribute different potential shares of the total benefit, as shown in Table 4.1.

Interestingly, the biggest chunks of benefits come from the most controllable capabilities, selecting projects and managing the portfolio. It was much easier for GE to identify and eliminate irrelevant or poor performing projects from the portfolio than it would have been to make every manager and team in the organization 15 percent more effective, more strategic, and of higher impact, in a fraction of the time.

Rule #4: Play Leapfrog

Textron had just begun a deployment to over 1000 users. It was a well-focused implementation targeting visibility, results tracking and a standard methodology, but with a very tight timeline—four weeks! The COO told us he wanted the average training time for team members to be *zero hours*—a stretch goal, indeed. Three weeks into this intense process—disaster. Textron announced a corporate restructuring at the deepest level, from six business units to three, with divestitures and planned acquisitions and lots of people changing chairs. Unfortunately, we had configured the data structure of the system the week before into a form that was now completely obsolete. The afternoon of the announcement our client services manager on the case manned two workstations with the client side administrator and together reconfigured the system to reflect the new structure in about three hours—much faster than the reorganization. This kind of enterprise-class flexibility has profound implications for how you can deploy a PPM system.

In the early days of systems development, we all learned not to pave the cow paths. Getting your processes right and then automating them with systems is generally still good advice, but the world has changed since every revision to a system had to be sent down to legions of programmers looking at green screens. All of the changes that our clients commonly need to make to PowerSteering are manageable through the administrator panel including data structure, reports, project methodologies, and custom fields—all configurable by the client.

This enables a continuous improvement approach to systems implementation. Your organization can start with the existing processes—or perhaps an incremental improvement on current processes—and add best practices, tweak methods and phases, and change data fields and reports in real time. Beginning with familiar processes and enhancing them over time greatly increases speed of adoption, ease of use, and ultimately the value of the system.

Many of our clients aspire to implementing a standard methodology for all kinds of projects across the enterprise. However, IT, R&D, operations, and marketing, all have different approaches and different requirements. The ability to start with a range of methodologies and data structures and a somewhat streamlined version of their existing processes allows the organization to build on the strengths of the past, address the weaknesses, and hit the ground running, without having to turn their organization upside down.

Summary

Successful PPM implementations with high customer satisfaction are in the distinct minority as illustrated in this chapter. There are many organizations like Paula's that start out with high hopes and buy the latest technology only to find that it doesn't work for business users outside IT and consequently delivers a fraction of the expected value. If you scope your project using these four principles—(1) crawl, walk, run; (2) focus on results; (3) build capability; and (4) continuously improve—you will find that you can avoid the six risks identified in the previous chapter, deliver better projects faster and more effectively than the competition, satisfy internal stake holders, and delight your customers. PPM is too important, too visible, and too big to fail. So embrace a measured, incremental, yet flexible approach that quickly gets users onboard and wins on the board.

Customer PPM Leadership Profiles

Product Portfolio Management at a Leading Healthcare Provider

A major healthcare organization that offers high-quality, affordable healthcare to 8.6 million members, turned to PowerSteering despite making a significant time, resource and financial investment in an installed, on-premises PPM application. The organization still needed an easy-to-use system to support portfolio management, demand capture, and project scoring.

PowerSteering was selected and implemented in a matter of weeks to work alongside the incumbent system. PowerSteering is used by nearly 150 people in the internet services and website workforce groups to capture new product requests, score and prioritize them, and integrate with the installed system. As shown in Figure 4.9, the business value derived from PowerSteering includes:

- Automated online demand capture (both ideas and product enhancement requests)
- Visibility of the prioritized demand
- Real-time updates and project tracking
- More accurate resource forecasting
- Improved product governance
- Flexible and extensive reporting
- Status reporting, issues, document management, detailed schedule management

Enterprise PPM at Ingersoll Rand

Following a failed *big bang* implementation of a traditional on-premises PPM solution, Ingersoll Rand turned to PowerSteering for top-down portfolio management across the organization. As a $13 billion global industrial company with such diversified brands as Club Car, Hussmann, Schlage, Thermo King, American Standard and Trane, Ingersoll Rand needed a flexible and highly configurable PPM approach that would allow them to introduce the most valuable capabilities in parallel including portfolio governance, project selection, prioritization and measurement processes. PowerSteering was selected as the standard for PPM in IT, HR, their PMO, NPD projects and for merger integration of their recent acquisition of Trane. In the words of Mike Macrie, Vice President of IT Architecture & Strategy, "By having one portfolio management tool, we're able to aggregate the information and provide our executives with

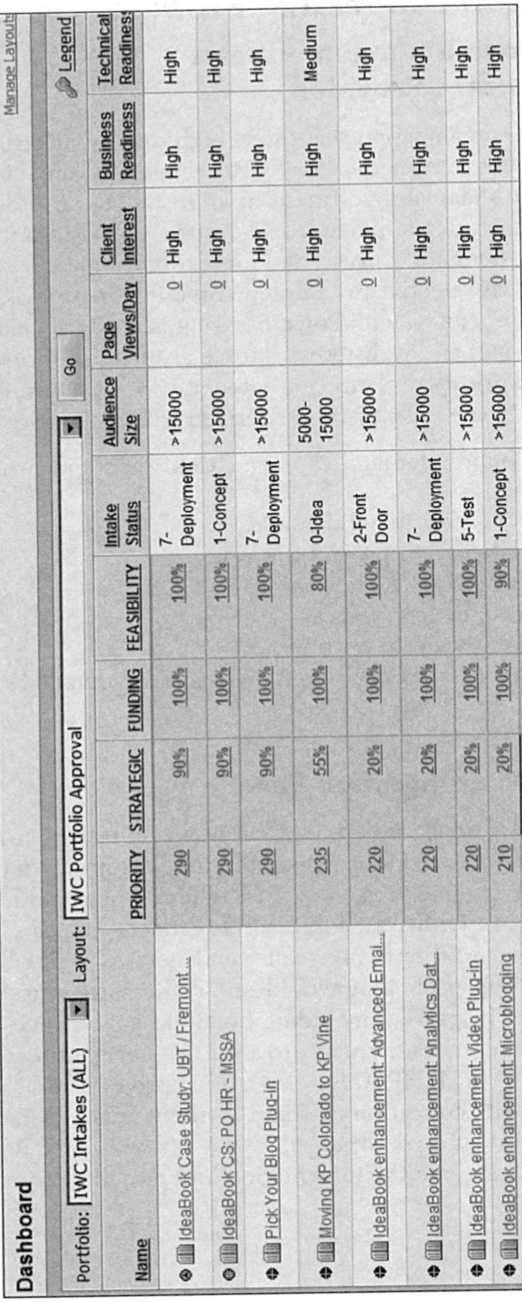

Dashboard

Portfolio: [TWC Intakes (ALL) ▼]   Layout: [TWC Portfolio Approval ▼] [Go]

Manage Layout

🔍 Legend

Name	PRIORITY	STRATEGIC	FUNDING	FEASIBILITY	Intake Status	Audience Size	Page Views/Day	Client Interest	Business Readiness	Technical Readiness
⊗ 📖 IdeaBook Case Study: UBT / Fremont...	290	90%	100%	100%	7-Deployment	>15000	0	High	High	High
⊕ 📖 IdeaBook CS: PO HR - MSSA	290	90%	100%	100%	1-Concept	>15000	0	High	High	High
⊕ 📖 Pick Your Blog Plug-in	290	90%	100%	100%	7-Deployment	>15000	0	High	High	High
⊕ 📖 Moving KP Colorado to KP Vine	235	55%	100%	80%	0-Idea	5000-15000	0	High	High	Medium
⊕ 📖 IdeaBook enhancement Advanced Email...	220	20%	100%	100%	2-Front Door	>15000	0	High	High	High
⊕ 📖 IdeaBook enhancement Analytics Dat...	220	20%	100%	100%	7-Deployment	>15000	0	High	High	High
⊕ 📖 IdeaBook enhancement: Video Plug-in	220	20%	100%	100%	5-Test	>15000	0	High	High	High
⊕ 📖 IdeaBook enhancement Microblogging	210	20%	100%	90%	1-Concept	>15000	0	High	High	High

Figure 4.9   PowerSteering portfolio management dashboard

visibility across any project area to help justify which portfolio investments to fund." Additional PPM capabilities that Ingersoll Rand realized:

◆ Rapid ROI
◆ Better user adoption
◆ Elimination of emails, spreadsheets and phone calls
◆ Streamlined, automated and standardized project management activities
◆ Increased portfolio visibility
◆ Lowered software cost of ownership
◆ Provided ample scalability

The top-down portfolio management allowed Ingersoll Rand to implement the software on their terms and not be required to capture an unreasonable amount of data that the competitive tools required. PowerSteering's SaaS model, flexibility, and configurability, allowed Ingersoll Rand to deploy the software quickly, at a more affordable price, and see immediate value.

5

PPM Risk #5: The Effects of Changing Processes and Measures

Once upon a time in the business world, the word "process" was viewed as a good thing and it invoked images of William Edwards Deming who advocated and made a reality of his conviction that 95 percent of the problem is process, only 5 percent is people. Though typically cited as a manufacturing and quality control expert, Deming and his teachings were actually centered on management principles for transforming business effectiveness. Deming's System of Profound Knowledge consisted of four relatively simple parts:

1. Appreciation of a system, understanding the overall processes
2. Knowledge and causes of variation and techniques of measurement
3. Theory of knowledge, the concepts of knowledge and the limits of what can be known
4. Knowledge of psychology and concepts of human nature. Deming believed that once an individual understood the system of profound knowledge, that individual would set an example, be a good listener, continually teach other people, and help people pull away from his/her current practices and beliefs and move into new, more effective ones

Those who are passionate about processes and measures, like Deming, usually have one after another real life experiences in the business world where adoption and commitment to processes and best practices lead to solving complex business problems, marked and measurable improvements, and business results that are sustained over long periods of time. However, it would be a

Illustration 5.1   PPM comics—process stuff

mistake to assume that passion for processes and best practices is common-place in today's business organizations, departments, and teams. In fact, one is far more likely to find disdain for processes and best practices for a number of reasons. Some of these reasons are of the same old change resistant mind sets, but more of these reasons emanate from bad experiences with processes and best practices as well as the current, and often hijacked, agile religion that more than a few agile enthusiasts erroneously cite as a reason to have no pro-cesses and best practices (project management that is) at all. As humorously depicted in Illustration 5.1, it is not uncommon to find processes, best prac-tices, and metrics being thrown under the bus due to misguided beliefs and understandings of what they actually are.

Understanding Perspectives on Processes and Metrics

Processes and metrics are a means to an end. That's all. In describing processes, business process guru Vadim Kotelnikov (2001, p. 1) advises that the processes are not ends in themselves, rather they help to create and deliver intended outcomes and results that customers care about. In essence, processes repre-sent and offer a structure for action. And in speaking of metrics in their book, *Advanced Project Portfolio Management and the PMO: Multiplying ROI at Warp Speed*, PPM experts Kendall and Rollins (2003, p. 315) quote Eli Goldratt, business management guru and originator of the theory of constraints, "The purpose of a measurement system is to drive the parts to do what is good for the system as a whole." Another perspective of processes and metrics comes from balanced scorecard expert, Howard Rohm (2008, p. 1), "Balanced Score-cards, when developed as strategic planning and management systems, can help align an organization behind a shared vision of success . . . A scorecard is more than a way of keeping score; it is a system, consisting of people, strategy, processes, and technology."

What these experts and many other advocates recognize is that processes and metrics enable an organization to improve on its capabilities and to achieve more predictable and consistent outcomes. For businesses that are truly committed to defining, using, and continually improving on them, processes and metrics enable companies to outperform their competitors and to achieve business results that are only limited by imagination.

Are processes and metrics easy to get right? Are processes and metrics always applied perfectly? Are processes and metrics a solution to every problem or an unknown that an organization faces? Are processes and metrics a guarantee that an organization will be successful? Of course, the answer to all of those questions is, "no." But these answers are not reasons to indict processes and metrics—rather just confirmation that complex systems like PPM are complex, difficult, involve the human element, and take time and effort to get right. To categorically dismiss the importance and value of processes and metrics represents, for most organizations and individuals, a missed business opportunity at best and bad, ineffective business thinking at worst. Nonetheless, a wide variety of perspectives, conceptions, and misconceptions on processes and metrics do exist, often making it a challenge for organizations seeking to more effectively manage the business.

To successfully develop, use, and improve on PPM processes and metrics, it is important to fully understand and appreciate the organizational and individual perspectives that weigh-in, shape, and influence adoption and success. Two useful constructs in understanding these perspectives are maturity models and attitude analysis models.

As a first step to establish, improve, and realize the benefits of PPM processes, best practices, and metrics, it is quite important to understand and acknowledge the true starting point for the journey ahead and it is a journey. When seeking to ascertain their starting point, many people intuitively think of and use the five levels of maturity commonly associated with the Carnegie Mellon University Software Engineering Institute Capability Maturity Model known and referred to as just CMM or CMMI, or the various organizational project management maturity models such as Harold Kerzner's model offered in his book, *Strategic Planning For Project Management Using a Project Management Maturity Model*, or the Project Management Institute (PMI®) standard called OPM3®. All of these models are of tremendous value, but they all overlook and fail to take into consideration one simple fact: just as there are positive levels of maturity, so too are there negative levels of maturity.

Most managers in organizations, especially large organizations, have witnessed firsthand organizational as well as individual negative levels of maturity. At IBM, I experienced this for nearly two decades, first as a willing participant and later as a victim. In my early career, I often enjoyed being a maverick, the first one to object to management processes that were seemingly wrong and out of touch with how real work was done. Of course, at that time my perspective was from that of a first line manager and minion that viewed most business processes and measurements as overly burdensome and time consuming. Only later as an IBM general manager with revenue, profit, and customer satisfaction responsibilities did I come to truly value processes and metrics as a key enabler of rapidly bringing new products to market, effectively growing the business, outcompeting rivals, and achieving higher levels of market share and customer satisfaction.

The concept of negative levels of process maturity is not hard to grasp. In working with a number of Federal Government CIOs and PMO Directors over the last several years, I have come to learn, and first wrote about in my book, *Business Driven PMO Setup: Practical Insights, Techniques and Case Examples for Ensuring Success*, that there is a widely known, somewhat informal, word of mouth process model for negative levels of maturity as depicted in Figure 5.1.

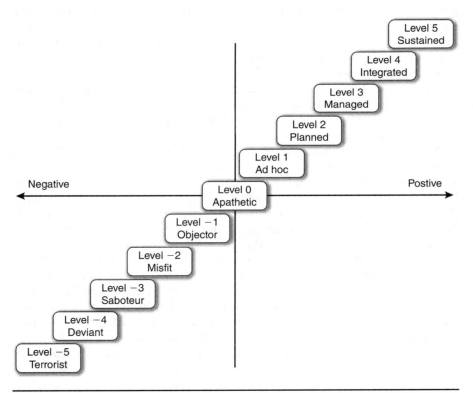

Figure 5.1 Levels of process maturity

Many people recognize and manage to the following positive levels of maturity:

- *Level 1:* Ad Hoc—There are no formal processes, methods, or procedures.
- *Level 2:* Planned—Processes, methods, and procedures do exist within areas of the organization, but they are not considered an organizational standard.
- *Level 3:* Managed—Processes, methods, and procedures exist throughout the organization and they are backed by formal documentation and management support.
- *Level 4:* Integrated—Processes, methods, and procedure are refined along with formal documentation and management support. Metrics are developed and used to collect performance data in support of project performance and proposed refinements.
- *Level 5:* Sustained—Lessons learned, best practices, and improvements are continuously applied. Metrics are used to enable the organization to evaluate capability improvement opportunities.

Also important to recognize and manage are the following negative levels of maturity:

- *Level 0:* Apathetic—There is no cognitive recognition or appreciation for the importance of processes. An apathetic (don't know, don't care) mindset regarding PPM processes, methods, and procedures is prevalent.
- *Level -1:* Conscientious Objector—There are individual and organizational entities that stand in the way of any attempt to change the way they work. The resistance to change is seemingly passive and sometimes not apparent, but in fact, the conscientious objectors can thwart even the best of organizational improvement plans. The conscientious objector has no real preference or "horse in the game" rather they object to whatever ideas and proposals are brought forward typically by making snide comments or suggesting there could be a better way though never offering one.
- *Level -2:* Misfit—Misfits are individuals and organizational entities that are unable to adapt to even the most simple of circumstances. Far worse than conscientious objectors, misfits set back organizational improvement tactics simply by not getting things right. Misfits are hard to work with and are often highly valued individual contributors or brilliant executives who vacillate from genius one day to a much lower form of intelligence and ability the next.
- *Level -3:* Saboteur—Saboteurs engage in sabotage. They take deliberate action to foil the plan. As there is nothing easier to derail than an effort to improve the PPM capabilities of an organization, saboteurs must be recognized for what they are and summarily dealt with. Regrettably,

they are difficult to identify. Saboteurs are much like professional, highly skilled, conscientious objectors who take the art form of derailing organizational change to the highest of levels.

◆ *Level -4:* Deviant—Deviants are usually individuals who are conditioned to diverge from the accepted standard, attaining immense pleasure in doing so. Deviants can be treated, cured, and converted into organizational PPM protagonists where they will heroically support the improvement efforts of the organization. It is widely believed that most process improvement gurus were once deviants who, on seeing the light, found their true calling.

◆ *Level -5:* Terrorist—In the context of PPM, terrorists are not the gun-toting, suicide bombers we hear about on the news; rather they are the ultra-early adopters of technology. They are the ones who seek to implement a technology solution for every problem without first understanding the processes, or lack thereof, and who led you to the set of business problems in the first place. Terrorists implement complex PPM applications but never have the time to plan for it; but they always have the time to do it over and over again. Obsessed with technology for technology's sake, terrorists no longer understand or care about the business that the company conducts and the customers they serve. The resulting problems they cause far more than frustrate the company; they institutionally terrorize it at all levels—employee, manager, executive. Where Deming lived by the motto, "Fix the process, fix the problem," these technology terrorists live by the motto, "Use enough technology, and the problem should go away." The terrorist level of maturity is the most dangerous level.

Evidence of negative levels of process maturity is not hard to find. For example, at the 2010 Scrum Gathering held in Orlando, Florida, I found myself in numerous discussions with agile enthusiasts who were frustrated with their PMOs. One such breakout session was billed as "I want to kill my PMO manager." The war stories of how the PMO worked with the agile development teams left nothing to the imagination, and for good reason, the agile developers were frustrated by a PMO mindset that forced traditional project management processes on those seeking to employ more contemporary and agile techniques such as Agile Scrum. But just as the PMO erred in imposing their view of best practices rather than collaboratively working with the agile development teams, so too did the agile development teams err in their objection to the mere existence of the PMO, not to mention trying to understand and find common ground that both parties could agree on with respect to managing projects and managing the project portfolio.

During one of the passionate breakout sessions, one such scrum master at a leading Fortune 1000 firm commented that their PPM tool and process was a joke. The development team staff simply entered their time as 100 percent utilized at the start of each week and that this was the unwritten truth of how most agile development teams use their PPM tools and participate in the PPM process of the organization. When asked what efforts, if any, were made to work with the PMO, the scrum master loathingly replied that they don't want to work with the PMO, rather they would just like to see the PMO and all of their tools and processes just go away.

In a similar vein, in his article "Five Symptoms of Mechanical Agile," agile enthusiast Daryl Kulak (2010, p. 1) quips, "If you see a best practice by the side of the road, kill it!" Though Kulak goes on to add that you can find a best practice and implement it effectively by taking the time to apply it to your unique situation rather than blindly adopt it as-is. This doesn't change the initial radical hyperbole and negative sentiment towards processes in general that only serves to add fuel to the fire, not put the fire out. Defending the PMO and processes is Glen Alleman (2008, p. 2) who in his article "PMBOK, Agile, and the Need for Theory" comments about the sport of PMBOK and PMI bashing. What seasoned IT, project management, and development veterans like Alleman understand is that processes are essential to maturing execution, improving individual skills and organizational capabilities, and increasing the probability of success.

In addition to maturity models that help to pinpoint the starting point of individuals and organizations with respect to establishing processes and metrics, also helpful in the effort are models and analyses of process biases both good and bad in the form of attitudes and dispositions. There are numerous factors that can contribute to an overall affinity to processes and metrics at one end of the spectrum or a complete disdain for processes and metrics of any kind at the other. Considerations such as position level in the organization, span of control, job duties, degree of specialization, degree to which individual contribution can be measured, degree to which compensation is based on end results achieved, knowledge, experience, and overall business acumen are but just a few of the factors that, in general, shape and influence attitudes toward processes and metrics. As depicted in Figure 5.2, two of these considerations that often directly correspond to and shape attitudes for processes and metrics are the job level of the individual and the degree to which the individual is compensated based on some kind of measurement of end results achieved.

At a high level, a consideration of job level and metrics-based compensation produces a simple 2x2 matrix with four quadrants:

- ◆ Quadrant 1—Highly committed. In this quadrant, the job level is high and the metrics-based compensation is high. An example would be an executive of a large organization who is held accountable for the success of the organization and is compensated based on specific results achieved. Typically, individuals in this quadrant are more inclined to

have an affinity for processes and metrics as processes enable the organization to exhibit higher levels of capability, more predictably achieve
outcomes, and sustain and improve on competitive vitality.

♦ Quadrant 2—Selectively committed. In this quadrant, the job level is
low and the metrics-based compensation is high. One example would
be a commissioned sales rep or sales and marketing manager with performance objectives that drive compensation. Typically, individuals in
this quadrant are selectively committed to processes and metrics. The
processes that help them achieve their compensation-based targets are
adhered to, and continually improved on, as a matter of self-interest.
The processes that may not directly benefit them are likely to be less
enthusiastically and selectively adhered to. It would not be uncommon
to find that a commissioned sales rep is keen to follow any and all processes that help advance a sale or help achieve a quarterly or annual
sales target while at the same time not particularly interested in following processes for sales activity, pipeline management, and forecasting
that may be viewed as bureaucratic overhead.

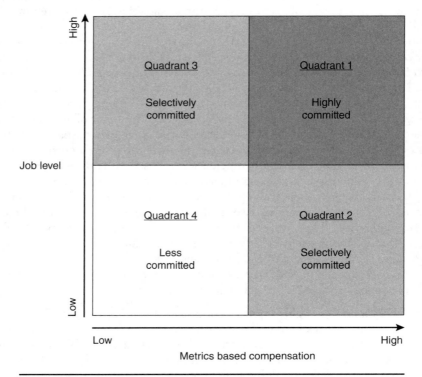

Figure 5.2 Processes and metrics attitude analysis

◆ Quadrant 3—Selectively committed. In this quadrant, the job level is high and the metrics-based compensation is low. An example could be a research and development executive or manager responsible for new product development who might have significant responsibilities by way of job position and level but not necessarily have a highly leveraged, metrics-based compensation plan. It would not be uncommon to find that such executives exhibit affinity for processes and metrics helpful to their own organizations and outcomes while at the same time are luke-warm to other processes and metrics that, though not viewed as particu-larly useful to them, may be of great help and value to other executives and members of the leadership team who have broader responsibilities.

◆ Quadrant 4—Less committed. In this quadrant, the job level is low and the metrics-based compensation is low. Examples of members of this quadrant are vast and could be represented by just about any individual contributor in an organization who is on a fixed salary with little, if any, effective incentive-based compensation. In a PPM context, members of this quadrant could include project team members such as developers, analysts, and support staff. With no responsibilities to manage people or to manage organizational capabilities, and no compensation that is directly tied to achieved and measured outcomes, it would not be un-common to find such knowledge workers, often experts in their fields, to just want to be left alone so that they can accomplish their jobs with minimal interference from others.

In just about any organization seeking to implement PPM, it is not difficult to discover the attitudinal differences to processes and metrics throughout the organization and the challenges that they present to management and the leadership team. At the executive level, members of the leadership team ac-customed to the "squeaky wheel gets the grease" decision-making approach and faring well under the old order, might be resistant to change and a new process and metrics-based approach to PPM. At the individual contributor level, subject matter experts and highly skilled knowledge workers such as software developers may be likely to have zero tolerance, not to mention af-finity, for any kind of PPM processes and metrics that aren't part of their de-velopment principles and work habits. Simply put, the leadership team with responsibility for PPM must understand these attitudes and the effects of changing processes and measures.

The Effects of Changing Processes and Measures

Many PPM experts suggest that PPM is a management activity that is concerned with doing the right projects and doing projects right. Similarly, as defined by the PMI (2008, p. 6) in *The Standard for Portfolio Management*, "The goal of portfolio management is to ensure that the organization is doing the right work, rather than doing work right." At a high level, these definitions are correct and helpful as a starting point in any discussion about PPM. However, for most organizations, PPM soon becomes not just a discussion, theoretical model, or even set of processes and metrics, but a management activity that is all about the management of the change that is required to exhibit better organizational and individual capabilities and to achieve better product of the project outcomes. As shown in Figure 5.3, supporting this management of change perspective is the Office of Government Commerce (2008, p. 1) of Her Majesty's Treasury of the United Kingdom stating, "Portfolio Management is a coordinated collection of strategic processes and decisions that together enable the most effective balance of organizational Change and Business as Usual."

To many, including those at the Office of Government Commerce, the real challenge of PPM is not so much the understanding of what it is in terms of the knowledge areas of a portfolio management standard but rather how to actually do it in terms of the management of change that adopting the standard entails.

Changing Processes and Measures—Bottom-up Evolution

To many people, PPM is viewed to be the result of a natural evolution of project management. As organizations adopt, use, and mature their project management processes, techniques, and best practices at the singular project level, a logical next step for improvement and change is addressing all of the management related activities that span multiple projects and that holistically

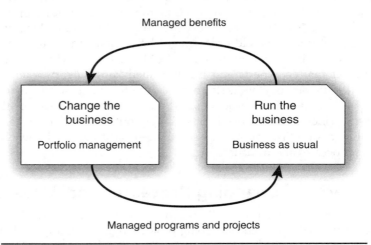

Figure 5.3   Change the business—run the business

take into consideration the needs, priorities, budget, and resources of the organization. This view of PPM is far more than a pompous aggrandizing of the project management profession as some early cynics contended, rather it is a business-driven observation that no matter how well projects are managed at the project level, it is actually quite important to be taking on the right in the first place. As an organization gets better at project management at the single project level, the organization becomes capable of doing much more.

As shown in Figure 5.4, many organizations experience an evolution of changing processes and measures. Immediately, tremendous value is recognized as the organization adopts project management as a best practice. The move from informal project management where projects are often approached and managed ad hoc and as a set of tasks to formal project management and where projects are managed by way of a prescribed best practice, gives integrity to the project effort and creates a project management culture that is cognizant of the project management triple constraints—scope, time, and cost. Just as the processes change, so do the metrics. The traditional spend comparison associated with ad hoc project management gives way to budget vs. actual and earned value analysis and project performance metrics. The benefit of these more accurate measures of project performance for many project types has proven to be invaluable.

Such change, even at this level, although beneficial, is not met without many forms of resistance. There are those who view project management processes,

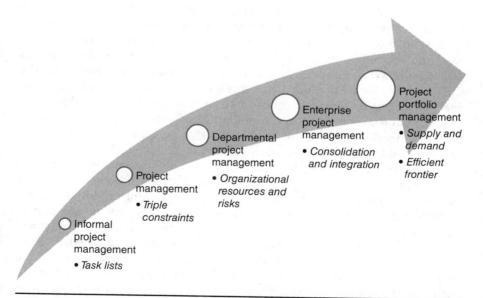

Figure 5.4   Changing processes and measures—bottom-up evolution

forms, tools, and training as time consuming and overly bureaucratic. Not all organizations do an adequate job of establishing effective best practices that provide project management discipline and rigor as well as the much-needed flexibility within structure to accommodate projects of different types and sizes within the project mix.

As the evolution continues, departmental project management, such as IT project management or new product development, quickly brings a focus to resource management and risk management. Resource management often brings about such changes as organizational reporting structure changes, establishment of a shared resource pool, implementation of a project and resource management system, and the development of management best practices, metrics, and policies to drive effective resource management. Resource management truly adds an additional dimension of integrity and complexity to the project efforts of the organization. For resource management to work, all involved must effectively participate in the process, and all cylinders have to be firing. Simply put, this means following the process and using the tools. If but just a few members of the department resist change and do not sufficiently follow the processes or effectively use the resource management tools, it will not be possible to obtain any kind of integrity to the management of projects, resources, and risks.

Enterprise project management (EPM) is often the next destination in the journey. While many people often use the terms EPM and PPM interchangeably, they are actually distinctly different. EPM is concerned with the integration and consolidation of project information at the enterprise level. Though the ultimate goal may be to align enterprise project investments to the strategic objectives of the organization, for many organizations the starting point for EPM and benefits are typically achieved by first obtaining a single view of all of the projects that are currently underway throughout the enterprise. Initially, this view may be a Microsoft Excel spreadsheet work product of a business analyst that inherently is manual and fraught with limitations and difficulties in preparation. Nonetheless, the resulting list of enterprise projects, even if produced manually, reveals tremendous insights into the project mix of the enterprise and opportunities for management.

The lowest hanging fruit for management decision making will be the redundant projects. These are projects that basically have the same product of the project outcome but are being performed by multiple divisions and departments throughout the enterprise. These projects represent an opportunity for consolidation into a program. The overall program will likely be redefined and improved on with some projects being kept and others cancelled. Another area for management decision making will be all of the projects that are in some way interrelated with one another. These projects represent opportunities for both consolidation and integration. Some of these projects will lend themselves to being redefined as a program, others might remain as stand-alone projects but with noted interdependencies or timings that can be better identified and managed.

Collectively, the ability to cancel unnecessary projects and to consolidate and integrate the remaining projects provides the enterprise with tangible benefits ranging from cost avoidance to better management of enterprise programs and projects. This is typically how EPM commences, but not what it is limited to. With the implementation of EPM tools to replace those spreadsheets and EPM processes and metrics to streamline and institutionalize the best practices for both selecting and managing the programs and projects of the enterprise, the leadership team is enabled to make EPM decisions with much better insights and supporting information.

The final leg of the bottom-up evolution is PPM. With EPM core capabilities in place, and often as a prerequisite, the organization is well positioned to formally engage in the management of the project portfolio. This means optimizing the mix and sequencing of proposed projects to best achieve the mission, goals, and objectives of the organization while at the same time being cognizant of management imposed constraints and external real-world factors such as economic and market conditions. As an example, the 2002 acquisition of Compaq greatly influenced HP's management of their project portfolio as did the Florida hurricanes of 2004 influenced the management of the project portfolio of several home owners' insurance providers that, because of weather trends, withdrew entirely from the Florida market.

At this level of evolution, PPM is far more than a million dollar spreadsheet; it is the ability to analyze complex sets of data and to make difficult organizational decisions. Modeling competing project opportunities, producing an efficient frontier analysis of portfolio alternatives, and managing supply and demand at the enterprise level requires far more functionality than a spreadsheet is capable of, even in the hands of a Microsoft Excel black belt. Required for success is a PPM application. Nonetheless, the real challenge of PPM is not just selecting and implementing the best fit PPM tool or even addressing all of the process and policy work that must be undertaken, rather it is the people considerations and resistance to change, especially at the leadership team level.

Commenting on this challenge is Australian PPM expert, Patrick Weaver (2005, p. 15), who writes, "The real challenge is managing the cultural change involved in training senior managers to make appropriate use of the new insights available to them and encouraging project, program, and portfolio management to work with each other in a spirit of openness and trust." Those resistant to change might incorrectly argue that business intuition and expert judgment are being replaced by software tools, processes, and metrics, but in reality it is the business intuition and judgment that is being supported by these things (PPM tools, processes, and metrics) and taken to higher level thought, analysis, and decision making.

Changing Processes and Measures—Top-down Evolution

To other people, PPM is still viewed as the result of a natural evolution but not of project management, rather of strategic business planning and executive decision making. In this context, this evolution starts at the top and drives downward through the organization. As shown in Figure 5.5, PPM is a driver of projects, not the other way around.

Management decision making enables and funds projects. Approved projects are managed according to the project management best practices of the organization, which include project processes and "go-no go" gating throughout the project life span. The product of the project is delivered to the customer and transitioned to operations. And to the extent that it is possible, product of the product benefit realization is quantitatively and qualitatively measured. As PMI Fellow, Harvey Levine (2005, p. 17), writes, "The basic elements of PPM are not new, nor is the environment in which it [PPM] is applied." Levine explains further that what is new is the emergence of PPM as a formally defined business management discipline including both operations management and project management groups.

Many people agree with PPM experts like Levine and find it overly simplistic to suggest that business management activities such as developing organizational strategy, evaluating and selecting project opportunities in support of the strategy, and managing projects through completion and delivery are

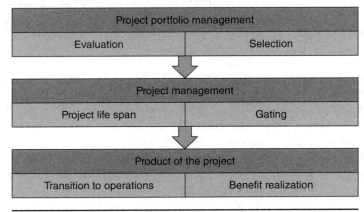

Figure 5.5 Changing processes and measures—top-down evolution

newly discovered techniques. But seasoned executives are not irritated or put off with the notion that PPM is some kind of new management technique, rather they welcome efforts to establish standards for it and they seek to embrace new tools and technologies that make analysis, decision making, and strategy execution easier and more effective to do. And in this context, one could argue that PPM is new in terms of being an accepted and formal discipline that is supported by industry standard best practices and metrics, newly developed technologies and applications, defined and accepted maturity models, and independent market research validating its value.

Summary

By its very nature, PPM involves a considerable amount of management of change. While one would expect that processes and metrics would be a key enabler of change, there are numerous factors that continue to make individuals and organizations resistant to it. Prior to any effort to introduce PPM to an organization, it is imperative to assess and truly understand the individual and organization perspectives on processes and metrics. The use of maturity models and an examination of attitudes and aptitudes for processes and metrics can help reveal numerous types of resistances that must be addressed for PPM to have a chance at success.

Adding to this challenge is the evolutionary aspect of PPM. At one level, this presents problems because of the fact that natural evolution, as well as planned maturity, involves a steady state of change as processes become more business-driven and agile and as measurements become more effective and real. Additionally, not all individuals and organizations mature at the same pace. This presents a real and pressing processes and metrics problem. On the one hand, you might have a new PMO seeking to establish project and portfolio management best practices aligned to, but one approach for selecting projects and managing project related work. This is often a reflection of a PMO that has yet to mature its set of best practices and policies for managing projects of different sizes and types. At the same time, a mature software development organization may already be adhering to the latest in advanced, agile-driven principles and techniques such as agile scrum. Naturally, a management decision to force traditional project management methods, tools, and reports on the development team, as opposed to jointly determining the most suitable going forward approach for both organizations, will certainly be met with resistance and possibly met with outright hostility.

The fact of the matter is that all organizations already have processes and metrics for portfolio management, project management, and software development. Absence of a defined, mutually agreed on, accessible, usable, and auditable process and set of metrics does not mean that they do not exist; rather that they exist in a low form and level of maturity. If the approach to the effort varies with the wind, and the measurement is but a mere feeling in the gut, then that is the process and metric. The only sensible debate isn't whether or not processes and metrics exist, rather what the processes and metrics should be and how the processes and metrics should change with time. As always, organizations that have had that debate and have met the challenges of PPM processes and metrics and the individual and organizational change that they entail are likely to exhibit higher levels of capability, achieve better PPM outcomes, and outcompete those that haven't.

Questions

1. What are the four parts of Deming's System of Profound Knowledge?
2. What are the five positive levels of process maturity?
3. What are the five negative levels of process maturity?
4. What level of maturity would a person be who advocates, "If you see a best practice by the side of the road, kill it"?
5. Why might certain groups in an organization such as software developers have a resistance to PPM tools and best practices?
6. What are examples of factors that influence attitudes towards processes and metrics?
7. How might job level and metrics-based compensation influence attitudes towards processes and metrics?
8. In what ways are changing processes and measures for PPM a bottom-up evolution?
9. From an evolutionary perspective, how is enterprise project management different from project portfolio management?
10. In what ways are changing processes and measures for PPM a top-down evolution?

References

Alleman, Glen. 2008. "PMBOK, Agile, and the Need for Theory." http://herdingcats.typepad.com.

Kendall, Gerald, and Steven Rollins. 2003. *Advanced Project Portfolio Management and the PMO: Multiplying ROI at Warp Speed*. Fort Lauderdale, FL: International Institute for Learning and J. Ross Publishing.

Kotelnikov, Vadim. 2001. "Business Processes." http://www.1000advices.com.

Kulak, Daryl. 2010. "Five Symptoms of Mechanical Agile." http://www.methodsandtools.com. Project Management Institute. 2008. *The Standard for Portfolio Management*. PMI. Newton Square, Pennsylvania.

Levine, Harvey A. 2005. *Project Portfolio Management—A Practical Guide to Selecting Projects, Managing Portfolios, and Maximizing Benefits.* San Francisco, CA: Josey-Bass.

Rohm, Howard. 2008. "Using the Balanced Scorecard to Align Your Organization." http://www.balancedscorecard.org.

The Office of Government Commerce. 2008. "Portfolio Management Guide." http://www.ogc.gov.uk.

Weaver, Patrick. 2005. "Effective Project Governance—The Tools for Success." http://www.mosaicprojects.com.au.

Showcase #5: Planview

The Effects of Changing Processes and Measures

Terry Doerscher, Vice President, Chief Process Architect, Planview

Introduction

Implementing most forms of portfolio management is about improving how your organization measures operational performance and manages change. Objectives for the initiative are usually associated in some way with increasing the level of confidence in your change management decisions and improving the effectiveness and efficiency of how those decisions are acted upon. As a result, the supporting information and measures you use, and the processes you employ, are necessarily affected by a PPM initiative—it is simply a matter of degree.

Preparing and guiding the various stakeholder groups to adopt and apply these changes in a way that actually realizes the added value you set out to achieve is one of the most routinely underestimated, yet debilitating, risks to successful PPM implementation. Drawing on experience gleaned from hundreds of PPM deployments, a consistent observation is that project team members and sponsors tend to naturally focus on those aspects of the project that they understand the best—most commonly, the technological elements of deploying a new supporting application and the functional design of target processes. Managing the cultural aspects of change is usually not a primary concern (or core competency) of the implementation team or sponsors.

However, the use of processes and measures goes to the essence of how an organization interacts at a humanistic level. And the cultural consequences of making changes to PPM-related processes and measures are often pervasive, whether intended or otherwise. These changes have the potential to impact how you interact with your customers, develop strategies, make investment decisions, allocate and manage demand and capacity, and plan and perform your work. As we illustrated in *Taming Change with Portfolio Management*, all of these functions are interrelated; even a seemingly contained scope of implementation can have unanticipated consequences that ripple through the entire cycle of change.

In practical terms, the cultural and social impact of changing processes and measures is a high probability, high impact risk to a successful PPM implementation. Integrating the human aspects of change management as a core component of your overall planning and execution of the initiative will do much to mitigate this risk and help you to realize the immense potential that portfolio management offers. The subject of how to manage cultural change related to deploying and using portfolio management is complex and multi-dimensional. A full exploration would rightfully fill a book on its own and would include topics such as communications, setting new expectations and promoting accountability, adjusting to new levels of organizational transparency, handling informal influencers, the role of the sponsor, conducting effective pilots, adult learning methods, and ongoing skills development, just to name a few. However, situational leadership is one particular technique that we want to explore as an effective method of mitigating PPM Risk #5. It is particularly useful because it can be applied throughout the life of the initiative to support all of these topics, as well as to provide an overall perspective of how changing processes and measures affect different stakeholders at different times.

Adapting Leadership Methods to Change Dynamics

Specific to its use as part of a PPM initiative, *situational leadership* is the practice of applying different management approaches and techniques that are most appropriate for the changing dynamics that occur as you proceed through your implementation. Situational leadership is particularly useful for helping to manage organizational change. PPM implementation typically follows a well-understood maturity cycle, allowing you to adjust how you collaborate with different constituent groups, as well as to anticipate and defuse a few known danger zones along the way.

The concept of situational leadership was formally codified in the mid-1970s by Paul Heresy and Ken Blanchard, however, we routinely apply the general practice as a basic aspect of human interaction. For example, you naturally adjust how you communicate with co-workers based on their relative experience and skill sets, their role within the organization, and according to your level of personal familiarity.

To demonstrate how you can apply this practice in conjunction with managing changes that result from a PPM initiative, we will consider four basic forms of leadership behavior:

- Directive
- Coaching
- Supportive
- Delegation

Directive behavior is the most aggressive form of leadership interaction; it is characterized by setting clear expectations for others to follow. For example, once a decision is made to implement portfolio management, an executive might call a meeting of key stakeholders to communicate that decision, establish specific objectives, and assign responsibilities for the initiative. A training instructor might direct students to perform a defined sequence of actions to accomplish a specific function. Directive behaviors are most successful when followers are willing to be led.

Coaching leadership offers a combination of both direction and encouragement to build on a foundation of existing capabilities while facilitating a specific approach or outcome. No doubt readers are familiar with the coaching leadership style from sports and other activities. A good coach builds self-confidence as he improves skills.

Supportive leadership involves reinforcing or restoring confidence and faith in the direction being taken or approaches that are being used. Supportive behavior can help others through a rough patch or mitigate periods of doubt.

Delegation is the most passive form of leadership. It reflects confidence that others have both the skills and motivation to achieve expected outcomes and is applied to signal that a given change has matured to a functional level.

Each of these leadership styles provides a preferred approach based on the different circumstances that are present at any time. Two key stakeholder attributes that vary significantly over the course of a PPM implementation are competence and commitment.

Competence and Commitment

The levels of competence and commitment that people exhibit are primary indicators of their general capability, either as individuals or as a collective group. Both of these elements are necessary to achieve intended results. Having the skills and aptitude necessary to perform a certain task is of little use if the individual is unwilling to apply them. Conversely, while enthusiasm is always welcome, it alone is of little value unless a functional degree of competence is also present. Perhaps more so than any other traits, the ability of each of the primary stakeholder groups to demonstrate appropriate levels of competence and commitment are prerequisite to accomplishing the objectives of your PPM program.

As the initiative progresses through its various stages, different levels of competence and commitment are often reflected in the attitudes that people display. For example, at the onset of your PPM endeavor, attitudes of excitement and hope may reflect a high level of commitment to the new program. However, they are also indicative of low levels of competency; you do not yet know what you do not know! Conversely, you may have also witnessed how teams can sometimes suffer a loss in morale once they are deep into a project. Perceived competence levels steadily increase as a result of greater familiarity with the work but as the sobering realities of the initiative becomes more apparent, it has the effect of extinguishing any lingering unrealistic optimism. This can dampen their commitment to reaching a successful conclusion.

Table 5.1 Leadership approaches

Attitude	Knowledge and buy-in	Leadership approach
Unrealistic optimism, hope	Low competence High commitment	Direct
Informed permission	Some competence Low commitment	Coach
Realistic acceptance	Low competence Variable commitment	Support
Informed optimism	High competence High commitment	Delegate

With all of this in mind, application of the leadership behaviors identified in the preceding discussion can be mapped as to how they are used to address varying levels of competence and commitment of stakeholders, as reflected by their attitudes. These relationships are shown in Table 5.1.

Mapping Leadership Approaches to PPM Implementation Phases

The next element of applying situational leadership to reduce the risk of changing measures and processes is to map how different attitudes, levels of commitment, and differences in competency relate to different phases of your PPM deployment. For purposes of this discussion, we will describe a PPM implementation using five general phases: concept, design, development, deployment, and operation. These phases represent shifts in the levels of competency and commitment for each different stakeholder group. For example, a profile of the competency and commitment of the project implementation team might look like the one shown in Figure 5.6.

As pointed out earlier, those involved in the earliest stage of the initiative will most likely display some degree of unrealistic enthusiasm or hope, depending on levels of commitment and confidence. For example, if you are procuring a PPM software system as part of your initiative, the selection team will probably feel confident about what the solution offers and in their choice of a vendor to partner with. The sponsors will express optimism over funding the investment and eagerly anticipate positive results. The project manager will probably be excited to get started with the initiative as the implementation team is selected and initial plans are drawn. At a more distant level, outside stakeholders will feel hopeful now that a decision has been reached to move forward. End users may feel relieved that better tools and processes are on the horizon. The conceptual stage is, for all intents and purposes, the honeymoon phase of the program—commitment is high, and attitudes are almost euphoric.

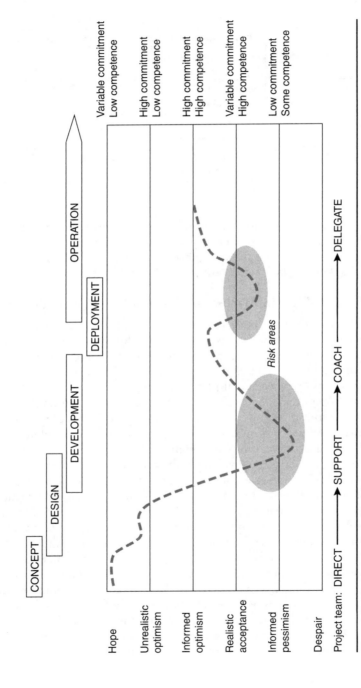

Figure 5.6   A typical profile of the project team over the phases of a PPM implementation

It is equally likely that, with the exception of a few individuals who might have direct prior relevant experience with PPM implementation, general levels of organizational competency specific to the initiative are quite low. For example, ability to configure or use a new software system, understanding of how process improvements need to be designed and integrated with the technology, and awareness of the cultural implications of the implementation are all knowledge areas that will only be developed as work progresses.

During the initial phase of the implementation, do not be surprised to find that the leading vendor consultant or system integrator is being direct with the project manager, the sponsor, and the team in the leadership approach. The consultant is likely working to channel all of the early enthusiasm into a proven implementation approach to ensure the initiative gets started on the right path. This is where you need to have a good deal of trust and confidence in your chosen partner. A high-quality solution provider will supply a solid implementation framework and level of leadership that reflects many years of related experience to fill in your initial competency gap. Think of your implementation consultant as your harbor pilot; their job is to initially steer the implementation into safer waters. Although it may seem uncomfortable at first, it is important that you have enough confidence in your expert advisor that you allow him to lead you early in the process.

As the initiative moves forward into the design and development phases, all of the implementation details will begin to emerge as real work that needs to be done. An initial process assessment might reveal a current level of organizational capability far below internal perceptions. The project team will be quickly immersed in new terms and capabilities and will face a large number of decisions about the implementation, from how to define and structure various forms of information to how to accommodate different stakeholder needs. Some details of the software functionality may not match prior assumptions. Technical or performance issues might arise. The vision of a comprehensive solution will collide with the need to control implementation scope within the capacities that are available. And the team will begin to realize that the degree of near term improvement that is realistically achievable is inherently constrained by the current process maturity level of the organization.

Other challenges during this period will include reconciling detailed design and development of reports and dashboards with available information, making trade-off decisions between ease of use and more sophisticated options, dealing with time and budget pressures, and a host of other unanticipated issues.

For the project team and functional sponsor, this is perhaps the most challenging period of the implementation. The team has developed enough competency and knowledge to clearly grasp the magnitude of the undertaking, and if not well-prepared, they can find themselves getting overwhelmed and disheartened. This is where a more supportive leadership style is applied to help motivate the team to continue to press forward. We have seen a few instances where implementing organizations simply weren't prepared to implement, either in ability to provide enough support or leadership, or in terms of not being culturally ready to make the transition to more structured and consistent management approaches. In those rare cases, the PPM implementation stalls in mid-development, placing it in jeopardy of simply fading away. We show this period in Figure 5.6 as the first of two risk areas, as attitudes of informed pessimism reflect some level of competency but potentially not much commitment.

It is important that the engagement consultant, sponsors, and project manager realize the potential for this situation to arise and be prepared to provide the necessary motivation to move development activities forward. Revisit the scope of work, compared to the capabilities of the team, and be prepared to reset expectations or provide additional support if necessary.

The vast majority of implementation initiatives are able to work their way through the development process and begin to see the light at the end of the tunnel. Using a coaching leadership model will continue to build skills and knowledge levels, and members will reestablish their commitment to the initiative as attitudes shift to accept the realities of the project. Once the majority of the development effort is complete and the team begins to see the results of their effort in the form of testing and preparing to deploy tangible improvements, it is not unusual to see attitudes improve further. Again, referring to Figure 5.6, the project team now has developed new skills and confidence in their own abilities, and they are able to recognize the value in what has been accomplished.

At this point, it is crucial to recognize that the levels of commitment and competence of the implementation team, while important to the PPM solution, are not highly relevant in an operational sense. The team represents only a handful of users compared to the hundreds, or perhaps even thousands, of people who will ultimately deploy the new processes, tools and measures. It is also important to understand that the project team is weeks, if not months, ahead of those end users who will also undergo changes in their own levels of commitment and competency with the PPM solution, as shown in Figure 5.7. As a result, the project team may again be tested during the initial deployment and operation phases.

As each group of end users is exposed to the new PPM solution and receives basic training, it is not uncommon to see general attitudes initially plummet, for a few reasons. First, general stakeholder expectations for the system are typically inflated by internal marketing and communications associated with the initiative, while the magnitude of change associated with implementing PPM is downplayed. Second, as is the case with nearly any type of change, new processes and tools will at first seem awkward and unfamiliar, thus creating frustration and stress. Third, the vast majority of PPM implementations result

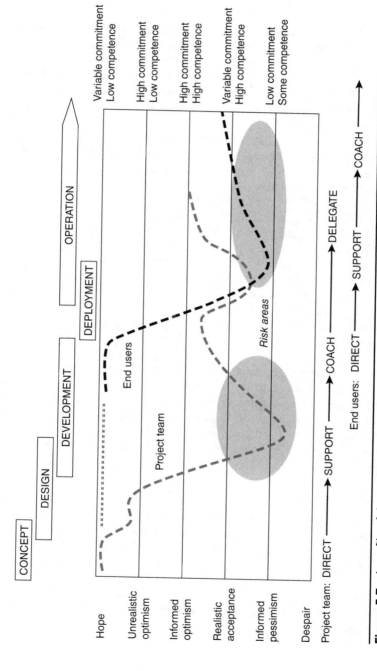

Figure 5.7   A profile of the end users during initial deployment and operation of the PPM system

in changing expectations and developing new behaviors among the affected groups, which is usually perceived as additional workload.

Predictably, this will dampen the attitudes of the project team. Their familiarity with the solution and pride of development will collide with the relatively low competency levels of first-time users who may question the design (or necessity) of the end result. In some cases, user feedback may result in making significant adjustments to processes, software configuration, etc. This can extend the deployment timeline and lengthen the project, which will have an effect on the team as well as end users.

At this point, it is easy to see that the entire leadership team, including the sponsor, project manager, consultants, training staff, and managers of end user groups, needs to be keenly aware of the competency and commitment levels of each constituent group they interact with so they can adjust their approach. The project team will need additional support and coaching, end users will need to be directed on how to apply the solution and then coached to build their skills, and line managers will need support to help them see the value that will be gained.

Assuming that a functional solution has been provided, you should see a steady increase in both competency and commitment over a period of several weeks. By then, the project team will have reached a point where they can see progress being made, while their own skill sets are sharpened by interacting with and coaching the end user groups. They have reached the point where leadership authority can be delegated to them to continue to support initial operations or to close out the implementation project.

End users will lose their initial anxiety as they become more confident in their own abilities with the new solution. Continued coaching and support from their respective managers over the first few months is critically important to firmly establish new norms and proper behaviors. If all goes well, all of this change ultimately results in the availability of new types of information and operational insights that will profoundly affect yet another group of constituents.

Managing with New Information and Measures

We will refer to those who use the information extracted from the solution to make strategic or operational decisions but are not directly involved with the tactical aspects of PPM implementation or use, collectively, as "external stakeholders." These include senior managers and executives, and in some cases, such as when implementing PPM in an IT department, representatives or liaisons for internal customers. This group of constituents, like those previously discussed, will also experience different levels of commitment and competency, as the example in Figure 5.8 illustrates.

Even among more mature and sophisticated organizations, the effects of new information and measures on the senior management team are rarely adequately anticipated. Most organizations pursue a PPM initiative as a top-down strategy to alleviate one or more chronic and significant management issues. Symptoms usually include inability to accurately manage demand and capacities, a reactive work environment, lack of visibility into actual value or results, and poor project performance in the form of missed delivery dates, low quality, and cost overruns. There are underlying problems, but current methods and tools are making it difficult to find, understand, and resolve the root causes. Sometimes, abruptly exposing operational realities with new information and measures can be the most surprising challenge of a PPM implementation.

To explain this phenomenon, consider the analogy of being deep in a dark cave. Visibility is extremely limited. Cobwebs brush against your face. The floor is slippery. You hear rustling sounds not too far away. Occasionally, something drips on your head. All things considered, there is a palpable sense of anxiety over your situation, yet the specific nature of your concerns cannot be defined. Exposing the information gained during the first few months of PPM operation can be comparable to turning on the lights in the cave—and sometimes the true nature of what is found can be more traumatic than dealing with the unknown.

The senior stakeholders—those who will need to address newly identified challenges and opportunities—are as vulnerable to making cultural adjustments as any other constituent group. I still vividly recall an event that occurred early in my first PPM implementation as a PMO manager; the department head physically threw the first resource utilization report out his office door and into the hallway in disgust and disbelief. Much like the newly lighted cave, the initial response to specific operational information might include shock or skepticism.

One of the first obstacles to overcome during initial implementation is to establish the credibility of the resulting information. Because this information has a high likelihood to paint a different picture compared to assumptions, you should expect initial reports and measures to be carefully scrutinized and heavily questioned by external stakeholders. In addition to being a perfectly natural response, it is often warranted. It is also how the leadership team raises their level of competency, by gaining a better understanding of how information is collected and interpreted.

Bear in mind that early PPM data can be riddled with questionable inputs as end users work through their own initial learning curve, so it is incumbent on the PMO or other responsible party to ensure that initial reports communicate rational results. It is much better to delay initial reporting than it is to publish suspicious or knowingly erroneous information. Once the credibility of system information is called into question, it is difficult to restore trust and support.

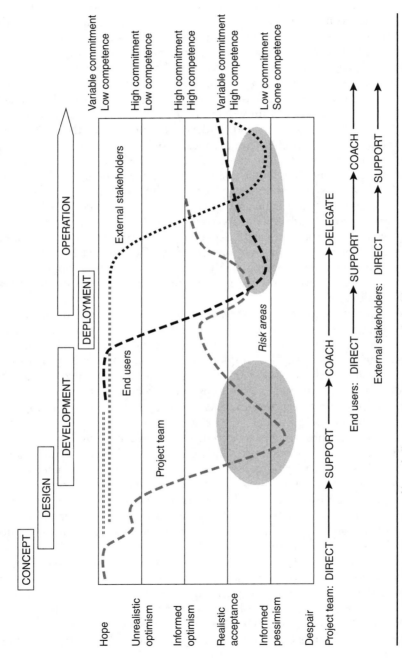

Figure 5.8   Constituent profiles of all major PPM system stakeholder groups

After the true nature of your work and resources is quantified, presented, and accepted, the next phase of the implementation is to analyze the situation and determine what actions are to be taken. Since that information can sometimes offer an opportunity-rich environment to make improvements, there is the potential for an organization to become overwhelmed and to freeze up with inaction. We call this situation "observation to failure." The leadership team continues to review measures and various trends but cannot reach consensus on how to best respond to make strategic (or even incremental) improvements.

All of these considerations will affect how you should interact with this critical stakeholder group. Since that highly directive behavior will likely not be an option, those responsible for championing the initiative will need to patiently coach and support senior management through their initial exposure to PPM results. Providing analytical interpretations and specific recommendations on suggested next actions will help to bolster their confidence, skills, and commitment to the program.

Incorporating Situational Analysis into Your PPM Program

The concepts presented here were developed as a way to assist and inform project teams, implementation consultants and sponsors in response to commonly observed issues across many different PPM implementations. In the field, they have proven useful to prepare the organization for what will occur over the course of the implementation—forewarned is forearmed. On a number of occasions, when the project team was in the mid-development risk zone, simply pulling out a copy of Figure 5.6 and reminding the team that we had talked about this, and that it is not an unexpected situation, helped them to recognize that this too shall pass and aided in bolstering spirits.

In our experience, you cannot over-emphasize the importance of systematically managing the cultural implications of a PPM initiative. If you are fortunate enough to have a group within your organization that specializes in assisting in this area, you would be wise to integrate their support into your overall project plan. There are also consulting groups that specialize in this area; in several large PPM implementations, customers have remarked that getting this kind of support was one of the most important aspects of ensuring their success. Even if you do not have access to specific organizational change management resources, it would be wise to designate one of the team members to specifically focus on addressing this area of the project.

As these concepts illustrate, it is important that communications with all stakeholder groups be forthright and realistic; creating overly optimistic expectations for results or masking the level of commitment that will be needed by those involved will eventually prove to be problematic.

Vendors can provide you with all of the technology that money can buy. Process architects can develop and automate highly sophisticated approaches to accomplish any type of business function. But, ultimately, it is the ability of the organization to accept, adopt, and assimilate change that is often the most limiting factor in how much you can accomplish with any given phase of your PPM implementation.

Changing the Approach to PPM

*Nayan Patel and Lenore Caudle, Portfolio
Management, Baylor Health Care System*

Baylor Health Care System is a non-profit organization located in the Dallas/
Fort Worth area and is comprised of 25 affiliated hospitals. With $3.4 Billion
in total operating revenue, 20,000 employees, 4,500 physicians and 120,000
admissions per year; it is a daunting task to track just the Information Technology (IT) projects necessary to keep this system moving forward. In 2005,
Baylor implemented their first Project Management Office PMO to track IT
projects. Their IT department, consisting of over 350 resources and an unknown number of projects, had no project management Methodology or formal governance project approval process. Similar to many other organizations,
they operated on the squeaky wheel philosophy that resulted in inefficient
operations.

Without any existing PMO processes, they were still able to purchase a
portfolio management tool. This decision was backed by upper level executive stakeholders but there was little input from the mid-management level
stakeholders. The tool was installed, and they proceeded to gather project information using an interviewing process—talking to resources and managers
about what was being worked on. The projects were entered into the tool, and
a single time reporting bucket was created in each project. Project Managers
were trained how to enter basic project data elements. Other training on how
to report time was also conducted. Processes and templates were created, but
it became apparent that they were too complex, and without the governance
to support the process, this initial PMO did not experience the success they
had envisioned. The PMO decided they needed to step back and re-evaluate
the implementation.

Second Rollout

The second implementation of the PMO process at Baylor had to include
some of the elements of the first rollout while considering the lessons learned.
One major requirement was the support of the executive stakeholders. Having learned that they would be unsuccessful with only that support, the PMO
re-branded itself as an enterprise portfolio management entity and included
much more input from the middle management.

The decision was made to use the existing tool. A new governance process for approving and entering projects into the system was developed and
existing projects were grandfathered into this process. The new simplified

methodology included only the Gates 0 and 1 components of request and charter. This was later expanded into Gates 2, 3, and 4 for scope of work, Go-live, and sign off. Data collection was limited to a small set of data elements (listed at the end of this paragraph) and a weekly communication strategy for distributing project status reports was implemented. A major factor for the success of this communication strategy was that the process was embraced by the CIO through his constant referral to the weekly project summary report.

Data elements collected:

- Project name (work more than 40 hours effort)
- Basic stakeholders
- Start/finish date
- Percent complete
- Single project cost

While time reported had been a part of the first implementation, it was not consistent and departments were not made accountable, thus, mandated weekly time reporting was implemented and communicated. Reports were developed and distributed to validate compliance.

A significant part of the second rollout came nearly two years later with the participation of the financial department. Over time, they started to ask about the project methodology, including what data elements were being collected. After reviewing the reports, they saw how the data in this central repository would add to the systems already in place. So while some of the financial components of the project management tool had not been used up to this point, requirements were defined to enhance the information currently provided.

Reports

Report development was a key component to the success of the EPM process re-implementation. Customized reports were designed to be consistent with the look of the project management tool. The EPM department felt this continuity would improve the acceptance of the new processes and methodology. One of the elements used in the reports was to make them look professional and present the data in a visual manner that was easy to comprehend. This was done by using conditional formatting to clearly highlight projects that needed attention. The reports are pushed out via emails and SharePoint links. Many reports are scheduled, but customers also request ad hoc queries. Over thirty reports for resource time, project time, project summary, status, budget, and governance are available. Shown in Figure 5.9 is an application screenshot of a sample report.

ID	Project name	Sponsor	BIS director	Project manager	Project stage	BIS estimated cost	Customer estimated cost	BIS estimated hrs	Rported hrs	% of est. hrs	Sched. finish date	% Comp
05672	Ambulatory EHR	Nancy S.	Alice S.	John L.	Initiation	Labor Only	$180,113	1116	610	55	6/30/10	35 %
06616	ANSI X12 5010 implementation	Donna C.	Michael P.	Neil A.	Initiation				2		7/26/10	2 %
05590	ARMS upgrade	Steve B.	Joe C.	Sam T.	Planning	Labor Only	$8,001	319	264	83	6/18/10	97 %
03757	Cancer center	Liz N.	Alice S.	John L.	Planning	Labor Only	$1,000,000	3963	1648	42	5/6/11	61 %
05806	Cath lab expansion	Joe W.	Michael P.	George F.	Initiation	$757,000	$0	3260	1346	41	1/14/11	27 %
04577	Phase 2: IT asset management	Steve B.	Alice S.	John L.	Execution	$250,000	$848,818	6000	6062	101	6/25/10	94 %
06297	Core SL 100 phone switch	Robert T.	Robert T.	Brian P.	Initiation	1.650.000	$0	652	18	3		100 %
04811	Desktop messaging	Joe W.	Pete S.	Robert R.	Execution	$570,000	$0	1190	924	78		100 %
06367	Patient preregistration	Michelle L.	Gregg L.	John H.	Initiation	$180,150	$0	618				0 %
06180	Perioperative documentation	Robert T.	Robert T.	John W.	Initiation	$813,484	$0	313				0 %
05844	Platform upgrade	Steve B.	Alice S.	John L.	Initiation	Labor Only		40	15	36	5/31/10	10 %
03335	RIS implementation	Nancy M.	Leslie A.	Linda M.	Execution	$157,000	$0	10,000	53,402	534	12/8/09	12 %
06168	Software implementation	Liz N.	Alice S.	John L.	Initiation	$156,188	$871,600	3250	689	21	8/9/10	10 %

Figure 5.9 EPM sample report

Successes

By changing the approach to project and portfolio management and continuously communicating the governance process, the image of IT being a black hole has been changed to one of being a productive and contributing departmental member of the hospital community. The level of trust the hospital staff has of IT is steadily increasing. Data accuracy is better, leading to an increase in the level of trust in the information provided by the PMO.

How to Build Your Own Successful PMO

Building a successful PMO is not an easy task, and it is not built in a short amount of time. There is a lot of culture change that has to be considered, as well as process change management. Management must see the value of the portfolio system. The Baylor system is both a project and a portfolio management system and was defined and supported by the CIO. You must define your requirements and objectives—then re-evaluate those requirements. You will probably find that they are much too complex. Changing the goals to the basic KISS principle of *keep it simple somehow* has a much better impact on the kind of data collected and a better acceptance of the processes necessary to collect that data. Understand this will not happen overnight. Take your original schedule and double it—and that is after the requirements are simplified. Be patient with your customers—you will get push back.

Lessons Learned:

- ◆ Have stakeholder support at all levels
- ◆ Establish a portfolio team—who owns it, who manages it, define dedicated technical and analyst staff for report writing and managing the governance process and maintaining the tool
- ◆ Have the methodology drive the tool, not the other way around
- ◆ Keep the process and methodology simple
- ◆ Reports (keep them simple, visual, easy to understand)
- ◆ Establish training of the governance process and templates and tool
- ◆ Don't try and implement everything at the beginning
- ◆ Don't try and automate everything (visualize you are here process map)
- ◆ Deliver great solutions not perfect projects
- ◆ Be patient, be flexible—the process and culture change takes time
- ◆ Have reasonable expectations for process implementation
- ◆ Project governance—three to six months
- ◆ Application install and time reporting—six months
- ◆ PM methodology—nine months
- ◆ Maturity and compliance—two years

Today, Baylor still focuses on the main data elements of cost, effort, finish date, and percent complete. It is important to establish your process and stick to it. When you do, this compliance will come. Make the system *usable* for *users*, otherwise it is *useless*.

6

PPM Risk #6:
Timeframe for Analysis
and Decision Making

Though visions of an executive sitting in a corner office on the top floor of an office building skyscraper often come to mind, most executives do not spend a great deal of time in their offices. And they certainly do not come to work in the morning, sit behind their computers all day waiting for the phone to ring. Critical to the success of PPM is an understanding of, and support for, the timeframe for analysis and decision making of the executive and leadership team. As playfully depicted in the cartoon in Illustration 6.1, this is far more than simply implementing a PPM system and providing the executive team with a login to it. Four key factors to consider for ensuring effective analysis and decision making by the executive and leadership team include decision timing, decision style, organizational level, and decision criteria.

Decision Timing

When are PPM decisions made by the executive team—annually, monthly, quarterly, over multiple years, on demand? For many organizations, prior to implementing PPM, projects and programs are envisioned, initiated, and approved in a somewhat haphazard, best-effort fashion. Often, the strategic planning cycle and activities and project planning cycle and activities are loosely coupled if not disconnected altogether. PPM provides the foundation and catalyst for better decision making and linking project investments to strategy, but a requirement of this better decision making is a better-planned and organized sequence of events that supports making decisions about the project portfolio.

Illustration 6.1   PPM comics—executive reporting

This is decision timing. Every organization has its own unique decision timing, and no matter which PPM system an organization implements, decision timing must be fully understood and addressed by way of the organization's business planning process and policy. If not, an organization implementing PPM is likely to end up with an expensive spreadsheet of projects, not a system for categorizing and optimizing project investments based on specific goals and strategies of the enterprise.

Determining the unique decision timing for PPM that is best for an organization can be done in a number of ways. One technique that many organizations use is a three-step approach. First, develop a high-level schematic of your PPM model. This schematic can be based on standards organizations like the Project Management Institute (PMI®) portfolio management standard or the United Kingdom's Office of Government Commerce portfolio management standard or based on PPM provider models that often extend on such standards to provide a practical approach for PPM adoption that marries industry best practice standards with tool functionality. Additionally, market analysts like the Gartner Group and Forrester Research and leading project management consulting firms like PM Solutions, Pcubed, and many others provide best practice models for PPM. As shown in Figure 6.1, a high-level schematic of a PPM model aligned to the PMI standard for portfolio management is depicted.

The next step in the process involves assigning dates, timeframes, and any other relevant information to each of the PPM model process activities. Let's take vision as an example. One company or organization may meet once a year, each fall, to formally establish their vision. Another may do this once every three years and at a different time of the year. After assigning dates and timeframes to each of the PPM model process activities, an initial view of PPM decision timing comes into view. An example of this is shown in Figure 6.2.

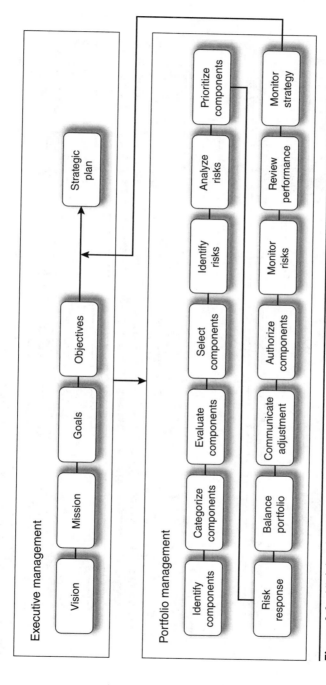

Figure 6.1 High level PPM model

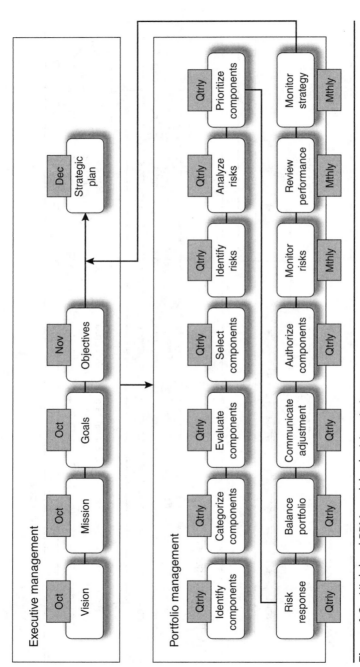

Figure 6.2 High level PPM model—decision timings

The third and last step in the process for determining the decision timing for PPM is to create a calendar version of the high level PPM model based on the assigned dates and timeframes for executive management and portfolio management decisions. As shown in Figure 6.3, this becomes the PPM calendar of regularly scheduled planning sessions, reviews, and control reporting for the executive team.

In this example, executive management develops the vision, mission, and goals of the organization in October for the following year. In November, specific objectives are established. In some businesses, objective setting involves a degree of organizational and executive team negotiations. Such negotiations may be related directly or indirectly to performance-based compensation, commissions, and stock options. In December, prior to year end, the strategic plan for the following year is established offering a reasoned and well tempered strategy for achieving the objectives of the organization. As indicated in the PPM calendar, portfolio planning and review first commences in January and regular PPM planning and review meetings are conducted on the first month of each subsequent quarter. Supporting the quarterly planning and review meetings and decision making, PPM control reporting is provided to the executive team on a monthly basis. Naturally, in addition to the regularly scheduled calendar of PPM meetings, additional meetings to review the portfolio and make decisions in light of changing market conditions, portfolio performance, and business opportunities and priorities can be scheduled and conducted at any time.

This is but one, high level example of PPM decision timing. A regimented approach to PPM has many advantages and need not be viewed as overly bureaucratic. For most organizations, the time and effort to manage the project portfolio effectively cannot be left up to chance and ad hoc best efforts. Nor should PPM be viewed as an activity that a group of people can do on a moment's notice. As strongly cautioned by the United Kingdom Office of Government Commerce (2008, p. 14) "PfM [Portfolio Management] must integrate seamlessly within the organizational governance decision-making process, align to the strategic planning process and ensure the engagement with many departments, including IT, HR, finance, performance and commercial."

Decision Style

Every organization and executive team has its own decision style, and typically senior executives analyze and act on issues and opportunities much differently than do lower level managers and staff. This can create tension and difficulties in implementing PPM merely as a result of differing decision styles being exhibited by all of the participants who are involved in the PPM processes and activities. As a part of the initial PPM implementation and ongoing activities,

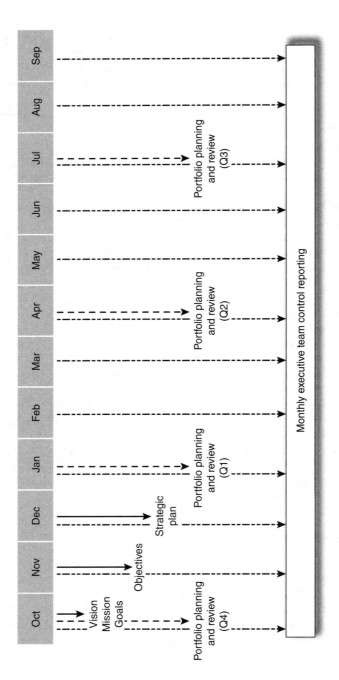

Figure 6.3   PPM calendar—decision timings

it is helpful to understand and define the decision style of the organization as exhibited by members of the senior leadership team.

Have you ever worked with an executive who quickly and decisively makes decisions with seemingly little information and analysis on hand? Sometimes the results of such decisions are brilliant and at other times, the consequences are less positive. And conversely, have you ever worked with an executive who, despite all of the information and analysis on hand, seems to be unable to make a decision without further review, continued analysis, and long, quiet, periods of contemplation? Sometimes such deliberation is necessary and at other times, it can be perceived as mulling about and taking too long to act.

Now imagine having a dozen executives who make up the leadership team, each with their own decision styles, and having to discuss, debate, and make decisions as a group. For many organizations, PPM decision making difficulties first arise not because of PPM tool functionality or lack of processes but because of the way people communicate and interact with one another. Adding to this complexity is the fact that executives and managers don't necessarily make decisions the same way as a group as they do individually.

In 2006, executives at Decision Dynamics, a firm specializing in the development and application of behavioral assessment technology, and Korn/Ferry's International Leadership Consulting Business published an article in the *Harvard Business Review* based on extensive research and entitled "The Seasoned Executive's Decision-Making Style." In this article, Kenneth Brousseau, Michael Driver, Gary Hourihan, and Rikard Larsson (2006, p. 113) suggest, "Approaches to decision making at the executive level differ in two ways: in the way that people use information and in the number of options they generate." Arguably, there are no two better variables from which to model decision making with respect to the complexities and participants in PPM. As shown in Figure 6.4, four decision styles are identified by mapping low and high use of information against single vs. multiple options.

The resulting four styles are decisive, flexible, hierarchic, and integrative. Characteristics of these styles include:

◆ *Decisive Style*—The decisive style decision maker values action, speed, and consistency. Once a decision is made and a plan is put in place, they stick to it. The fewer the options the better. In dealing with people, decisive style decision makers value honesty, loyalty, clarity, and brevity. In this style of decision making, time is precious and always limited.

◆ *Flexible Style*—The flexible style decision maker, like the decisive style decision maker, values speed, but here the emphasis is on ability to change and adapt. The flexible style decision maker wants just enough information to consider options and quickly make a decision or quickly correct a course of action.

◆ *Hierarchic Style*—The hierarchic style decision maker operates with a "haste makes waste" mind set. Rather than rushing to judgment, the hierarchic decision maker will analyze a great deal of information and expect others to so do as well. The hierarchic decision maker wants to hear all sides and perspectives and will challenge other people's views and analysis. From the hierarchic perspective, decisions should be lasting, not up for continual review and debate.

◆ *Integrative Style*—The integrative style decision maker values examining a solution from a wide holistic perspective. Their tendency is to frame situations and options broadly and to take into consideration multiple elements that overlap and relate to each other. Integrative style decision makers may opt for an alternative that may not be the best point or single solution, but that will have long range potential and encompassing synergies with other needs. Integrative style decision makers seek to obtain as much information as possible and are open to exploring multiple scenarios and options before making a final decision.

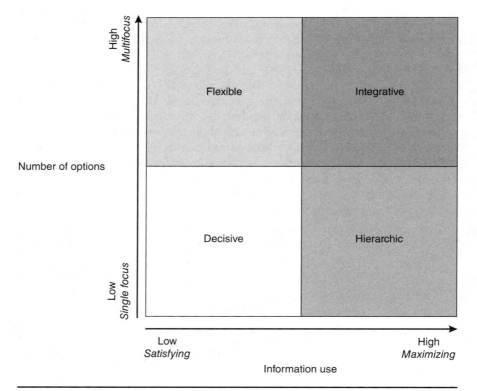

Figure 6.4   Four styles of decision making

Without too much difficulty, it is possible to understand and accommodate the decision styles of all those involved in the PPM process as well as the group as a whole. PPM tools inherently lend themselves to the integrative style of decision making. In fact, they are required for it. But also, the use of PPM tools and the careful adherence to the PPM process can equally meet the other decision styles that may be in play, such as making decisions with *just enough* information. In the event that the executive team experiences difficulties with the PPM process and tool usage, it might be a good idea to examine the prevailing decision-making styles to ensure that they are supported by the PPM tools and process, rather than being frustrated by them.

Organizational Level

In practice, PPM can be applied at many different levels within an organization. For example, though much of the prescribed guidance for PPM focuses at the organizational level of business change management in terms of the totality of organizational change throughout the enterprise, there is no reason why PPM cannot be effectively applied at other directorate levels within specific business units and even within individual programs. For a given company, it would not be uncommon to find PPM being applied at the organizational level of business change management, within the IT organization, and within the organization responsible for new product development, to name a few. But in the context of *Timeframe for analysis and decision making*, organizational level refers to the organizational construct required to support PPM governance and decision making. As advised by the United Kingdom Office of Government Commerce (2008, p. 4), "Portfolio Management is not a group of 'project people' that sit in isolation and produce a plan every year."

Does this sound like the PPM experience and environment that you are seeking to establish for your organization? *The commitment from our Executive Committee was critical to the adoption of PPM within our organization. Once the Executive Committee began to participate in the PPM process, they realized that not all of the current and proposed project initiatives could be undertaken. Additionally, the committee realized that the projects were not adequately aligned to or driven by the strategic goals of the company. The Executive Committee also realized that this work could not be performed in a vacuum and that there was a strong need for working together and making decisions more collaboratively and a standardized approach for evaluating options and alternatives.*

As shown in Figure 6.5, to arrive at this state of PPM, the organizational level factors are important to identify, configure, and manage.

At a high level, the organization level factors provide a visual representation of the required organizational components and how they work together. From

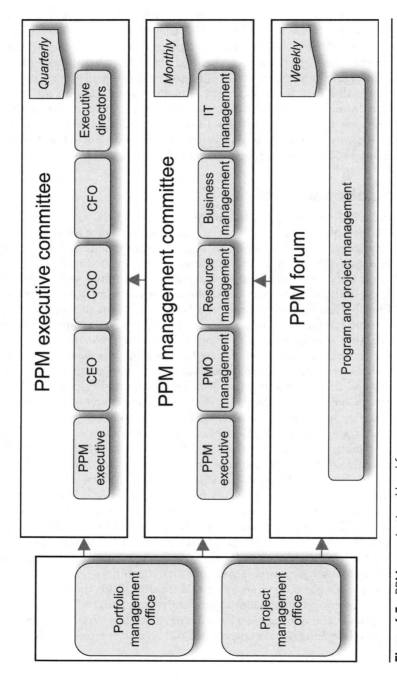

Figure 6.5 PPM organizational level factors

this high level construct, the PPM process and governance can be enunciated enabling all involved to speak a common PPM language, follow a common PPM process, and collaboratively work together using the prescribed tools and techniques required to support effective and healthy debate and decision making as well as to ensure the integrity and consistency of the resulting program and project work efforts.

Decision Criteria

Decision criteria, in the context of PPM, is all about knowing which criteria is important to the organization, how to weigh that criteria to establish a common currency, and how to assess a particular component, such as a program or project, against the set of criteria. In determining a set of decision criteria for PPM, it is wise to follow the adages, *If everything is important, then nothing is important* and *keep it simple, stupid*.

Over the years, numerous forms of PPM scoring models have been used effectively. Some of these are simple, spreadsheet-style models with a handful of criteria that produced a weighted average score for a component. Others are far more complicated, with indicator groups and criteria within each indicator group that collectively produced an overall weighted average score for the component as well as scores for each indicator group. Can you imagine a scoring model that has ten indicator groups and ten criteria for each indicator group? Altogether, such a model would result in one hundred distinct criteria that would not only need to be assessed but that would also need to be defined in a sensible way to be measured in the first place.

The fact that PPM tools, and even Excel spreadsheets, can do this is not a debate, but, that this level of complexity in terms of the number of distinct criteria is. For most organizations, four to seven distinct points of criteria are more than enough to effectively use. Some PPM experts prefer more, such as PM Solution's Bruce Miller (2002, p. 2) who suggests, "Twelve to fifteen criteria are the maximum required to appropriately model your IT project selection decision-making process." However, even experts such as Miller do not advocate overly complex models and models with too many distinct points of criteria.

In determining the decision criteria, the first place to look is the strategic plan of the organization. The strategic plan will likely outline vision, mission, goals, measurable objectives to be achieved, and critical success factors and dependencies. Most organizations are driven by common business measures such as customer satisfaction, market share, profit, competitive vitality, and corporate brand image as well as other supporting measures and factors. Of course, no two organizations, even in the same industry and geographical market, will necessarily have the same sets of priorities with respect to these measures.

Table 6.1 PPM weighted average scoring model

	Customer satisfaction (30%)	Market share (25%)	Short-term profitability (20%)	Competitive vitality (15%)	Core competency (10%)	Total (100%)	Weighted rank
Project 1	9 (2.7)	6 (1.50)	6 (1.20)	9 (1.35)	9 (.90)	39 (7.65)	1
Project 2	4 (1.20)	7 (1.75)	6 (1.20)	8 (1.20)	8 (.80)	33 (6.15)	5
Project 3	4 (1.20)	5 (1.25)	9 (1.80)	8 (1.20)	8 (.80)	34 (6.25)	4
Project 4	6 (1.80)	8 (2.00)	9 (1.80)	5 (.75)	4 (.40)	32 (6.75)	2
Project 5	10 (3.00)	5 (1.25)	5 (1.00)	5 (.75)	3 (.30)	28 (6.30)	3
Project 6	3 (.90)	5 (1.25)	5 (1.0)	4 (.60)	9 (.90)	26 (4.65)	6

Even the simplest of decision criteria can be effectively used to advance collaborative discussions and encourage healthy debate in support of decision making. As shown in Table 6.1, the PPM weighted average scoring model enables portfolio components, in this case projects, of differing merits to be evaluated against one another. In a similar fashion, as shown in Figure 6.6, a PPM two-criterion comparison grid can be used to facilitate comparison portfolio components with respect to significant or leading decision criteria.

A common technique in two-criterion comparison grids is to provide labels such as *pearl, oyster, bread and butter, white elephant* or *blockbuster, high wire act, cash cow, dud* that serve to provide descriptions of the characteristics of each of the resulting four quadrants. For the PPM two-criterion comparison grid shown in Figure 6.6, examples of such descriptions are:

◆ *Pearl*—Components in this category have high amounts of benefits realized and a low degree of risk. This category represents the most attractive PPM components for the organization. Generally, these PPM components should be selected.

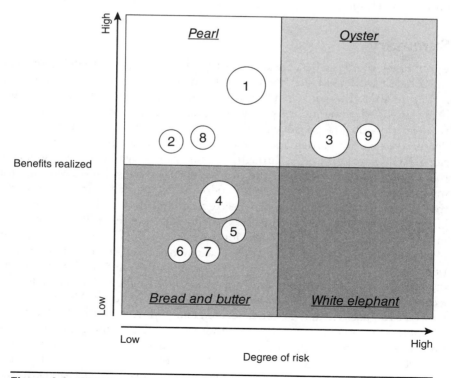

Figure 6.6 PPM two-criterion comparison grid

◆ *Bread & Butter*—Components in this category have fewer amounts of benefits realized and a low degree of risk. This category represents the attractive PPM components for the organization.

◆ *Oyster*—Components in this category have high amounts of benefits realized and a high degree of risk. This category represents the potentially attractive PPM components for the organization assuming that levels of risk are manageable and acceptable.

◆ *White Elephant*—Components in this category have fewer amounts of benefits realized and a high degree of risk. This category represents the least attractive PPM components for the organization. Generally, these PPM components should be terminated, unless mandated or required.

It is important to note that PPM decision criteria can, and should, change over time and with respect to changing economic, market, and business conditions. Additionally, sensitivity analysis can, and should, be applied to the decision criteria and their weighted values. Such analysis should have integrity and be conducted not to arrive at a desired model in support of a desired outcome, but to understand how slight changes in the PPM decision criteria might affect portfolio outcomes.

Summary

Often times, there can be a tendency by high-level executives to delegate all of the difficult work associated with PPM to the capable hands of director level management and to participate only periodically in the process, usually after being provided a bouquet of pretty charts and reports for review. Seldom is there an individual responsible for the PPM function that does not want a high degree of executive participation. To the contrary, project management professionals who have progressed through the ranks of management to a leadership role responsible for managing the project portfolio are all too aware of the many fine nuances of this craft. They, perhaps better than anyone else, know that an organization cannot be half-heartedly committed to PPM and the work effort involved, nor can executives expect to just let a few folks lower down in the organization give PPM a try for a while to achieve attention-grabbing results as a precondition for further discussions about organizational adoption. Yet this is what happens time after time, and as cautioned by the leading project management standards organizations, providers of PPM tools, and experts in the field, this is how *not* to do PPM. Simply put, PPM must not be viewed as an activity that can be delegated and performed in the back office.

There are numerous factors to consider when determining the most appropriate and effective approaches and techniques for an organization with respect to PPM analysis timeframes and decision making. Four of these include decision timing, decision style, organizational level, and decision criteria.

Decision timing is critical. Decision timing answers the pressing question, when are PPM decisions made by the executive team? Some view decision timing as merely a PPM calendar of events, activities, and key decision dates and can quickly put together an approach that is acceptable to the leadership team of the organization. Others, especially in larger and more complex organizations with existing governance and functional management processes already in place, are likely to experience greater difficulties in getting decision timing established to best meet the needs and timeframes for all involved. One technique that can help is the three-step process of first, developing a high level schematic of your PPM model; second, assigning dates, timeframes, and any other relevant information to each of the PPM model process activities; and third, creating a calendar version of the PPM model based on the assigned dates and timeframes for executive management and portfolio management decisions.

In addition to decision timing, decision style is an important factor to consider. Executives make decisions, but as research has shown, executives make decisions differently when in a group than when made on an individual basis. It is not uncommon to find difficulties in implementing PPM merely as a result of differing decision styles being exhibited by all of the participants involved in the PPM processes and activities. A helpful model of decision making relative to PPM is one that takes into consideration the degree to which decision makers like to use detailed information and like to consider multiple options as part of their decision-making process. This is the *four styles of decision making* model as developed by researchers at Decision Dynamics and Korn/Ferry International. This model identifies flexible, decisive, hierarchic, and integrative as four distinct styles that are exhibited, often situationally, by executive decision makers. Failure to understand these decision styles represents a risk to effective and successful PPM decision making.

Organizational level is also a key PPM consideration and it refers to the organizational construct required to support PPM governance and decision making. It is essential to identify the organizational entities that participate and influence the management of the project portfolio. These entities span across organization reporting structures and consist of all levels of management and individual contributors. It is helpful to depict organizational level factors graphically and to show interrelationships and how and when the various entities collaborate and work together.

Decision criteria is another important PPM consideration. Often times, decision models can be made too complex and can have too many distinct criteria that exist merely for the purpose of creating a numeric score of some kind. Models for decision making and the number of distinct points of criteria should be only as complex as needed. Said in another way, decision-making models should be as simple as possible to get the job done. Decision criteria will often be directly related to the strategy and key priorities of the organization. Effective PPM decision criteria and effective analysis of both portfolio components via two-criterion comparison grids and of the criteria, itself via criteria sensitivity analysis enables better PPM decision making and helps to reduce PPM risks.

Project portfolio management (PPM) is not easily achieved because of the fact that there are so many moving parts and the timeframe for analysis and decision making is one of those moving parts. Therefore, as part of the adoption of PPM standards, development of PPM processes, and use of PPM tools, it is essential to take into consideration the PPM risk factors. Taking the time to understand, discuss, and plan for these risk factors will not automatically guarantee the success of PPM for any organization, but overlooking these factors will likely result in unnecessary and unhelpful PPM execution difficulties.

Questions

1. What is decision timing and how does it relate to PPM?
2. What are the three steps that can be taken to establish the PPM decision timing for an organization?
3. With respect to number of options and use of information, what are the four PPM decision styles?
4. Consideration of a high number of options and a high use of information is characteristic of which decision style?
5. Consideration of a low number of options and a high use of information is characteristic of which decision style?
6. Consideration of a high number of options and a low use of information is characteristic of which decision style?
7. Consideration of a low number of options and a low use of information is characteristic of which decision style?
8. In terms of organizational level factors, what is the benefit of providing a visual representation of the required organizational components for PPM and showing how they work together?
9. What is the benefit of using scoring models to establish a common PPM currency?
10. In a PPM two-criterion comparison grid that provides a matrix of benefits realized compared to level of risk, what would be the labels used to describe the characteristics of each quadrant?

References

Brousseau, Kenneth, Michael Driver, Gary Hourihan, and Rikard Larsson. 2006. "The Seasoned Executive's Decision-Making Style." *Harvard Business Review*. http://www.hbr.org.

Miller, Bruce. 2002. "Portfolio Management—Linking Corporate Strategy to Project Priority and Selection." http://www.pmsolutions.com.

Office of Government Commerce. 2008. "Portfolio Management Guide— Final Public Consultant Draft," http://www.ogc.gov.uk.

Showcase #6: UMT

Project and Portfolio Management Go Mainstream:

Financial Management Improves Organizational Agility

Gil Makleff, Founding Partner and CEO, UMT

General

Enterprise project and portfolio management (EPPM) techniques and the tools that support them have now matured to the point where they are no longer leading edge, nor is it risky to embrace them. EPPM is now considered an established discipline that offers benefits and value. In fact, the argument can be made that operating without EPPM today borders on negligence. Without visibility into the planned initiatives and the impact of ongoing cross enterprise initiatives on attainment of strategic goals, or financial resource utilization, the enterprise will squander scarce resources and miss opportunities. While identifying the importance of initiatives relative to strategic goals is already part and parcel of any successful EPPM implementation, the recent addition of portfolio financial management to the traditional EPPM capabilities is the *missing link* that enables management teams in any firm to improve their control of deployment activities and fundamentally improve their organizations agility. Making better informed management decisions and being able to follow them up with fact based action plans when external events change strategic priorities requires EPPM with financial management.

The purpose of this showcase is to describe how adding project and portfolio financial management to the discipline of EPPM makes it an essential must-have management tool.

The Gartner Group refers to Enterprise Program and Portfolio Management, however, we will be using the term EPPM in its broadest sense to identify the end-to-end project and portfolio management process, including ideation, business case development, selection, planning, execution, and benefits realization. Project and portfolio financial management is contained within EPPM.

How Market Forces Relate to Deployment Activities

In Figure 6.7, we show how market forces, as originally presented by Michael Porter, influence the development of business strategies for the enterprise. Once the business strategy is developed, a strategy deployment plan needs to be devised. This will include all the tactical steps needed to successfully deploy the strategy including allocation of financial resources (for example, budget cuts and budget increases) across different parts of the organization.

As a simple example, a firm may decide that, given current external conditions, the best path is to align all efforts to the goal of becoming the low-cost provider in a particular market and reduce investments in innovation and research. The links between external forces and enterprise strategy and tactics must be explicit, which requires integrated systems and procedures.

Once the strategic goals are set, all project proposals and management decisions should be based on the expected return of the continued investment toward attaining those goals. In this example, portfolio management appears as a set of discrete, dependent, static decisions. However, in its simplistic form, this approach overlooks the fact that the original market forces are rarely static. It is not uncommon to embark on projects based on assumptions that are no longer valid. The goal is to implement systems and controls to ensure that, as conditions on which assumptions are based change, tactics and operations change as well, to reflect the updated reality.

A Three-Tier Framework

Organizations that are able to align their project portfolio with dynamic business conditions use a three-tier model with work, enterprise, and portfolio management tiers. In Figure 6.8, we see how the concepts from Figure 6.7 map to projects and organizations within the enterprise. Although market forces are external, strategy changes should be reflected in the behavior of an agile organization at varying levels. In this diagram, we see a model of the typical complex enterprise, mapped to the three fundamental components of a "complete" EPPM solution. People, processes, and technology support the business at different levels of abstraction, from the concrete (projects) to higher-level initiatives and portfolios. Business as usual (BAU) ongoing activity is not explicitly displayed in this diagram, although must be part of any complete solution.

At the bottom, or work management level, tools and techniques for management are mature and well understood. The scheduling techniques first introduced in the 1950s are mature and have been in the mainstream of corporate American thinking as important planning tools. From PERT and CPM tech-

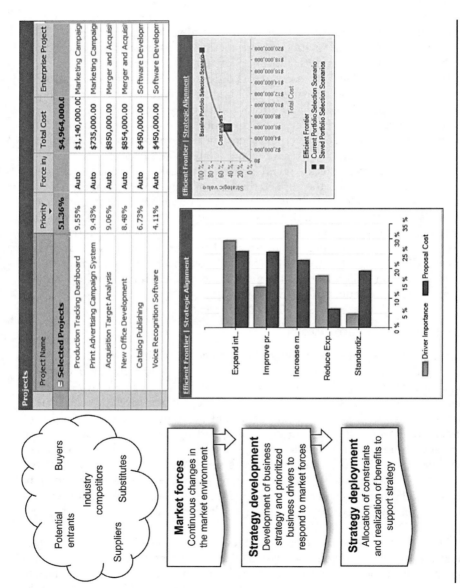

Figure 6.7 Response to market forces

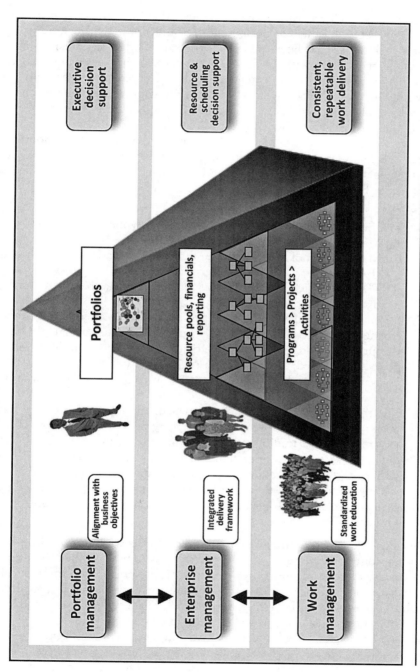

Figure 6.8 Enterprise view of project and portfolio management

niques to activity based costing, managing an individual project that doesn't have to interact with others or compete for resources is straightforward.

These techniques have been refined over decades, and no significant project should be embarked on without developing a plan, so that it can be managed to that plan. Today, the de facto standard toolset for project management begins with Microsoft Project, which facilitates the capture and monitoring of project-level planning and operational data. At this level, the enterprise must identify the appropriate standards and codify tasks.

Before we move to the next (middle) level on this chart, it is important to note that many organizations lack transparency between these views—the links that enable better decisions are not maintained or shared, leading to management by outdated assumptions. The middle level (enterprise project management [EPM]) consists of three "engines."

1. The first is the resource management engine, which includes:
    a. Management of skilled resources
    b. Management of the demand for discretionary and business as usual (BAU) projects across the enterprise
    c. The tracking of time—resource management has been a maturing discipline for the past decade
2. Several attempts have been launched to tie the resource management engine to the second engine, the scheduling engine, so that planning the project is done in a more efficient way. For example, when a project is initiated, the resources associated with it are not assumed to be available, and when the project is completed, the resources can be released back to the pool of available resources.
3. The third engine is the financial management engine. This engine has been quite elusive, as it relates to managing the portfolio of project investment and has traditionally resided in the domain of the CFO, who did not focus on the operational side of portfolio management but rather on the organizational side. Budgets were often prepared without regard to the fact that many enterprise investments are funded by several cost centers (organization units and sub units) and categories (expense, capital, etc.).

At this level, things become more complex, and this is where many firms begin to lose control as they grow their application asset base. While it is natural to view a chart like this from the top down, in reality projects are often developed in isolation, and the impact of cross-enterprise integration is just an afterthought. This leads to wasted effort, duplication of data and processes, and loss of visibility into the real costs as well as the value being created.

At each successive level—and indeed within levels as they become more complex—the need for standards and effective governance increases. Many organizations initially use a brute force approach to rolling up the information and it is at this level that many begin to add financial management support as part of EPPM processes and toolsets.

A Common Language Is Needed

Managing a complex enterprise effectively requires ongoing alignment of business strategy with the portfolio of projects that deploys this strategy through a repeatable decision-making process. Such a process enables rapid response when external market conditions change. Decisions that result in adding or changing people, projects, locations, and processes increase complexity and risk unless explicit steps are taken to manage the associated information. It is therefore critical to be able to continuously trace and realign the allocation of resources to projects and processes. In a large enterprise, that means strong measurement and tracking capabilities which will allow these changes to be monitored.

It is critical to understand the financial impact of implementing specific projects on the enterprise as a whole, beyond the impact to specific departments or divisions funding the projects. A common language—the financial component to enterprise project and portfolio management—is required to gain this visibility and translate it into management insight.

Adding financial management to the scheduling and resource engine makes this information useful to a much broader audience. Management outside of the IT organization becomes strongly interested in the management of the portfolio for cost efficiencies and for benefits realization.

Change Is Always Difficult

Most firms have difficulty with the transition from an ad hoc environment of loosely coupled projects to the discipline required in a complex enterprise. Eventually, however, all large firms require a factoring of assets, and an approach to prioritization of projects that reflects a strategic alignment of systems and subsystems with business objectives. This can be a painful transition, but with a little discipline and modern approaches to governance, workflow management, and financial management as a component of project/portfolio management, the goal of optimal allocation of resources with manageable risk can be attained. The resulting visibility into costs and associated benefits more than offsets this investment.

Financial Management—A Game Changer

Project financial management (PFM) is a discipline that provides financial data and guidance for its use to ensure optimal allocation of capital to projects and portfolios within a set of constraints. It merges the two historically independent disciplines of project management and financial portfolio management. PFM helps an enterprise to synchronize project and BAU work planning with financial planning to provide an integrated view for more effective management and allocation of resources and tracking of benefits realization, which enhances organization knowledge and self-correcting portfolio management mechanisms.

Every project has associated financial data that becomes more comprehensive and accurate as the project progresses through its lifecycle. Failure to link financial data to specific projects and business outcomes increases risk of project failure, and makes it impossible to calculate the true business value of project success. PFM ensures that the right financial data is captured, monitored, and managed so that the right projects and BAU work are built correctly.

A financial workflow tool that captures cost and benefit information should be used during project planning and development to help manage the process, and after completion to track the benefits of the system during the operational phase. This is an area that typically gets lost since the project team has dispersed, and tracking benefits have been shifted to PMO groups or other organization units, which in many cases are not vested or knowledgeable about the benefits realization expectations. Additional complexity is introduced by the fact that a project could be funded by multiple organizational units to achieve a result that will benefit the whole enterprise. This shared services model complicates the funding and tracking model but with EPM, this paradigm becomes part of the norm.

Together with scheduling and resource management, financial management is the third dimension of project and portfolio management. Its importance should draw the attention of corporate executive teams and even the CEO, who have traditionally relied on the financial organization perspective alone. Why is this so fundamentally exciting?

In Figure 6.9, we see a financial management component that facilitates alignment of cost and benefit financial data by project, added to the more traditional resource and scheduling engines familiar to project managers for decades.

This addition enables general and financial management to narrow the field of ideas and projects to be considered by providing ongoing impact analysis based on alignment with strategic goals. When the market forces change, resulting in a need to modify strategy, the impact of deploying the new strategy can be evaluated if everyone is using the same enterprise tools that help the organization compare different projects using a common language. With financial management, this transparency can be traced to cost centers and cost categories in dollars and cents—the common language accessible to all stakeholders. The alternative of looking at gantt charts and surplus and deficit resource skill charts does not foster the right level of discussion around portfolio value as change is being considered.

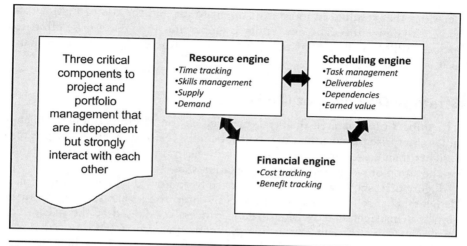

Figure 6.9   EPPM major components

PPM has, for the last ten years, focused on evaluating the effectiveness of a project portfolio. Basically asking the question, "Is the portfolio aligned with the enterprise yearly operational drivers?" The only way to answer this question is through understanding the strategic value of each project. Strategic value is the empirical value that describes the affinity of a project investment to the set of business drivers that are critical to achieve the corporate strategy. In addition to strategic value, we are now introducing the other key dimension—the financial value of the project investment—to obtain more information for improved decision making. Adding this dimension will help us understand the cost and the benefits realization potential of the portfolio in a more comprehensive context. It makes project portfolio information useful to a much broader audience. Management outside of the IT organization becomes strongly interested in the management of the portfolio for cost efficiencies and for benefits realization—this could include R&D, capital budgets, manufacturing and new product development areas. Once the link between cost and benefits becomes visible, the enterprise will see more participation from stakeholders who were implicitly excluded in the past.

As an example, when two Fortune 500 competitors merged recently, the combined entity had new priorities and a reduced field of competitors. One firm had already embraced a financial engine in its IT planning and management function, and was able to quickly evaluate, prioritize and justify existing projects, while the other part of the combined firm had to rely on outdated justification documents that were not aligned to the new strategy. It quickly became apparent that the group with better information was making better IT decisions that resulted in more investment to expand the use of PFM across the entire new entity. The new entity is embarking on an enterprise effort to include EPPM in all IT activities going forward. Knowledge is power, as long as it is current.

Strategy Deployment Models

The impact of integrated financial management on EPPM is dramatic. It enables enterprise management to monitor benefits realization, providing greater insights than cost management alone and a far more effective allocation and re-allocation of resources across organization silos.

Figure 6.10 shows a traditional approach to strategy deployment, once fundamental change in the market prompts an enterprise level response. The first step is a management decision-making process conducted at the executive level. Next, deployment of the financial consequences of the selected strategy is implemented traditionally through the office of the CFO where budget

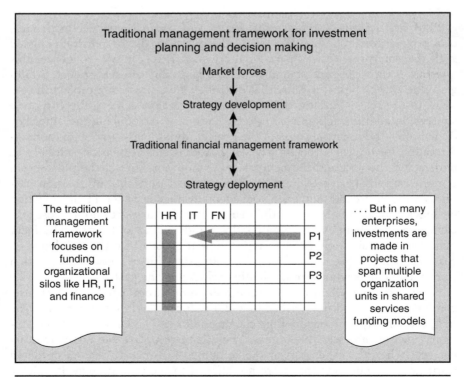

Figure 6.10   Traditional deployment framework

decisions that support the new strategy are communicated to lines of business and implemented. The funding cuts and budget increases are typically done at the business silo level. However, in many organizations much of the yearly investment goes to projects that span outside the business silos via different models, such as a shared services model. Here, one silo cannot make an independent decision to stop funding a project simply because the project spans multiple organization areas. Stopping the funding in one silo would simply increase the waste related to the implementation of this project in other silos, and this could potentially cause more chaos than benefit.

The Combined Model for Deploying Strategy

The addition of financial management to EPPM, as noted previously, allows the enterprise to shift resources based on changes in the enterprise environment. Once an event that requires a shift in strategy occurs, the executive team can make decisions based on the planned implementation, the status of current projects, and the sunken costs, as well as identifying the projects that are most associated with the preferred strategy. As shown in Figure 6.11, moving from a traditional or legacy management framework to an EPPM framework allows greater insights and flexibility.

When changes in priorities occur, perhaps spurred by changing market forces, it is a straightforward exercise to reallocate resources to maintain optimal investments based on the current priorities rather than being locked into misguided investments based on outdated assumptions.

Using the Right Tools

Businesses frequently start with the implementation of EPPM efforts with spreadsheets, but as they scale up to capture data across projects and portfolios, it becomes necessary to evaluate purpose-built tools that can serve all constituents. For project and portfolio management, Microsoft has achieved a significant market leadership position with Microsoft Office Project Professional for project management and Microsoft Office Project Server for EPM support. However, what has been lacking in these tools is the traceability of accurate, accessible cost and benefit data to specific projects, with departmental/divisional, product line or business unit consolidation. UMT, in close collaboration with Microsoft, fills out the suite required for full EPPM and addresses these requirements with its new project financial server, which is seamlessly integrated with Project Server 2010.

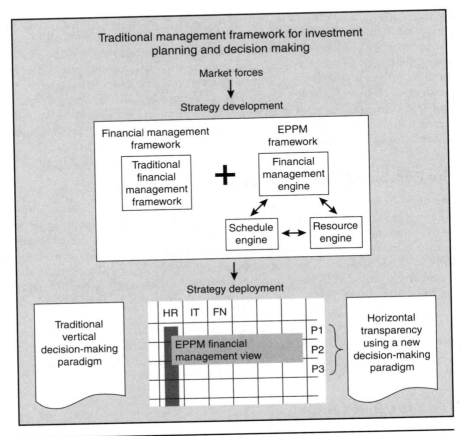

Figure 6.11   New strategy deployment framework

Making Better Decisions with EPPM

EPPM enables increased participation from new stakeholders within the enterprise. For example, using UMT's Project Financial Server 2010 provides benefits to the different levels of the organizational hierarchy, levels that previously did not have the ability to exploit these benefits.

◆   C *level executives*—who need to make decisions on how to best allocate funds across the organization get a single source of truth for project and portfolio financial data, which, in turn, enables better funding decisions and provides the ability to respond effectively to changes in the business environment.

◆ *Business managers*—who need to know if their portfolio of projects will enable them to meet their project financial benefits targets, get real time data and early warnings to make go/no-go decisions.

◆ *Project managers*—who need to effectively manage and collaborate on all project and portfolio financials, get fast access to reliable data coupled with the ability for effective collaboration throughout the project lifecycle.

◆ *PMOs*—who need to drive and enforce standards and governance, get easy-to-use and configurable templates, as well as configurable workflows that can ensure consistency across the organization.

◆ *Project team members*—who need to be able to easily create and update project costs and benefits data, get appropriate and pertinent access to team members, enabling them to participate in the project financial management activities without taking their time away from their primary project tasks.

EPPM data includes any financial data associated with a project or portfolio throughout its lifecycle (from conception through evaluation/prioritization, implementation, and ongoing evaluation). Whether the enterprise focuses on DCF measures such as ROI and IRR or takes a real options approach (or a hybrid mix of both), EPPM data is created. How it is captured and used is the difference between a financially mature organization and one at a lower level of maturity.

EPPM with Financial Management Impacts All Stakeholders

The effectiveness of EPPM has an impact on every member of an enterprise— when done well it can improve profits and reduce waste, but done poorly, even good projects may not be recognized as such.

> *. . . EPPM has an impact on virtually every member of an enterprise . . .*

As shown in Figure 6.12, stakeholders throughout the enterprise can benefit from contributing to, and using, data from the financial engine in EPPM. In this figure, we show typical roles of users of the UMT project financial server.

As a general rule, each participant in the specification, evaluation, selection, implementation, and execution of a project generates or uses EPPM data. It is critical, therefore, to have a system that facilitates the capture of this data in a standard form and makes it available to the right people at the right time to make good decisions about the ongoing viability of the project. Visibility of

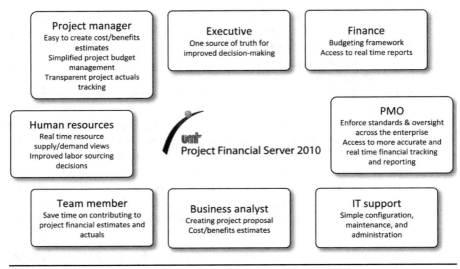

Figure 6.12   Usage of financial management across the enterprise

EPPM data throughout the lifecycle is critical to success. Formalizing EPPM as a discipline allows an enterprise to:

◆   Create business value
◆   Create governance support with templates and BPM
◆   Enforce standards through workflow governance

Consistent EPPM processes deliver repeatable results that are critical in a learning organization—one that can learn from past experience and continuously improve performance based on analysis of historical EPPM data.

Tools

EPPM is clearly a powerful combination of data and workflow, and for all but the simplest of enterprises, it will require automation to ensure complete and consistent processing. Fortunately, new tools are available that can capture data from all the relevant stakeholders and make it available to their counterparts at the right time and in a standard format to ensure that there is one financial truth at the project and portfolio level. Such tools must:

◆   Help enforce standards and processes
◆   Use templates to simplify processes and reduce effort
◆   Use processes that embody best practices and lessons learned

◆ Establish sources of truth (important for governance and to increase confidence in the efficacy of EPPM)
◆ Bring transparency and drive expectations for better data
◆ Gain operational efficiencies
◆ Aggregate information so that the right level of detail is available when needed
◆ Capture and report on projects, programs, portfolios, organizations, cost centers, and categories
◆ Facilitate team, workgroup, and enterprise collaboration
◆ Workflow automation
◆ Support reporting in formats appropriate for each stakeholder
◆ Provide a range of analytics suitable for each stakeholder, with supporting evidence (similar to a financial bill of materials)

Why Invest in EPPM Now?

There is a temptation to delay introducing a discipline like EPPM when money is tight, but the fact is that failure to introduce EPPM prolongs exposure to uncertainty and its inherent risk. In a litigious climate, one cannot afford to be seen as negligent. As a test, ask yourself these questions:

◆ Can your management team respond effectively to a market change?
◆ Can you reallocate resources effectively?
◆ Do you have the right level of transparency?
    ◇ To project status?
    ◇ To portfolio status?
    ◇ To project and portfolio financials?
◆ Do you have the right reporting tools to plan effectively?
◆ Can you get live/on-demand updates?

A single "no" answer makes the case for EPPM. Multiple "no" answers indicate clear danger.

Findings and Recommendations

PPM at the enterprise level has evolved over several decades, most recently to include financial management. More recent EPPM integrates data from resource, scheduling, and financial engines to provide project visibility for enterprise management. From humble beginnings as a tool for scheduling and tracking resources to a comprehensive general management tool that keeps the enterprise on track with strategic objectives, even when external business drivers change, EPPM has become indispensable to management.

The need for better financial information is driven by more rapid external changes, and the need to report and fine tune operations as a matter of better governance. Real time access to information is inherently better than periodic reports. Summary data on a quarterly basis may be required for reporting purposes but relying on it for internal management is similar to flying a plane with no real time instruments. At this point, if you haven't started an EPPM program, you are already behind the leaders in many industries. Fortunately, with new tools from UMT and Microsoft, the path to effective EPPM is clear.

7

PPM Risk #7: Quantifying Business Value

How do most organizations go about measuring the success of the project portfolio? Do they measure the manner in which the projects of the portfolio meet their planned and agreed to scope, budget, and schedule? Or do they measure the quantified business value as evidenced by the delivery of tangible benefits to organizations of the actual products of the projects? Traditionally, most organizations such as project management offices (PMOs) and their constituents tend to measure the former, but it is the latter, quantified business value, that is the truer and more important measure for project and project portfolio success. This measure is useful for initial project portfolio evaluation, selection, and ongoing management and review purposes, as well as post-project benefit realization assessment and verification purposes. Today, more and more project performing organizations are seeking to understand and place greater focus on business value. As humorously depicted in Illustration 7.1, quantifying the business value of project portfolio components is not easy to do and is often done in a manner that involves far more educated guessing and exaggerated hopes than the application of a sensible model and repeatable process.

Project Success Perspectives: Enabler or Impediment?

Most project managers are familiar with the project management triangle and its constraints, such as scope, time, and cost, along with the more recent inclusions of quality, risk, and resources. The concept of time, cost, and output is

Illustration 7.1   PPM comics—quantifying business value

centuries old and is said to have even been applied some 4500 years ago by the Egyptians in the construction of their pyramids. I can vividly remember my IBM class instructor, nearly three decades ago, bringing the concept home to us by saying, "If you have a lot of scope and want it quick, it won't be cheap. If you want it cheap and fast, it won't be good (referring to scope). And, if you have a lot of scope and want it cheap, it won't be fast." He then proceeded to educate us and entertain us with one project example after another that served to demonstrate this concept from fast food preparation, home construction, wine making, and eventually back to projects to convert business processes and functions like GLAPPR (general ledger, accounts payable, and payroll) and BICARSA (billing, inventory control, accounts receivable, and sales analysis) from manual and batch operations to online applications. Of course, it was the business benefit that first justified the project but once justified and underway, it was as if business benefits were no longer part of the discussions regarding management of the project and project success. Rather, project success was viewed and discussed as on time, on budget, and conformance to scope.

Who can argue with the project management triangle as a measure of project success? It is accepted project management theory and the foundation of today's project management standards. Certified project management professional and project management blogger Samad Aidane (2010, p. 1) writes, "We all grew up with the iron triangle. It has been drilled into our psyches from the day we took our first Project Management course . . . PMI, after 50 years, has killed the iron triangle in its latest PMBOK edition. So we should too." Also commenting on the project management triangle and its absence in the fourth edition of the *PMBOK® Guide* is certified project manager Kurt Clemente (2009, p. 1) who writes, "As we teach project management principles to today's new project managers, we need to take off the blinders and realize that tomorrow's modern project manager needs to come to grip with more than just the traditional 'triple constraints', plus Quality." Also weighing in are project management experts Dr. Ginger Levine and Dr. Parviz Rad (2006, p. 1) who caution on focusing too much on the project management triangle of triple constraints, which concentrates on technical project management areas without consideration of people issues and motivations that greatly impact project success.

A new book on project management by Aaron Shenar and Dov Dvir (2007, p. 7), *Reinventing Project Management: The Diamond Approach to Successful Growth and Innovation*, discusses why we need a new framework and a new approach for project management, and suggests that most project problems are not technical, rather, they are managerial. The authors advocate that the triple constraint theory is a key impediment to project success and that projects should not be defined in terms of scope, cost, and time. Rather, they should be defined in terms of quantified business value, such as business results and customer satisfaction.

Having attended a Project Management Institute (PMI®) Chapter meeting to hear Aaron Shenhar speak about the book, Dave Garrett (2008, p. 1), CEO of gantthead.com and project management industry servant-leader blogs, "It (the book) cuts to the core of why there is so much controversy around PM-BOK-based approaches and Agile approaches. In his presentation, given mostly to PMPs mind you, he says, 'PMI has given us a great foundation. However, it's time to leave that foundation and go to the next level.'" Agreeing with this premise is Ross Pettit (2008, p. 1), a former COO and frequent speaker on Agile, who in his article "Management-Driven Metrics Versus Metric-Driven Management" cautions on the poor alignment of project metrics to the way work is actually performed in Agile practices. Pettit advises that metrics are indicators of the project, not the project itself, and they do not tell the entire story of the state of the project deliverable in success measure terms that are meaningful to the business.

Offering leadership and a new PMO model are project management gurus Gerald Kendall and Steve Rollins (2003, p. 65). In their project portfolio management (PPM) book, *Advanced Project Portfolio Management and the PMO: Multiplying ROI at Warp Speed*, they provide a Deliver Now PMO model that extends on enterprise PMO concepts and focuses on throughput of the project portfolio as a strategic vehicle to drive bottom line value as opposed to the more traditional PMO focus on cost and efficiencies in the actual technical management of projects. Kendall and Rollins advocate the importance of accelerated project delivery and faster benefit realization. Though this will likely negatively impact traditional project management success measures, the advantage of the Deliver Now model for the PMO is that earlier project delivery will result in earlier benefit delivery and increased capacity to perform more projects.

Perhaps the greatest confirmation of the need to expand the view of project management from the technical side of project management (scope, time, cost) to that of the business context comes from the acting head and COO of PMI, who in his keynote address on June 8, 2010, at the Gartner Group IT Governance and PPM Summit said, "If we only speak this dialect (scope, time, cost), we will fail." He further advised that project management is an evolving model and that future leaders will need to embrace an iron triangle of not just scope, time, and cost, but (1) technical project management skill, (2) leadership, and (3) strategy and business management acumen.

What these business-driven executives, certified project management professionals, agile enthusiasts, PMO and PPM experts, industry stewards, and many others recognize is that managing project constraints and achieving project success should not be viewed as, or limited to, a discussion of scope, time, and cost. Yet for many organizations, these have been the primary measures of project and project portfolio success.

Caveats of the Two Dimensions of Project Success

In defense of traditional project management, the premise that there are two dimensions of project success—product of project success and project success—is technically correct. Commenting to this effect is project management subject matter expert and primary author of the original version of *A Guide to the Project Management Body of Knowledge*, William Duncan (2010, p. 1) who states, "Gosh, I thought we put this issue to bed years ago!" As illustrated in Figure 7.1, Duncan explains the two dimensions of project success and gives four examples of the possible outcomes that these dimensions represent.

Each of these success dimensions must be supported by documented best practices and success criteria including good change control processes. According to Duncan, "PM (project management) is responsible for meeting PM success criteria and for ensuring that project decisions do not adversely affect the product success criteria." In his article, "Defining and Measuring Project Success," Duncan (2004, p. 4) wisely advises, "As with any other tool or technique, project success measures can be overdone." Duncan also suggests that after all is said and done the project will be measured, usually by stakeholders, and someone will also decide the degree to which the product of the project was, or was not, successful.

I would like to add one final perspective of project success—a practical one. Though project management traditionalist are technically correct in defending the premise that there are two dimensions of project success, project and product, in real life practice this is ill advice. There should be no distinguishing from project failure and project management failure. The project is only successful if the product of the project is successful, period. To think otherwise, no matter what the project performance metrics are for scope, time, and cost management would be much like saying, "The patient died, but the surgery

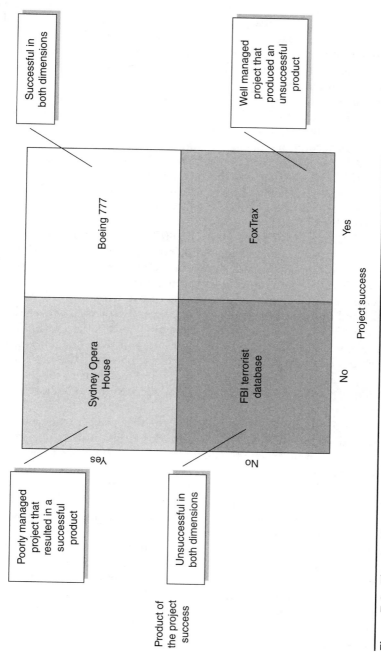

Figure 7.1   The two dimensions of project success

was a success!" More important, it lets the project manager and the PMO manager off the hook and creates a *staff-oriented* project management profession and mindset, one that is not accountable to product of the project success, and one that is likely to be compensated for mere efforts, not end results achieved. Simply put, there are differences between success and failure, and there must be consequences.

Imagine an account sales manager telling the sales VP, "We were successful in our sales effort, we just lost the sale." Or a customer service engineer reporting to his boss, "I told the customer everything I know, we just couldn't fix the problem." Or an accounting manager telling the CFO and sales VP, "Our team worked great last week. We just had a lot of end of quarter orders and could not process them all. Sorry about the missing revenue." Nobody would dare make any of these statements. Everyone else in the organization knows the difference between success and failure and so, too, should those who manage projects and PMOs.

In *Business Driven PMO Setup*, I wrote quite a bit about business-driven vs. theory-driven approaches to managing projects and managing the PMO. Consider the two project schedules as shown in the Microsoft Project screenshot in Figure 7.2. Both of these projects started and completed as indicated by the tracking Gantt chart. The first project ran its course without incident, finishing on time and on budget. It seems that the second project, however, did not go as smoothly. Two of the tasks took more time and budget to finish than originally planned and the project finished late and over budget. From the perspective of all involved, including the project managers, the project team members, the stakeholders, the PMO manager, and members of the leadership team, which of these two projects was more successful? Look closely. What action should be taken?

At first glance, most would conclude that the first project went quite well, and the second project did not. So let's reward that first project manager and team and wouldn't it be great if the next time around the project manager for that second project could plan and manage their next project with less difficulties, perhaps this time having nothing but *good* status indicators for every task of the project? Well, as it turns out, these projects were the exact same project. Now, take another look at the project schedules in Figure 7.2 and ask yourself, "Which project really was more successful?"

In Project 1, the project manager had a traditional project management mindset and thought of the project in terms of scope, time, and cost. The project manager accepted overly conservative estimates allowing and planning for more than ample time and budget. Once the project commenced, tasks were scheduled and managed according to plan. All tasks completed on time and on budget, the project completed on time, and all involved thought that a good job was done. Hooray!

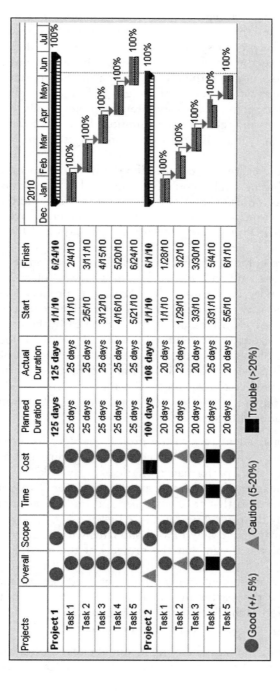

Figure 7.2 Project schedule comparison—business value focus

In Project 2 the project manager had a more contemporary, business-driven and agile mindset and thought of the project in terms of business value. Working closely with the project sponsor, project manager 2 understood that the product of the project would produce immediate business value and that earlier delivery of the product of the project was far more important to the business than managing to a perfect set of project performance indicators. Rather than accepting overly conservative estimates, the project manager for Project 2 challenged estimates and set aggressive durations for each of the tasks, twenty days as opposed to twenty-five days as planned by the project manager in Project 1.

With these more aggressive task deadlines, time was squeezed out of the schedule so that business value could be recognized as soon as possible. Some of the Project 2 tasks finished on time, others finished late, and though Project 2 completed late compared to its initial schedule baseline, overall Project 2 finished earlier than Project 1 by seventeen man-days and by twenty-three calendar days.

Let's add more color to the picture. The benefit stream of the product of the project is one million dollars a month. Hence, Project 2, by finishing twenty-three calendar days earlier than Project 1, produced an additional seven hundred and fifty thousand dollars of hard dollar benefit to the organization. Additionally, by finishing nearly one month early, the project manager and project team resources are returned to the PPM shared resource pool facilitating the start of the next project in the portfolio pipeline. Now what do you think? Which project, Project 1 or Project 2, best served the company? Without a doubt, Project 2 best served the company as measured by delivered business value as opposed to project status indicators. Let's consider the management implications of this example:

◆ Should management reward the project manager for Project 1 as the project ran so smoothly, not once having anything but a good status indicator for every performance metric of every task?

◆ Should management encourage project manager 2 to better manage future projects so that task schedules and budgets are not overrun as indicated by the project performance metrics?

◆ Should management view PPM dashboards with nothing but good status indicators as a sign that the projects of the portfolio are running well?

◆ Or should management view nothing but good performance indicators as a sign that there is too much padding in the projects of the portfolio and that there is the likelihood that business value, benefit delivery, and PPM throughput will be negatively impacted?

One could easily argue that management should expect to see and encourage a healthy balance of all project performance status indicators (good, caution, and trouble) as a natural consequence of a business-driven focus placed on product of the project success and business value. In fact, one could argue that business value should be one of the indicators dashboarded in a meaningful way along with traditional technical project management measures such as scope, time, and cost.

It is when we speak in terms of two dimensions of project success (project management success and product of the project success) that we take our eyes off the ball and allow, and sometimes even rationalize, project failure while at the same time praising the management of the project effort. Though unintended, for some projects and of course not all, excessive focus on measurements of technical project management and the attainment of those metrics can result in (1) less priority given to business value, (2) actions taken to meet project metrics that may be harmful to product of the project success, and (3) a reinforcement of *the patient died, but the surgery was a success* syndrome that only serves to add risk to the management of the project portfolio and to widen the gulf between project management traditionalists and those with a more contemporary business-driven and agile mindset.

Quantifying Business Value

Quantifying business value is all about observing, measuring, and translating. It is difficult, but not impossible. Let's start with observing. Just as it is helpful to move away from thinking in terms of technical project management success to product of the project success, it is also helpful to move away from thinking in terms of *calculating numbers* to *measuring observations*. Instead of making a calculation, we are making an observation.

One of the most memorable examples and business lessons that I learned about the power of observation occurred years back in Asia. At the time, I was the Asia Pacific Managing Director of a software firm and we were working with telecommunications providers throughout the region. In one particular week, I had executive meetings with leading telecommunications firms in Hong Kong, Kuala Lumpur, and Singapore. As customary in the region, business meetings started with gracious hospitality, a cup of Chinese tea, and discussions about the state of business in general. In Hong Kong, when discussing the state of business, the senior executive at Hong Kong Telecom with whom I was meeting expressed caution and worry about the economy and overall business climate. By way of rationale, he cited that the Hong Kong taxi queues were far too long and that long taxi queues meant that business was slowing down. To him, it was a bad sign of things to come.

The following day I was in Kuala Lumpur having a breakfast meeting with our Malaysian business partner and executives of Telekom Malaysia at the Mandarin Oriental Hotel. When the customary discussion of the economy and general state of business came up, the friendly smiles of all at the table turned downward. The top executive at the table commented how quiet and relatively empty, by local standards, the restaurant was. He added that when business is good, you have to wait thirty minutes to even be seated for breakfast. But now, the restaurant was quiet, only partially occupied, and with far too few expats and business people engaged in business discussions and deal making. To all at the table, the lack of hustle and bustle of the restaurant at this leading hotel was an omen and sure sign of a weakening economy and unappetizing times ahead for business.

Two days later I was in Singapore to meet the executives at Singapore Telecom. From the conference window of the high rise in the downtown business district, we had an extraordinary view of the port of Singapore. The quiet, emerald green sea with a spattering of container ships and vessels that were floating about could have easily been mistaken for a Thomas Kinkade puzzle. But when I commented about the picturesque view, all in the conference room displayed the same countenance and expressed the same concern; there weren't enough ships in the port, a sure sign of troubled *business* waters ahead.

The three meetings in the three different countries with the three different executive teams provided a lesson in observation—taxi queues, restaurant hustle and bustle, and ships on the sea. But it wasn't until nine months later that I truly learned this lesson of observation. By then, the Indonesian currency had collapsed, the Asia Pacific region had entered a period of financial and economic crisis, and I was back at our US headquarters working to correct our Asia Pacific business plan and to explain to our results-oriented CEO how we failed to take earlier notice of the changing market conditions.

The number of taxis in a queue, the amount of time it takes to be seated for breakfast at a swank hotel, the number of container ships in a port—if it is observable, it is measurable. In his article "Everything is Measurable," Douglas Hubbard (2007, p. 4) advises, "If a process produces an exact number (such as an accounting formula), that is a good indication that it is not a measurement at all. It's just a calculation. Measurements are pragmatic observations and observation never eliminates uncertainty."

For many IT and project management professionals, measurement is a widely misunderstood concept and misapplied activity. A process that produces an exact number is a calculation and this is exactly what many IT and project management executives want to have when it comes to discussion of value and benefits. In a business context, such things as revenue, expense, and profit are calculations. If a business had $6m in revenue for the month and $4m in expense for the month, the resulting profit (or some form of gross profit) for the month is $2m. In a project context, if a project had ten billable contractors for a week at $1k per day each, then the cost of the contractors for the week would be $50k. These are calculations produced by mathematical means, not measurements produced by observational means.

Measurement is an approximation that is arrived at by way of observation. Hence, measuring business value is an approximation. But, how many times have we heard someone say, "There is no way to measure business value because you can't put an exact number on it." So at the end of the day, the organization does not believe the measurement of quantified business value, or worse gives up on the idea of quantifying business value altogether. These people have a fundamental misunderstanding of what measurement is and are often unaware of, or not willing to, entertain concepts and approaches for observation and measurement. At a basic level, this is incorrect thinking, and it can impact how project portfolios are viewed and managed. As well known author, software development expert, and frequent lecturer, Tom DeMarco (1999, p. 58), advises, "Anything is measurable in a way that is superior to not measuring at all."

Do other managers and executives throughout the enterprise struggle with the concept of observation and measurement? Not nearly as much as in IT. For example, marketing executives are all too well aware of concepts and techniques for measuring such things as market share, customer satisfaction, and brand loyalty. These are not calculations at all; they are well-reasoned observations from which a measurement can be made. Likewise, human resource executives routinely measure employee satisfaction and management effectiveness. And of course, CFOs, CEOs and experts in mergers and acquisitions are finely in tune with the measurement concepts and techniques for assessing the valuation of a company. But in IT, measurement of the seemingly intangible, such as benefit realization, is often summarily dismissed as even possible. For those governing IT and managing the project portfolio, the end result can often be measuring least the things that matter most and measuring most the things that matter least.

In quantifying business value, for some organizations, there are some initial hurdles in terms of mindsets that may need to be overcome. First, the problem of quantifying business value is not as unique as you think. Often times, there can be a prevailing sentiment that the problems to be solved, the project, the company, and the overall environment are just too complex and unpredictable to be measured. But in fact, nearly always, someone else has done it before.

Second, you have more available data than you think. Data comes in many forms that can be observed and measured. Part of the measurement process involves identifying that which is helpful to observe and measure. Once you realize what is observable, many forms of data become measurable.

Third, you need less data than you think. Many observations can go into a measurement. Always, a few key observations will stand out as most significant areas to be measured and sufficient for establishing values and making decisions.

Fourth, there is a useful approach and measurement that is much easier than you think. The trick is to limit measurement to high value things that can be easier to observe, as opposed to attempting to measure all areas of value of which some may not be as easy to assess.

And fifth, there are more resources that can help with observation and measurement than you think. As always, measurement is best when performed by the person closest to the measure. In addition to that person in your organization, experts as well as practitioners with prior experience can be of great help in the establishment of a measurement approach to quantity business value. Once these initial hurdles are overcome, an effort to quantify business value can be commenced.

In terms of knowledge related to measuring business value, the concepts of benefits management and benefits realization are addressed at a high level in the various program management standards by both the PMI and the United Kingdom Office of Government Commerce (OGC). But these standards don't tell you how to actually go about it, by way of a prescribed methodology and step-by-step set of guidelines, nor is there one categorically correct industry approach or de facto standard, by way of popularity and adoption, that is universally accepted for how to do it. There are, however, numerous models and approaches that are readily available and can be adopted without a great deal of difficulty. From process improvement methodologies like Six Sigma to the wide variety of business model and methodologies such as business systems planning, business process management, organizational development, organizational change management, organizational and capability maturity, there is no shortage of approaches from which to choose.

One particular approach offered by Jeffry Smith, a Six Sigma Black Belt who has completed more than 20 Six Sigma and Lean projects, involves establishing areas of benefits to observe and then measuring those observations of benefits in terms of real dollars. In his article, "Five Ways to Measure Six Sigma Financial Benefits," Smith (2010, p. 1) provides practical guidance that can be applied to just about any product of the project assessment of benefits. As shown in Table 7.1, five areas of benefit (time, people, inventory, errors, and revenue) are observed, measured, and expressed in terms of a dollar value. Let's examine each of these benefit areas:

◆ *Time*—The time needed to perform a task or operation should be measured in terms of the before and after improvement states. The net savings in time can be multiplied by a measure of cost, such as the hourly pay rate for personnel. This can be measured as a savings each time the task or operation is conducted. If the task or operation occurs many times, even a small savings per occurrence can lead to significant benefits overall.

◆ *People*—If an improved process only requires one person, rather than ten, the product of the project can claim those people costs such as the

Table 7.1 Measuring areas of benefits

Benefit area	Observation	Measurement	Dollar value
Time	Net savings in time multiplied by the hourly pay rate for personnel	10,000 hours saved x $50 per hour	$500,000
People	Reduction of people multiplied by annual wages and benefits	10 people × $100,000 per year	$1,000,000
Inventory	Reduced inventory as a one-time benefit	$5,000,000 inventory × 50% reduction	$2,500,000
Errors	Reduction in errors multiplied by the cost per error	1,000 fewer errors × $1,000 per error	$1,000,000
Revenue	New, additional revenues as an ongoing benefit	10% revenue growth × $50,000,000 existing revenue	$5,000,000

total cost of compensation as benefits. The people may be redeployed elsewhere in the company, which is fine, but for the improved process they are no longer needed and represent a tangible benefit.

◆ *Inventory*—When the product of the project results in a reduction in inventory, a one-time benefit can be measured as well as amounts saved annually because of having less inventory carrying costs.

◆ *Errors*—Certain improvements lead to the reduction of errors, such as software and hardware products malfunctioning while under warranty. The reduction in errors times the cost per error provides an overall measurement of the benefit for the proposed improvement.

◆ *Revenue*—If the product of the project results in sales growth or sales of new units, this measurable revenue can be claimed as a benefit.

Many experts in process improvement projects advocate the limiting of the stated benefits to just the first year or first two years starting from the acceptance of the product of the project. This is sage advice and focuses the project efforts of the company on opportunities that deliver benefits sooner, rather than later. This also mitigates benefit realization risks that may be associated with, or affected by, time.

Up to this point, we have observed and measured benefits in terms of dollars and many people make the mistake of stopping there, but in reality, we are far from done. Consider the following two projects. As shown in Table 7.2, Project A has a cost of $500,000 and a benefit of $2,500,000 in reduced operating expense to the organization, and Project B has a cost of $500,000 and a

Table 7.2 Translating benefits

Project	Cost	Benefit	Rank
Project A	$500,000	$2,500,000	2
Project B	$500,000	$5,000,000	1

benefit of $5,000,000 in increased revenue to the organization. With all other considerations, strategic alignments, and risks being essentially the same, which project is the better investment for the organization?

The answer to this question involves an understanding that not all dollars to an organization, such as a for profit company, are the same. For example, operating expense dollars are not the same as sales revenue dollars. I first learned this years ago when I became a general manager with IBM and had for the first time in my career performance plan responsibilities, measurements, and compensation for expense and profit goals in addition to the customary, and lofty, revenue goals.

In reviewing my compensation plan, I suggested to my boss that the compensation associated with making expense targets seemed out of proportion to the compensation associated with making revenue targets—seemingly by a large multiple. My boss showed me the income statement for the organization and explained that, based on our business model, one dollar of revenue correlated to twenty cents of profit. As a reduction in expense flows directly to the bottom line, one dollar of reduced expense correlated to five dollars of revenue. Hence, within my operating budget, making a small reduction in expense as a percent of revenue was comparable to selling and installing a new mainframe data center. I quickly got the picture.

Every organization has a unique business model and internal measurement and management systems. Therefore, it is essential to involve the finance and accounting department in any kind of discussion about financial measurements such as revenue, cost (product cost), expense, and profit as they relate to observing, measuring, and translating benefits into a common currency. Using the example previously cited, which equated one dollar of expense to five dollars of revenue; we can update our comparison and rank of Project A and Project B as shown in Table 7.3.

Table 7.3 Translating benefits to a common currency

Project	Cost	Benefit	Multiplier	Revenue equivalent	Rank
Project A	$500,000	$2,500,000	5	$12,500,000	1
Project B	$500,000	$5,000,000	1	$5,000,000	2

Now, in light of this analysis of the quantified business value, which project is the better investment for the organization? The answer is Project A. This also serves to reveal why finance executives are so keen to reduce cost and expense. We may call them bean counters in a not so flattering way, but what finance executives realize is that a reduction in cost and expense has a tremendous impact to an organization, especially for organizations that operate on thin margins.

Imagine a company with a 5 percent profit margin. For every dollar of profit, twenty dollars of sales is required. Hence, project opportunities that reduce cost and expense may be far more important to the head of finance than project opportunities that generate additional revenue. And conversely, organizations with large profit margins would have a need to model the quantified business value with a different multiplier for profit to sales to reflect a common currency and to rank the projects of the portfolio accurately.

Summary

Quantifying business value is critical to the management of the project portfolio. Yet many IT and PPM executives scoff at attempts to measure business value or don't even try. Is quantifying business value difficult to do? Yes, but it is not as difficult as most people think. As with any complex endeavor, it is helpful to first understand the perspectives of all who are involved in the effort. It is imperative to leave behind the traditional measures of technical project management; scope, time, and cost. Focus on these measures nearly always results in a desire to achieve project management performance success by way of those status indicators as opposed to a desire to ensure product of the project business value and benefit realization—real success.

Experts in project management correctly advocate that there are two dimensions of project success. One dimension is represented by how well the project was managed. This is a form of project management success. Another dimension is represented by the success of the product of the project and this is referred to as product success. Though technically correct, the problem with this way of thinking is twofold. First, it inherently results in behaviors and actions to achieve project management success; sometimes to the detriment of, and other times oblivious of, product of project success. And second, the notion that the product of the project can be a complete failure while the project, as a project management activity, can be a success leads to a *the patient died, but the surgery was a success* mindset. There is little, if any, benefit to this mindset, and there are many kinds of disadvantages and patterns of poor business behaviors and decisions that this mindset produces. Though technically correct or correct in theory, for most organizations this is a mindset that simply should not be tolerated.

Quantifying business value as a measurement is not about having a mathematical formula that produces a value. That is a calculation, not a measurement. Quantifying business value is all about observing, measuring, and translating. The first step in the process is realizing what measurement is all about and overcoming the initial hurdles and barriers that prevent people from trying to do it in the first place. Once commenced, quantifying business value becomes an effort to understand that which should be observed, to determine ways to measure that which is observed, and most important to translate the measures of observed benefits into an *apples to apples* common currency. The benefits of quantifying business value are manyfold. When done properly, quantifying business value helps to ensure the effective management of the project portfolio. When done improperly, or not at all, this activity, or lack thereof, represents a significant risk to effective PPM and risk to the business.

Questions

1. What is the project management triangle?
2. What are the disadvantages and potential negative consequences of the use of traditional project management measures such as scope, time, and cost?
3. How is the focus of the Deliver Now PMO model different from traditional PMO models?
4. What are the two dimensions of project success?
5. What is likely to be more important to an organization: increasing project throughput and realizing product benefits sooner or ensuring that metrics of technical project management success such as scope, time, and cost are met?
6. What is the difference between a measurement and a calculation?
7. How can a reduction in time benefit be measured as a dollar value?
8. How can a people reduction benefit be measured as a dollar value?
9. How can a reduction in errors benefit be measured as a dollar value?
10. In what ways are dollar amounts, such as revenue and expense, different and how can they be measured as a common currency?

References

Aidane, Samad. 2010. "Is Project Success a Superior Value." http://pmstudent .com/.

Clemente, Kurt. 2009. "Triple Constraints Model." http://projectmanagement blog.globalknowledge.com.

DeMarco, Tom, and Timothy Lister. 1999. *Peopleware—Productive Projects and Teams*. New York, NY: Dorset House Publishing Company, Inc.

Duncan, William. 2004. "Defining and Measuring Project Success." http://www.pmpartners.com.

Duncan, William. 2010. "Is Project Success a Superior Value." http://pmstudent.com/.

Garrett, Dave. 2008 "Is the Triple Constraint the WRONG way to Define Success." http://www.gantthead.com.

Hubbard, Douglas. 2007. "Everything is Measurable." http://www.cio.com.

Kendall, Gerald, and Steve Rollins. 2003. *Advanced Project Portfolio Management and the PMO: Multiplying ROI at Warp Speed.* Boca Raton, FL: J. Ross Publishing and International Institute for Learning.

Levine, Ginger, and Parviz Rad. 2006. "Successful Motivation Technique for Virtual Teams." http://allpm.com.

Pettit, Ross. 2008. "Management-Driven Metrics Versus Metric-Driven Management." http://www.agilejournal.com.

Shenar, Aaron, and Dov Dvir. 2007. *Reinventing Project Management.* Boston, MA: Harvard Business School Press.

Smith, Jeffry. 2010. "Five Ways to Measure Six Sigma Financial Benefits." http://www.isixsigma.com.

Showcase #7: Outperform

Project Culling

Mike Ward, Operations Director, Outperform UK Ltd

No matter which industry sector you are in, or whether you are a private, public, or not-for-profit company, the things you invest in should have some bearing on achieving tangible benefits aligned to the strategy of the organization. Techniques such as ordered-ranking of projects do not always produce the right answer for the sponsor—*my project is the most important*—especially when their pet project ends up *below the line*; therefore a more objective approach may need to be performed.

Reviewing data such as delivery cost, benefits expected, resources required, risks envisaged, or some other combination based on key project or program data may yield more objective decision making regarding projects' investments, rather than the emotional-style of *you can't stop this project—it's mandatory*! To do this, you must first understand the business objectives and their associated measures. Useful background reading on this topic is provided by Shenhar et. al. (Shenhar). The benefits of this approach are:

- ◆ Showing whether the benefits from your investments are having the intended impact on the business strategy
- ◆ Having clear links between the portfolio office, strategy office, and corporate performance management
- ◆ Understanding more clearly what can maximize your return on investment
- ◆ Ascertaining the correct level of assurance to be applied

In difficult times, it is easy to focus on cutting costs when survival drives strategy, but how do we know which costs are the necessary ones to cut? The answer is surprisingly similar to prioritizing and commissioning new projects. Culling projects (this term was coined by Outperform during a PPM conference in the UAE, just after the Dubai economic collapse) requires a structured approach of valuing each project in terms of its contribution to strategic objectives and assessing the impacts should those projects be stopped, deferred, slowed down, or accelerated. This is the realm of portfolio management.

Where Do Projects Fit into the Business?

I have been asked to analyze a number of project portfolios in various sectors (local government, education, nuclear, energy and transportation), and each time I wonder whether the business sponsor really knows what the business objectives really are and what targets they are trying to achieve. All too often, I am presented with a list of projects being managed by what can only be described as *simple* metrics, that is, are they being delivered to time and cost? Occasionally these parameters are shown as *earned value*, but my faith in this metric collapses when I hear that the project was re-baselined at the start of each financial year!

Portfolio Managers should ask three key questions when putting together a portfolio analysis:

1. What are the projects and how are they characterized against the business objectives?
2. What are the objectives by which the projects' successes will be measured?
3. How will the progress of each of the projects be monitored

Before we can get answers to these questions, we need to know *what the business is trying to achieve*. In our experience, projects can exist in one of two parts of a business:

1. *Running the business*—Projects such as asset renewal, developing a new product for sale, improving an order fulfillment process, and other operational improvement projects would fit into this category.
2. *Changing the business*—Projects such as the one that local councils in the United Kingdom are being asked to do: cut 25 percent from the budget without losing core delivery staff, safeguarding operational metrics, and not suffering a mortal wound

It is important to know which parts of the business the projects contribute to because the objectives and measures will be quite different. But note here that some organizations may split the portfolio into two parts, and other organizations may exclude "running the business" projects entirely. One place you would expect to find the objectives and measures is in the *business plan*—you should be looking for five strategic objectives, with a couple of measures allocated to each objective—this is likely to be sufficient for most business areas looking ahead over the next three years.

Before I go into measures in more detail, I want to step back. Earlier in this chapter, Perry uses three analogies to describe aspects of business value and the measures adopted (lack of ships, lack of bustle, and number of taxies available), which are all sound measures, and interestingly, none of these measures is about project or business performance but all are about looking at operational performance in some way. So is there confusion about what we mean by measures? From now on, I will use the following terms:

- ◆ *Objectives*—the goals of the organization or business
- ◆ *Measures*—the quantification of the business objectives (sometimes called targets)

- *Contribution*—the part or portion of the business objective that a particular project addresses
- *Key performance indicators*—showing how the business is doing, that is, its operational performance (such as Perry's examples previous cited)
- *Metrics*—information to show how the projects are doing (for example, RAG status, cost-to-date, estimate to complete, earned value, and others)

What Projects Do We Have?

When characterizing the portfolio, or more simply put, tagging the project list with some useful data, it is most helpful to understand what type of project you have. I am a great fan of multiple tags and find spreadsheets particularly unhelpful here (the pictures that follow have been reproduced with kind permission from ChangeDirector, with whom we have been working for the past two years).

The most helpful form of tagging is a scoring system based on a number of dimensions. The primary dimension I use is a rough estimate of how each project contributes to the objectives of the organization. Table 7.4 is an example in which 1 is a small contribution and 9 is a major contribution. The four categories are: (1) financial sustainability, (2) flexible and responsive

Table 7.4 Project tagging

Projects	I	II	III	IV	Alignment score
Project 1	3				**3**
Project 2		5	5	3	**13**
Project 3	3	5	9	5	**22**
Project 4	5	1	3	9	**18**
Project 5	9				**9**
Project 6	1	5	5	1	**12**
Project 7	7		3	3	**13**
Project 8	7	3			**10**
Project 9			3		**3**
Project 10	5		1		**6**
Project 11		1	1		**2**
Project 12	7	5	3	3	**18**
Project 13			7		**7**
Project 14		9			**9**
Project 15			7		**7**
Score	**47**	**34**	**47**	**24**	

services for customers, (3) efficiency savings, and (4) high performing teams and individuals.

This scoring system enables me to see (a) if all objectives are being covered—in this example the portfolio manager should be concerned about the last objective, which is not being addressed much; and (b) if there are too many projects tackling the same objective. Projects 1, 5, 9, 13, and 15 also need to be examined to see if they are required or could be combined with other projects. We now carry forward the alignment score in the next phase of the analysis.

The secondary dimensions that make up the *version score* are defined by the client, but here is an example of the set I used recently:

- ◆ Objective alignment score (see previous text)
- ◆ Delivery risk
- ◆ Benefit risk
- ◆ Investment cost
- ◆ Remaining cost
- ◆ Business resources

For each project, I now quantify the five items above, using the client's method of assessment. Once this is complete, I can now analyze the portfolio and also produce scenario portfolios when new projects are being proposed.

Analysis is best done graphically. For this example, in Figure 7.3, I have plotted the remaining cost of projects against the value score. This is just one way in which I can examine projects to see whether they *fit* my business profile. In one organization, we showed the delivery risk against the value score to identify the most risk/highest value project, only to find a junior project manager was assigned to deliver it.

A coarse view of the portfolio has now been captured and analyzed. I would expect to have discussions with the directors about the projects identified above to see if the decisions suggested are correct and acceptable. Using this sort of approach, observations can be made easily, thereby shortening decision-making time—A major consultancy organization spotted that their Madrid office was delivering the best results world-wide; an insurance company's board moved a project from being high priority to abandoned in five minutes following a presentation at the executive level.

We carry out the type of analysis illustrated when we deliver our investment decision support service (which we colloquially refer to as *project culling* since this approach can be used when pruning projects from a portfolio).

Measuring Success

It is all very well producing a coarse *score* against objective, but what we need to do during project execution, and after the project has been completed, is

Projects	I	II	III	IV	Alignment score
Project 1	3				3
Project 2		5	5	3	13
Project 3	3	5	9	5	22
Project 4	5	1	3	9	18
Project 5	9				9
Project 6	1	5	5	1	12
Project 7	7		3	3	13
Project 8	7	3			10
Project 9			3		3
Project 10	5		1		6
Project 11		1	1		2
Project 12	7	5	3	3	18
Project 13			7		7
Project 14		9			9
Project 15			7		7
Score	47	34	47	24	

Figure 7.3   Future investment appraisal chart

to track our understanding of whether or not benefits will be realized in the agreed timeframe—these benefits are the contribution I spoke of earlier. Suppose Company A wishes to reduce its operational expenditure by 25 percent in three years. Table 7.5 shows an example of what this profile might look like.

Two improvement projects, shown in Table 7.6, are planned to achieve this objective.

Please note that the sum of the planned, forecast, and actual from the two individual projects make up the overall picture; that is, these two projects are contributing to the overall objective, noting also that the overall planned result does not have the same profile as the target.

Without this sort of information, no quantitative assessments of project contribution can be prepared. In the past we have stated "just because the

Table 7.5 Benefits realized score

	Definition	2010	2011	2012	2013	2014
Target	What is required	5	10	15	20	25
Planned	What we plan to do	5	9	15	15	25
Forecast	What we think we can do	3	9	13	15	20
Actual	What we have done	3	4			

project delivers to time and cost, it will be OK." This just does not stand up to scrutiny, and relies heavily on the original business case analysis. What we need to have are regular updates of the benefit projections of each project against the strategic measures so that we can see if the project is having the intended impact on the strategy (Jenner). The portfolio office should be singularly responsible for tracking progress of these measures.

It is also worth noting that key performance indicators are an excellent way in which to monitor progress—the use of balanced scorecards and indices for customer satisfaction, response times, and such can all be used to detect trends and are the analysis toolkit for the organization along with the measurement data set I have defined above.

Monitoring Progress

So what about project progress metrics. Gone are the days of having just time, cost, and quality, and in comes scope, risk, and benefits to add to the mix (OGC). From a portfolio perspective, we clearly need the earlier indicators of time and cost to show us whether or not the project is ahead or behind where it should be, but what we really want to know is how any changes to plan will affect the overall benefit profile. The next time you get a progress report from your project manager that has a red flag on cost, just ask them to update the business case and see what reaction you get! The business case needs to be made into a living document; its constituent parts make up the portfolio's costs, resources, risks, and contributions to strategy that we estimated in an earlier phase.

Table 7.6 Improvement projects planned to achieve objective

Project 1	2010	2011	2012	2013	2014	Project 2	2010	2011	2012	2013	2014
Target	5	10	15	0	0	**Target**	0	0	0	20	25
Planned	5	9	11	0	0	**Planned**	0	0	2	15	25
Forecast	3	9	11	0	0	**Forecast**	0	0	2	15	20
Actual	3	4				**Actual**	0	0			

I would like to add a short note on tools here. I have seen and used many project management tools that have a strong focus on the project metrics. Some vendors are now moving toward the portfolio space, but beware, many are just rolling up data from multiple projects—unfortunately, the measurement and tracking systems needed for showing contribution and measurement against strategic objectives are not derived from rolled-up project data alone.

Conclusions

In summary, there are three things I would like to highlight:

1. The portfolio must address the strategic objectives necessary to run the business and change the business.
2. The business value of the portfolio is about being able to state what benefits the projects in the portfolio will bring to the organization and when they will be forthcoming.
3. Having progress metrics and KPIs that show a healthy project progress does not necessarily mean that you will have a profitable business.

In this showcase, I did not discuss risk. I have assumed that readers will be happy with the concepts of delivery risk (that is, the failure to deliver to time, cost, and scope) and benefit risk, (that is, the failure to deliver the contribution to the organization as stated). In portfolio management, I am mostly interested in the latter and will save further discussion for another time.

References

Jenner, Stephen. 2009. "Realising Benefits from Government ICT Investment—a Fool's Errand?" API.

OGC. 2009. "Managing Successful Projects with PRINCE2™." TSO.

Shenhar, Aaron, Dragan Milosevic, Dov Dvir, and Hans Thamhain. 2007. "Linking Project Management to Business Strategy." PMI.

8

PPM Risk #8:
Ensuring Data Integrity

Many project portfolio management (PPM) experts advocate that implementing PPM is all about data integrity. Others go further and suggest that it is entirely about integrity and that PPM data, in whatever form the organization is capable of producing, is but a mere side-of-the-road bystander. As the cartoon in Illustration 8.1 reveals, organizations implementing PPM will come face to face with a wide variety of data integrity challenges and opportunities, from the friendly fire casualties of not having adequate processes and tools to the organizational mischief caused by those accustomed to, and good at, gaming the system. Ensuring data integrity is critical to the success of just about any leadership team seeking to adopt a business management system and PPM is no exception. Three management considerations for the leadership team that help in getting started with PPM, working with one another fairly, and ensuring an acceptable level of PPM data integrity are: understanding data integrity, producing data integrity, and improving data integrity.

Understanding Data Integrity

What is data integrity, and why is it important? Most people can put these two words, data and integrity, together and intuitively, if not cognitively, arrive at an accurate understanding of the term. Technical definitions of data integrity are abundant and with little time and effort, one can easily search the internet and find the following kinds of views:

- *Wikipedia (2010, p. 1)*—"Data integrity is data that has a complete or whole structure. All characteristics of the data, including business rules,

Illustration 8.1   PPM comics—ensuring data integrity

rules for how pieces of data relate, dates, definitions, and lineage must be correct for data to be complete."

◆ *The American Health Information Management Association (2010, p. 1)*— "The assurance that information has not been modified between the time it is sent by the sender and received by the intended recipient."

◆ *Virginia Tech Certification Authority (2008, p. 1)*—"Assurance that the data are unchanged from creation to reception."

◆ *Microsoft (2005, p. 74)*—"The verification that a message has not changed in transit."

These definitions and many others provide good examples of data integrity from a technical point of view. As shown in Figure 8.1, the technical view of data integrity is primarily concerned with a correct and whole definition of the data itself and the assurance that data will not change, be lost, or modified in any manner when sent and received.

If the data is whole and complete, and if the data remains unchanged from time of creation to time of reception, then the data has integrity. Hence, this is the technical view of data integrity.

Another view of data integrity that is important to consider is the trusted view. At its most basic level, data integrity is all about trustworthiness, and four considerations determine the extent to which data can be trusted by the business to make complex, strategic decisions. As shown in Figure 8.2, these

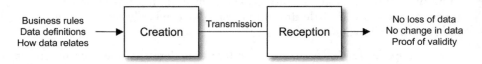

Figure 8.1   Technical view of data integrity

as a natural progression from having first used Excel spreadsheets, a marked improvement in data integrity is immediately recognized. Of course, this is the technical view of data integrity. To move beyond mere technical data integrity to produce a trusted view of data integrity, three things are required—purpose, people, and process.

Why not *people, process,* and *tools?* For many years I have written about, presented, and staunchly advocated the premise that no three words have contributed to more execution difficulties and outright project management office (PMO) failures than the words people, process, and tools. I still stand behind that conviction, and more resolutely than ever, because of witnessing firsthand so many organizations that initially went about setting up their PMO or commencing PPM with a knee-jerk rush into a people, process, and tools strategy and an all but blind adoption of a project management methodology prior to first discussing, gaining agreement, and then codifying the vision, mission, goals, and objectives to be achieved by the PMO—the purpose. That these things (people, process, and tools) are useful is of no debate. That they are the means or the ends, in terms of the purpose of the PMO, should not be debated but, regrettably, it is, as evidenced by the track record. With that disclaimer out of the way, let's talk about the importance of purpose, people, and process as a slightly different model and means to produce PPM data integrity.

As shown in Figure 8.4, for businesses to successfully implement PPM and achieve a high level of data integrity, it is necessary that the three dimensions of purpose, people, and process are aligned and work effectively throughout all levels of the organization.

When the *purpose* of PPM is clear to everyone, and that purpose is relevant to the needs of the business, all those that need to be involved are more likely to be actively engaged and committed to giving their best possible effort to the success of the enterprise. The result is an understanding of strategy, critical success factors, and informational needs and a willingness to effectively participate and contribute. When *people* are energized through the inspiration of a shared vision, they come together and develop their own team awareness and self-directed patterns for effectiveness and communication. When *processes* are defined, understood, and adhered to, then organizational capabilities are improved on, and better outcomes are more consistently and predictably achieved. This in turn results in the ability to systematically capture value and to achieve a people and process-driven focus on tools and technology aimed at achieving higher levels of efficiency and effectiveness.

A focus on purpose, people, and process is not a new way of thinking. James Womack (2006, p. 2), management expert and founder of the Lean Enterprise Institute, suggests that organizations should examine their purpose, process, and people as a simpler formula for evaluating their lean efforts. Similarly, in their book, *Corporate Branding,* Schultz, Antorini, and Csaba (2005, p. 133) emphasize the core themes of purpose, people, and process as critical to the success

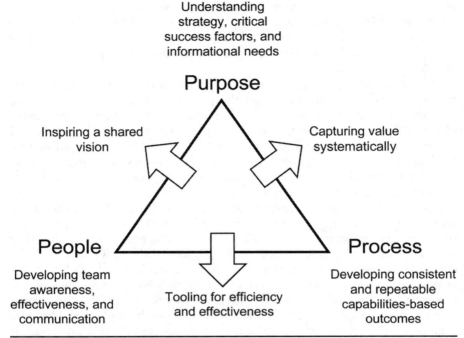

Figure 8.4   Producing PPM data integrity

of corporations seeking to create and manage their brands. Also commenting about purpose, people, and process is Matt Linderman who warns against approaches that companies use to manufacture confidence and a false sense of security, such as the over reliance on, and use of, specifications, documents, and process as a crutch to lean on. Linderman (2006, p. 1) advises, "If you trust the people, the process, and the goal, you don't need all the bullshit trust-builders like specs, documents, and promises to make you feel secure." What these experts and many others realize is that purpose is essential to any discussion of people and processes and that collectively these three dimensions interrelate with one another and serve to create an environment of high performance and high integrity.

If but one of these dimensions is not in place, it is all but impossible to achieve any kind of PPM data integrity. If the purpose of PPM is not understood by all involved, there can be numerous areas of breakdown. Sponsors may not appreciate the need to provide complete, accurate, and realistic estimates of the end product of the project benefits, costs, risks, and other considerations for not just selection of their project but optimization of the project portfolio of the organization. If the people required for PPM are not put in

References

American Health Information Management Association (AHIMA). 2009. "Electronic Signature, Attestation, and Authorship. Appendix D: Glossary of Terms." http://library.ahima.org.

Linderman, Matt. 2006. "Confidence in people, process, and purpose." http://37signals.com.

Microsoft. 2005. "Web Service Security." http://msdn.microsoft.com/practices.

Schultz, Majken, Yun Antorini, and Fabian Csaba. 2005. *Corporate Branding: Purpose/People/Process*, Copenhagen Business School Press. Copenhagen, Denmark.

Virginia Tech Certification Authority. 2008. "Glossary." http://www.pki.vt.edu/help/glossary.html.

Wikipedia. 2010. "Data Integrity." http://en.wikipedia.org/wiki/Data_integrity.

Womack, Jim. 2006. "Purpose, Process, People." http://www.ccat.us.

Showcase #8: Hewlett-Packard

The Four Starting Points of PPM

*Bruce Randall, Director of Product Marketing, Project and
Portfolio Management, HP Software & Solutions*

No two companies are alike; no two organizations are alike; no two PMOs are alike. But if the goal is effective project and portfolio management, the key business process requirements for success are the same. Traditional project management techniques are not working as well as expected. According to analysts, 70 percent of projects fail to meet their goals. And even when projects are executed successfully, all too often they still fail to deliver adequate business benefits.

So how do you get started? How do you prioritize which issues to address first? What are the risks and potential rewards? What can you do yourself and where can you find help? This chapter helps you answer those questions. It provides new insights into the root causes of project failures and misalignment with expectations, along with possible solutions. It illustrates the path to optimized project and portfolio management from four different starting points, and provides step-by-step advice to help you reach new milestones quickly. It is intended to help you make the transition from managing projects to managing the right outcomes of those projects.

Whatever the type and size of your business, whatever its level of experience with project and portfolio management, you can improve the effectiveness of your practices—at your own pace—without disrupting your current operations or increasing the level of heartburn among your current staff.

Symptoms of a Serious Problem

Despite significant investment by organizations, and the best efforts of highly trained and talented project managers, technical staff, and technology vendors, projects consistently fail to meet their original objectives. As an example, according to a recent report, only 30 percent of IT projects are successful, and 20 to 50 percent of projects are "challenged." This same report shows that IT projects have a 66 percent failure rate and 82 percent are delivered late. Analyst Research shows that 2 to 15 percent of existing IT projects are not even strategic to the business.

The result of unsuccessful projects is enormous pressure on the PMO. Executive management wants tighter alignment between business objectives and investments (projects); project staff wants better tools and processes for executing projects; project managers want technology that provides more meaningful insights into project status, resource usage, and so on.

At the same time, budget constraints continue to tighten, and executive management is hesitant to allocate more resources to internal organizations that appear to be underperforming. Thus, the PMO finds itself in a vicious cycle. No two companies are alike; no two organizations are alike; no two PMOs are alike; but if the goal is effective project and portfolio management, the key business process requirements are the same. The PMO must:

◆ *Establish the workload*—Capture the demand, evaluate and prioritize the project requests, and select and execute specific projects. In addition, project management processes and operational process controls (as established in ITIL, PMBOK, PRINCE2, CoBIT frameworks, and the like) must be applied.

◆ *Align roles with workloads*—Identify resources and apply them. The PMO must also apply organizational change processes such as the RACI model (responsible, accountable, consulted, informed).

◆ *Identify and apply measurements*—Examples include service level management in IT or Six Sigma, and balanced scorecard throughout the organization.

◆ *Achieve compliance*—The PMO must help the organization facilitate complete, consistent, and ongoing compliance with regulations, such as Sarbanes-Oxley, HIPAA, the Gramm-Leach-Bliley Act (GLBA), and the EU Data Protection Directive.

◆ *Provide financial transparency*—Gain early indication of budget deviations between plan and actual project costs to stay ahead of potential financial risks, and leverage cash flow analysis to increase accuracy of IT investment decisions and subsequent reporting to the business.

◆ *Ensure project outcomes*—Deliver as promised with key requirements of the business fulfilled.

Root Causes of Project Failure

Today's organizations struggle with project, time, cost, and resource management challenges at the aggregate level. Most of these organizations have time-reporting systems and project-scheduling tools, but with such tools, these organizations cannot take a step away from the trees to see the forest.

The lack of the *big picture* is at the heart of the PMO's challenge. There is no consolidated view into all the good ideas that could receive investment, so there is no structured way of prioritizing which projects to invest in across the organization. There is no integration of planning, financial, and resource data across the project portfolio, so there is no way to optimize the workflow and reduce bottlenecks. There are no enterprise-wide standards or methodologies, so there is no consistent way to measure or monitor success. Simply put, there is no easy way to align project activities with business priorities at all levels.

Four Starting Points

For most PMOs (and organizations for that matter), there is no question that better project and portfolio management processes are needed. The question is how to get started on the road to optimization. This section offers practical advice about next steps to take from any of the four areas of focus or *starting points*. Your starting point depends on your company's particular business issues, but it's important to note that all four starting areas have resulted in real-world success.

◆ *Demand/idea consolidation*—For many organizations, understanding all of the demands being placed on the organization is the essential first step in prioritizing the workload and determining the relative business value of various alternatives.

◆ *Portfolio management*—You cannot calibrate the business value of an individual project if you cannot see the big picture. A focus on portfolio management allows you to govern the entire investment portfolio and make apples-to-apples comparisons.

◆ *Project execution*—Delivering complex programs and projects on time and on budget is a major challenge for any organization. Focusing on project execution allows you to see which projects are in trouble at any given time and make decisions about how to get them back on track.

◆ *Resource management*—For some organizations, the top priority is the ability to analyze and compare skill sets, levels of proficiency, availability, and projected resource utilization while staffing projects as well as during the initial proposal evaluation process.

Setting Your Priorities: The Maturity Map

For each of the four starting points, this chapter can help you determine where you are on the *maturity map* so that you can set your next milestones realistically.

In general, there are five phases of maturity as shown in Figure 8.5:

1. *Informal*—Planning is ad hoc. There are no structured processes for any aspect of project and portfolio management. Projects come in the front door, the back door, or the side door. Budgeting is done in a *black box*. Visibility is non-existent, and there is no single source of truth.

Figure 8.5   The Maturity Map

2. *Defined*—This phase involves manual planning, but evaluation is based on seat-of-the-pants calculation. Pet projects of top executives get priority regardless of business value.
3. *Managed*—A project and portfolio management solution is typically in place with automated processes that support objective proposal ratings. A single system of record is used, enabling planned vs. actual budget comparisons and proactive management of projects and resources.
4. *Measured*—This is a KPI-driven stage, typically defined by advanced what-if analysis, benefits realization, and performing total cost of ownership (TCO) calculations on assets. Companies can perform supply/demand load balancing. Visibility into project baselines with earned value analysis offer greater specificity.
5. *Optimized*—Companies at this stage are performing real-time planning and full portfolio optimization. Scorecards are communicated to key business stakeholders. Advanced skills management drives efficient, cost-effective resource management. Overall portfolio planning leverages what is now a considerable knowledge base (see Table 8.1).

Starting Point Option 1: Demand/Idea Consolidation

The first step in consolidating demand is to identify a solution that is capable of aggregating and managing all the diverse demands placed on the business—operational projects, strategic projects, ideas, projects that come in through the front door (established processes), and projects that come in through the side door (such as, the executive's pet project). This gives you the information you need to determine which requests have the highest business priorities and how they match up with your staff and technical resources. You also need a solution that allows you to bring in existing project plans from Microsoft Project, Excel, Word, and other disparate project data sources, and you need to be able to create an aggregate view across all project types. Once all requests have been captured, requests can be processed based on your best practices and business rules for that type of request. We call this process of modeling, automating, measuring, and enforcing rules the "digitizing" of the management process. Every typical project, such as new product introductions, maintenance, upgrades, or routine service requests like provisioning a new cell phone,

Table 8.1 Demand consolidation—maturity phases

Maturity phase	Does this describe your organization?
Informal	Ad hoc handling of all types of requests and ideas. Phone calls, drop boxes and e-mails are the dominant type of communication.
Defined	Manual spreadsheets and other manual tools track projects. Operational and strategic projects are separate and reside in many different systems.
Managed	Operational and strategic projects are centralized into a single instance of truth
Measured	Reports deliver visibility into types of ideas/requests, costs and sources
Optimized	Quantitative measurement and nearly continuous process improvements are instilled and routine

can be evaluated, prioritized, and scheduled based on the digitization of your company's best practices and policies.

With digitized processes in place and a smooth flow of data about projects and resources, you have the information and real-time visibility necessary to effectively manage status, delivery or service contracts, and trends. Tracking the costs of an approved idea throughout its entire lifecycle can provide information needed for sound financial management. And for compliance requirements, you have reliable audit trail information needed to cost effectively meet government or industry regulations. As shown in the application screenshot in Figure 8.6, HP Project and Portfolio Management Center software provides a demand management view into cost, value, and risks of various investment opportunities.

You need a better demand consolidation solution if:

◆ You are using multiple systems to collect, track, and resolve problems, review/approve ideas or service requests
◆ You are only tracking strategic projects, not operational requests and work
◆ Requests frequently come in through the back door and are not formally managed
◆ There is no consistent prioritization—the squeaky wheel gets the grease
◆ The requirements for responding to and completing requests are difficult to track and report
◆ There is no audit trail for requests or actions taken

Starting Point Option 2: Portfolio Management

Many organizations continue to manage the project portfolio as a collection of individual projects rather than as a portfolio of investments. To be effective,

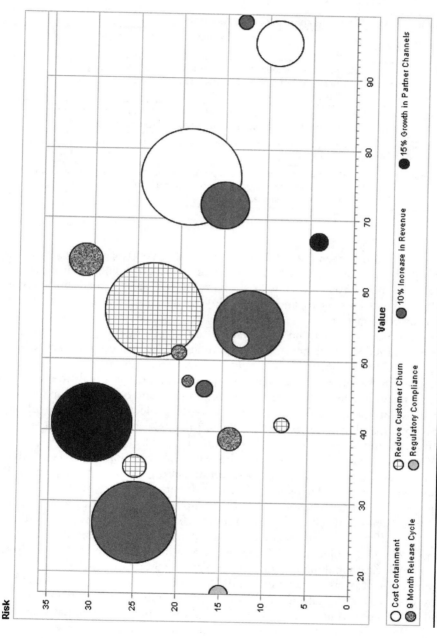

Figure 8.6 HP Project Portfolio Management Center

Table 8.2 Portfolio management—maturity phases

Maturity phase	Does this describe your organization?
Informal	Annual planning cycles are manual and present high-level business cases.
Defined	Manual spreadsheets and other manual tools track projects. Operational and strategic projects are separate and reside in many different systems.
Managed	Proposal processes are automated and include business prioritization. Detailed business cases and approval processes are in place.
Measured	Planning is KPI driven, supported by benefits realization, assets/TCO analysis.
Optimized	Portfolio *what-if* analyses are performed at the budget, resource and schedule levels. Sophisticated data is available from a knowledge base of experience.

your portfolio management solution should enable you to govern your entire portfolio by evaluating, prioritizing, balancing, and approving both new and enhancement initiatives to your existing product or service portfolio, analyze multiple what-if scenarios, and align with your business strategy using budget and resource constraints.

Your project and portfolio management solution should be designed to give you the unified and collaborative environment that is needed to let key stakeholders govern the portfolio. It should integrate and automate your strategic, financial, functional, and technical checkpoints and give you real-time visibility into resources, budgets, costs, programs, projects and overall demand. From proposal initiation, justification, and review—to project initiation, execution, deployment, and benefits realization—your project and portfolio management solution should keep all stakeholders involved.

Whatever stage of maturity describes your organization today (see Table 8.2), and whatever level of portfolio optimization you are striving for, HP Project and Portfolio Management Center software can help you take the next step quickly and with reduced risk or disruption to existing processes. Unlike approaches that only offer time-reporting systems and project scheduling tools, HP offers top-down planning capabilities that are supported with bottom-up detailed project plans. A top-down planning approach facilitates rapid portfolio decision making without requiring the creation of detailed, time-consuming project plans. For example, HP Project Portfolio Management Center allows you to create staffing profiles that enable you to accurately determine what resources and budget would be needed to support a new initiative.

HP Project Portfolio Management Center also supports the execution of projects and oversees the project methodology from the bottom up, allowing you to move from a reactive posture to a proactive, *management by exceptions*

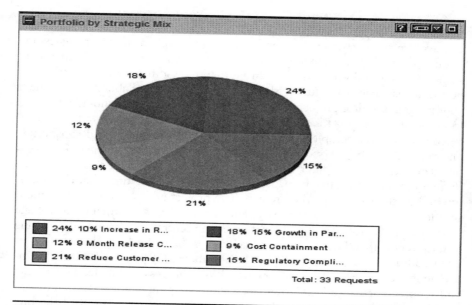

Figure 8.7 Portfolio by strategic mix

stance. Details of the day-to-day work of delivering projects bubbles up in real time with exceptions to the project plans clearly called out in the information that is presented. This allows project managers, program managers, and executive management to clearly see the impact that changes will have on their projects and align their decisions with business objectives. Either way, HP offers you the flexibility to make effective portfolio decisions in a process that works best for your organization as shown in Figure 8.7, an application screen shot of an HP Project Portfolio Management Center view into the current high-level portfolio mix with intended strategic organizational goals.

You need a better portfolio management solution if:

◆ You have no aggregate-level visibility into time, cost, and resource information for project and non-project effort
◆ In-flight projects, strategic projects, and operational work are all managed and maintained in different systems of record
◆ You are not able to get an objective analysis of the items in the portfolio; there is too much weight given to subjective criteria and *political* considerations
◆ You cannot do apples-to-apples comparisons of the expected ROI or net present value of requested projects in the portfolio
◆ Processes are not automated, and your staff is frustrated feeding data into the system

Starting Point Option 3: Project Execution

The average organization is constantly juggling multiple projects, processes, and resources. Conflicts are inevitable, and with so many variables, effective management of these diverse entities can be extremely difficult. Your project and portfolio management solution should enable you to collaboratively manage your programs and/or projects from concept to completion. It should allow you to automate processes for managing scope, risk, quality, issues, and schedules, so you can deliver complex projects with the highest quality and capabilities, on time and on budget (see Table 8.3). Each week, PMO staff members spend hours or even days compiling status reports from multiple data sources. This *fire drill* required by executive management consumes critical time that could otherwise be used to manage the projects. The project and portfolio management solution should free up staff time by capturing all of this information in a single repository and automatically rolling it up in one centralized dashboard. Creating a status report then becomes a small task rather than a looming chore.

In addition to addressing the challenges above, HP Project Portfolio Management Center provides best-practice PMO processes that let you model and enforce corporate PMO standards while keeping stakeholders and team members aligned at every step. It gives you the structure and out-of-the-box processes for managing scope changes, risk, quality, issues, schedules, resources, releases, and costs—so you no longer need multiple point tools and procedure manuals. You select which process workflows you want to use out of the box without losing the ability to adapt and extend these processes as your business changes. Figure 8.8 shows an example of a detailed status review of a project.

Table 8.3 Project execution—maturity phases

Maturity phase	Does this describe your organization?
Informal	Project status reports are manually aggregated. Projects are often initiated at departmental levels.
Defined	A departmental PMO is established and a project methodology adopted. The methodology is supported by manual processes and standard templates.
Managed	Standards and project methodology are closely adhered to. Projects often meet business and technical expectations.
Measured	Resource supply and demand load balancing is supported. Visibility is given into project baselines and earned value for projects.
Optimized	An enterprise PMO is established and projects consistently meet or exceed business expectations. Advanced skills management helps the organization leverage the right people at the right time and cost.

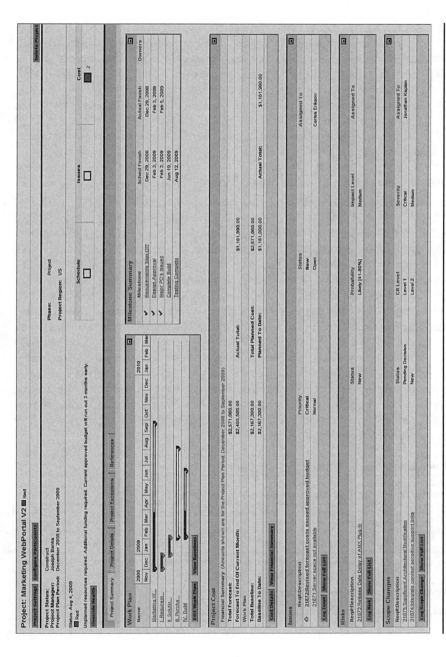

Figure 8.8 Detailed project status view

You need a better project execution solution if:

◆ Your company lacks a real-time status/health view into critical projects
◆ Projects are frequently late and over-budget, creating constant headaches, and the perception that the project staff *just doesn't get it*
◆ You are having difficulty keeping your current tools, such as spreadsheets, binders, and point tools, up-to-date and in sync
◆ Inadequate visibility into resource availability is impacting your staff's ability to manage projects effectively
◆ You are unable to offer management hard data to support your budgetary and resource needs

Starting Point Option 4: Resource Management

It can be extremely difficult for any organization to match the skill levels and availability of multiple professionals with specific project time frames and deadlines. The project and portfolio management solution should provide visibility into resource availability and utilization across projects and non-project work to allow for better planning, forecasting, and scheduling (see Table 8.4). In addition, it should allow for resource planning and tracking of actuals at multiple levels—the staffing profile level, the project level, and the task level.

HP Project Portfolio Management Center effectively delivers this visibility, managing resources from top-down planning through bottom-up execution. It balances your resource supply, giving you full visibility and control over resource demand. It also provides a clear picture of resource supply, including resource roles, skills, and level of proficiency at those skills, across the entire organization. And, it captures resource demand from projects and operational activities that drive the business in real time, so that you have visibility into resource requirements, and you can make better decisions about where staff members should spend their time.

Table 8.4 Resource management—maturity phases

Maturity phase	Does this describe your organization?
Informal	Ad-hoc resource management with no time tracking.
Defined	Point-in-time, manual resource utilization analysis. Time capture done at the project level.
Managed	Real-time visibility into supply and demand for all resource types. Time tracked at the phase/milestone level.
Measured	Resource supply/demand balancing. Time tracked at the task level. Project baselines exist.
Optimized	Comprehensive enterprise resource balancing at skill level and proficiency. Advanced skills management with planning leveraged off of knowledge base.

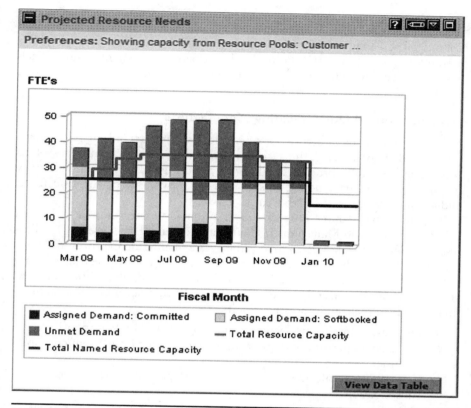

Figure 8.9   Projected resource needs

To fulfill demand, you can allocate resources by name, position, role, or group and then track the effort against any work item. As shown in Figure 8.9, CIOs and portfolio decision makers get real-time status displays and immediate access to detailed resource information on which to base decisions.

You need a better resource management solution if:

- ◆ You are not sure your staff is always working on the right projects at the right time
- ◆ You cannot pinpoint when a skill or resource can become available
- ◆ You do not know how much of your capacity is consumed by strategic projects, as opposed to operational activities
- ◆ You are not tracking what tasks people worked on previously
- ◆ It is difficult to determine what training is required for which employees

Customer Examples

Let me tell you about a few examples of actual customer experiences using HP's methodologies and tools (HP Project and Portfolio Management Center). Each has been successful although they began the process from a different starting point.

Demand Consolidation: Leading Manufacturer

A leading global manufacturer of scientific instruments and analysis equipment needed to increase the efficiency, visibility, and accountability of its project and portfolio processes. While they had a good overall methodology for managing requests, the use of spreadsheets proved inefficient, inaccurate, and a constant source of frustration.

To gain a single source of truth that is available to everyone, they selected HP Project Portfolio Management Center implemented by HP Software Professional Services. The HP Demand Management module captures all IT requests, giving stakeholders a comprehensive view of past, present and future demands. Requests can be prioritized, assigned, viewed, and *sliced and diced* across multiple dimensions to identify trends. Within six months of deployment, the firm realized impressive results:

- ◆ Decreased time from idea generation to approval by two months
- ◆ Rejected 40 percent of requests quickly, detecting insufficient corporate alignment
- ◆ Cut required information entries by 50 percent with request form consolidation
- ◆ Optimized use of corporate resources and reduced project overhead

Portfolio Management: drugstore.com

Drugstore.com, founded in 1998, is a leading online retailer of health, beauty, vision, and pharmacy products. With approximately 900 full-time employees, drugstore.com recorded $445.7 million in net revenue for FY07. Through its first few years, drugstore.com operated like many e-commerce pioneers—its business and technology processes were largely informal and ad hoc.

Company leadership recognized that to mature and grow their business, they needed to gain greater visibility of their technology operations, including automating the project and portfolio management process. Their main objectives were to optimize IT innovation and business growth projects while also increasing IT productivity and reducing operational costs. The company then turned to HP Project Portfolio Management Center for the solution. Working with HP Partner ResultsPositive, drugstore.com was able to:

- ◆ Increase innovation portfolio mix by 15 percent
- ◆ Increase visibility into technology demand, portfolio, and service performance

- Improve project on-time delivery
- Reduce employee on-boarding time by 50 percent
- Reduce the cost and time of annual Sarbanes-Oxley (SOX) auditing efforts

Project Execution: Birlasoft

Five years ago, Birlasoft, a global outsourcing company for software development, questioned how it could achieve Six Sigma and CMM Level 5 best practices without having any clear visibility into how well it was managing its processes. Executives decided to convert the company's manual project management processes into digital processes using HP Project Portfolio Management Center. Doing so would allow project managers and developers to conform to best practices as they gathered system requirements, built and tested applications, and deployed and supported them on an ongoing basis. An independent HP Project Portfolio Management Center ROI study performed by The Gantry Group demonstrated that instituting a standard framework for workflow processes yielded impressive results for Birlasoft:

- Improved project timeliness by 31.5 percent in one year, improving by 63.1 percent after three years
- Reduced labor expense by improved staff utilization, saving $2.7 million after three years
- Decreased the time per manager to generate a labor capitalization report by 35 percent after three years
- Saved 29.5 percent of their annual IT budget in one year, increasing to 68.9 percent saved after three years
- Increased customer transparency to project status, increasing customer satisfaction and reducing project overruns

Resource Management: Investment Management Company

In 2005, this company struck a deal with Citibank that changed its corporate business model dramatically. Virtually overnight, this investment management corporation became one of the largest asset management companies in the world. The assets under its management more than doubled. For the company's IT staff, the transaction meant the company's application environment became much more complex and distributed. In fact, the company went from averaging 70 to 80 changes per week to 150 per week. Using a system of spreadsheets to keep track of these types of changes, along with overall IT and business serviced relationships, was neither efficient nor sustainable.

In spite of the increased workload, the company needed to provide the same quality of information while increasing its change management success rate with nearly the same number of people. The company selected HP Project Portfolio Management Center, HP Software Professional Services along with other HP BTO software products to create a new automated platform to manage its applications environment. This would standardize processes and give much needed visibility to IT. The company has seen measurable payback by:

◆ Gaining a complete view into IT demand and resource availability
◆ Doubling the number of changes processed with only a low increase in staff
◆ Changing volume increased dramatically, change success rate improved to 95.8 percent
◆ Automating change tracking of 140 applications across several hundred production servers
◆ Being better able to respond to business requests for new projects and status of IT and application data (Hewlett-Packard)

The HP Approach to Project and Portfolio Management

HP believes that effective project and portfolio management requires a focus on the desired outcomes at the aggregate level, not just success at the project level. Solving the challenges of project and portfolio management does not require more and better project management tools; it requires an integrated, top-down view of all activities so that management has better visibility, more control, and greater flexibility. With this information comes transparency and reliable reports—enabling more productive, fact-based conversations between business stakeholders.

Better Visibility

Any organization needs complete visibility into the things being worked on, including project health metrics, non-project work, resource allocations, and overall costs against budgets. You need the ability to aggregate both strategic and operational projects and see the critical interdependencies among projects. This enables you to identify projects that have the greatest impact to the business quickly and optimize the project portfolio accordingly. In fact, The Gantry Group HP Project Portfolio Management Center ROI Benchmark Study determined that increased visibility into the portfolio enables firms to cancel projects that do not demonstrate sufficient value. Doing so saved study participants millions from their annual budget within one year, rising to three to four times that number after three years.

More Controls

Integrated, top-down project and portfolio management can help you cut costs by automating and enforcing project, program, and portfolio processes.

An effective solution can provide field-level audit trails for all changes to critical applications and projects, helping you maintain compliance with your goals. Once the PMO becomes more agile, processes can be adapted quickly to respond to changing market conditions with an easy-to-configure workflow process engine. Implementing standard project management processes will also help you gain transparency into critical financial data and allow you to quickly see how your initial estimations are holding up against project actuals. This enables rapid course correction and helps you keep more projects on time and within budget. Gaining early visibility into the potential impact of change yields significant savings. The Gantry Group HP Project Portfolio Management Center ROI Benchmark Study revealed that companies using HP Project Portfolio Management Center to automate the project and portfolio management processes saved millions.

Increased Agility

A project and portfolio management solution should be flexible enough to allow you to adopt either a top-down or bottom-up project planning approach. It should enable you to accelerate execution and usability with zero-client web-based project management. It should allow you to bring in project plans from Microsoft Project, Excel, Word, and other data sources and gain an aggregate view across strategic and operational projects. The Gantry Group HP Project Portfolio Management Center ROI Benchmark study also revealed that by giving IT managers visibility into the entire project portfolio and related in interdependencies, IT could lower IT labor expense by improving resource utilization and greatly reducing the need to hire additional in-house or external resources. In short, an effective project and portfolio management solution is expected to be flexible enough to allow you to aggregate all your project data into one place regardless of data source. It is also expected to be flexible enough to enable you to implement standards and methodologies across the enterprise in the way that best maps to your organization's maturity—so that you can get started quickly, accelerate adoption, and get great results sooner.

Reliable Reporting and Analysis

Automating and standardizing project and portfolio management processes helps verify that the data recorded by key stakeholders and project team members is consistent and reliable across all projects types. This provides the basis for apples-to-apples comparisons that drive effective decision making at the portfolio, program, and project levels. Operational reports can be easily printed to support rapid review of project budgets, and financial analysts can gain real-time insight into emerging trends with ad-hoc reporting. At the same time, analytical reports can be used by management to identify and resolve issues before they become significant problems. Delivering real-time reports and analytics, based on reliable information, can help you create an effective, on-going dialogue with all stakeholders. Importantly, it can help you develop and sustain momentum, as users at all levels can quickly see how their day-to-day work affects the big picture. The organization needs complete visibility into everything that it is working on, including project health metrics, non-project work, resource allocations, and overall costs. Integrated, top-down project and portfolio management can help you cut costs by automating and enforcing project, program, and portfolio processes. A project and portfolio management solution should be flexible enough to allow you to adopt either a top-down or bottom-up project-planning approach.

Summary

Effective project and portfolio management is an achievable goal. You can start at any of the four areas of focus described and derive significant benefits. You can start at any level of organizational maturity. You can start quickly, or you can phase in new tools and processes, one by one. But the key is to get started. Research and plenty of anecdotal evidence has shown that traditional methods of managing projects simply are not working—not for end users, not for staff, not for the company. Until the PMO stops managing projects and starts managing business outcomes, project failure rates are likely to remain high. It is time to break the cycle and evaluate new alternatives.

References

Hewlett-Packard, 2009. "Four Starting Points for Effective IT Project and Portfolio Management", www.hp.com/hpinfo/newsroom/press_kits/, p.10-11.

9

PPM Risk #9: Tooling and Architecture

For many organizations, determining which of the various tools, applications, and systems to use in support of project portfolio management (PPM) can be much like putting together the pieces of a complex jigsaw puzzle, blindfolded. A lot of pieces seem like they should fit, but in reality many don't, and the effort becomes tiresome. Often it is a good idea to approach the task in a more methodical manner, rather than haphazardly trying to piece the puzzle together. In the case of a complex jigsaw puzzle, this would be: first, identifying and aligning the straight-edged pieces that make up the border, and snapping those into place to create a completed frame; next, arranging all of the other pieces in a sensible way to get a grasp of what you actually have in front of you; and then, continuing the effort to evaluate the various pieces and put them where they belong, doing the easy pieces right away and then focusing your attention and efforts on the hard ones. The end result is soon a beautiful picture, and mission accomplished.

With respect to the challenges that PPM entail, the same way of thinking and approach can be applied. The various pieces of the puzzle represent the tools that are required—all of them. When viewed individually, it can be a daunting task to understand the importance of the tools, how they are used, and how they all relate. But when viewed altogether and in their correct context of use and value, the required tools come together to form a single picture that shows how they fit, relate, and work. This is architecture. And as comically depicted in Illustration 9.1, rather than merely implementing one tool after another, establishing an architecture can be tremendously helpful to meet the wide and diverse set of needs and challenges that organizations,

Illustration 9.1   PPM comics—PPM architecture

departments, teams, and individuals will face as part of the overall work effort that PPM spawns and encompasses.

Overcoming the Tool Mindset

There are many contributing factors that can result in a tool mindset rather than an architecture way of thinking. At first thought, one might conclude that the tool mindset exists because of all of the tool sellers out there marketing their offering as the one and only best-in-class, one-tool-does-it-all, solution that can address the full spectrum of your business needs, at least your important business needs. As depicted in Figure 9.1, with respect to providers of PPM offerings and the way in which they market their offerings, nothing could be further from the truth.

Generally speaking, all of the leading PPM solution providers provide rich feature sets for their own offerings as well as connectors, APIs, plug-ins, accelerators, and features for integration to the wide variety of other systems, applications, and tools that are needed and used by the business. These include enterprise resource planning applications, business intelligence tools, and IT management applications, along with collaboration platforms, desktop tools, web services, and other useful things. Though some providers may participate in the one-tool-does-it-all way of thinking, most simply do not. For one, they recognize that all of the required functionality is more than any one provider or tool can provide and for another, they are on the hook to get it all to work.

Though unintended, the analyst community contributes to the mindset of one-tool-does-it-all. The leading research firms, such as the Gartner Group, Forrester Research, and a host of others provide valuable analysis and research findings. Experts in IT technology, business systems, and best practices for IT governance and project portfolio management such as Michael Hanford, Matt Light, and Dan Stang of the Gartner Group and Margo Visitacion of Forrester

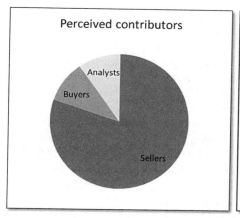 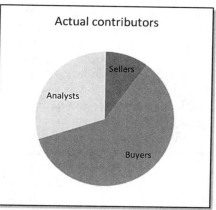

Figure 9.1 Contributors to the tool mindset—perceived and real

Research have provided real-world guidance to CEOs, CIOs, and IT executives for years. Many people advocate that their IT industry summits are must-attend events and that major IT investments should be made in light of their research and market views.

Often, this research will overview the market, position the various providers who serve the market, and make an assessment of the product offerings of the providers. Such assessments are always made after careful due diligence and unbiased examination, and they are intended to position the salient attributes of the providers and their offerings but not to be interpreted or used as a ranking or selection recommendation. In fact, on the first page of this year's Gartner Group "Magic Quadrant for IT Project and Portfolio Management" report, PPM expert and research analyst Dan Stang (2010, p. 1) advises, "Prospective customers of PPM applications should examine all the functional capabilities (including integration support to third-party products), and identify initial functionality that meets immediate needs." Nonetheless, despite such advice, report findings and research analysis are often taken out of their original context and used for the purposes of determining which product offering is the closest to meeting the one-tool-does-it-all promise.

The greatest contributor to the one-tool-does-it-all mindset is not unintended, and it emanates from the customer side of the house. Some of this thinking comes from the request for information (RFI) and request for proposal (RFP) efforts that tend to provide preformatted Excel spreadsheets requesting sellers to indicate how their product offerings meet, partially meet, or do not meet their specifications. How these specifications are even arrived at in the first place is worthy of discussion. But the broader point is that the resulting analysis nearly always favors the product with the most tick marks in the *meets* column. This is generally an architecturally unsound approach.

For example, an RFI or RFP for a PPM solution may have specifications for collaboration, document management, and social software features in support of the envisioned PPM activity. One provider may provide none of that by way of product design, preferring instead to allow the customer to choose from among existing capabilities or best-in-class offerings. Many organizations view such capabilities as enterprise-wide and not limited to a particular business area, let alone limited to but one application, thus, a product offering that recognizes that, and in fact anticipates it, need not be viewed as inferior.

Can you imagine an organization that has an enterprise strategy to use a particular platform, such as Microsoft SharePoint, IBM Lotus, EMC Documentum, or Intuit QuickBase, abandoning that investment simply because a point tool of some kind happens to have some amount of collaboration functionality? Of course not. And the same comparison can be made with a number of different cross enterprise components such as analytics, reporting, and wikis along with web services, applets, and mashups.

One could make the case that a provider who leverages best-of-breed enterprise components that customers already have, rather than providing redundant functionality, might well have a better understanding of the market, a better product design strategy, and a better product offering than a rival who is seeking to provide all of this functionality in one product. Rarely will that discussion and examination come up during those RFI and RFP efforts that are often carried out by well-intended procurement staff who are not necessarily familiar with the bigger picture of the enterprise's overall infrastructure and application architecture.

No doubt, there will be certain times when a tool mindset is needed, and a comparison of one point tool against another is appropriate to do. But PPM is not one of those times. Organizations seeking to implement, adopt, and improve on their PPM capabilities, and outcomes will be far better served with an architecture approach to understanding requirements, evaluating alternatives, and implementing components that best meet those requirements. In essence, taking the time to first understand what PPM is all about.

An Architecture Approach

The goal of architecture is to deal with, if not simplify, complexity, and there are few business environments more encompassing and in need of simplification than PPM. Consider the following capabilities that organizations seeking to implement PPM require:

◆ *Portfolio management*—The ability to interactively and visually assess, compare, and determine the optimal mix of proposed investments taking into consideration a wide variety of weighted criteria, such as

♦ *System Center*—A suite of IT infrastructure and server management products for systems, operations, data management, application availability, and service delivery

♦ *Visual Studio*—An integrated development environment for developing forms, applications, websites, web applications, and web services

The EPM solution layer of the Microsoft EPM solution architecture depicts Microsoft SharePoint, Project Server, and Microsoft Project. Microsoft Project Server is built on SharePoint, so it combines collaboration platform services with structured PPM capabilities. Project Server 2010 unites project management and portfolio management (previously provided as two separate products) to help organizations align resources and investments with business priorities and manage all types of project work. Project Professional 2010 builds on previous versions of Microsoft Project and delivers visually enhanced ways to plan, collaborate, and manage resources. Connecting Project Professional, the leading desktop project management tool, with Project Server provides organizations with a holistic view of the project portfolio and an ability to exhibit the capabilities and realize the benefits of effective, unified PPM.

Integration-Centric PPM Architecture

Another example of PPM architecture comes from Computer Associates, the software giant simply known as CA. CA is a recognized industry leader in providing integrated solutions for IT management and service delivery. EITM, Enterprise IT management, is CA's vision for providing a new level of management control across the enterprise by both integrating and automating the management of disparate systems and CA provides an integration-centric approach to PPM architecture. First, as shown in Figure 9.4, CA espouses the premise that IT organizations require an integrated management solution that can consolidate all demand from incidents to strategic and tactical demand.

Most PPM solutions provide integration with desktop tools used for project scheduling like Microsoft Project and Open Workbench as well as ERP systems. CA Clarity also integrates with change, service, and asset portfolio management. Years back, many within the project management community may have felt that this level of integration was not necessarily needed as project work was often viewed, to be distinct and different from operational work. The PMO as an organizational concept dealt primarily with projects. Ironically, as the importance of the demand management function emerged, this function, or at least the responsibility to figure how best to do it in terms of people, process, tools, and policy, was often given to the director of the PMO. By integrating these components, organizations can establish and achieve a complete end-to-end governance and track and manage business requests providing stakeholders with visibility throughout the entire lifecycle.

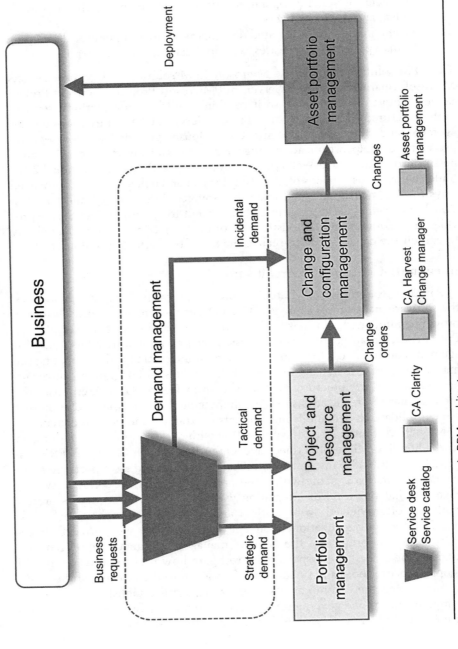

Figure 9.4 Integration-centric PPM architecture

Enterprise Performance Management Architecture

Another example of PPM architecture comes from Planview. Founded in 1989 by PPM visionary Patrick Durbin, Planview has been focused on PPM for over two decades. Too large to be called a *boutique company*, Planview remains as one of the top providers of PPM software that has not been acquired by one of the IT giants, such as IBM, HP, Oracle, and Microsoft. As shown in figure 9.5, the PPM architecture espoused by Planview is known as enterprise performance management architecture.

The Planview enterprise performance management framework recognizes the importance of an organization's enterprise business applications, desktop tools, collaboration platforms, business intelligence and financials, and IT infrastructure. And, it leverages the existence of these common and predictably existent tools, rather than duplicating or being oblivious to them. To develop such functions and capabilities that are already inherent to an organization's existing tools, applications, and infrastructure would only result in duplication of functionality and additional cost and complexity.

The Planview enterprise component of this architecture presents the applications and tools needed to effectively manage the project portfolio of the PMO. These are Planview tools:

◆ Enterprise Portfolio Management (EPM) enables the PMO to define and communicate organizational objectives and strategies, acquire a complete view of capacities and demand, and make optimal and transparent decisions to control costs, risks, and benefit delivery.

◆ PPM provides tactical execution of integrated work and workforce management, supporting workflows, and daily reporting at the project level.

◆ Service Portfolio Management enables the organization to catalog, quantify, and manage the resulting products and services.

◆ PRISMS enables the PMO to establish and integrate the supporting network of business processes, best practices, and supporting tools.

◆ Business Process Manager automates these processes with a user friend interface that can also track work as it traverses these processes as well as measure compliance using gates and supporting checklists.

◆ Insight Analytics enables the organization to monitor performance of all activities with meaningful drill-down metrics and graphics. And supporting functions help the organization to manage resources and money, collaboration capabilities, and data and request management.

The Planview EPM framework enables the PMO to establish an architecture approach grounded in the customer-centric reality of heterogeneous IT environments. This enables the integration of PPM with the other components of the overall architecture such as business service management, application

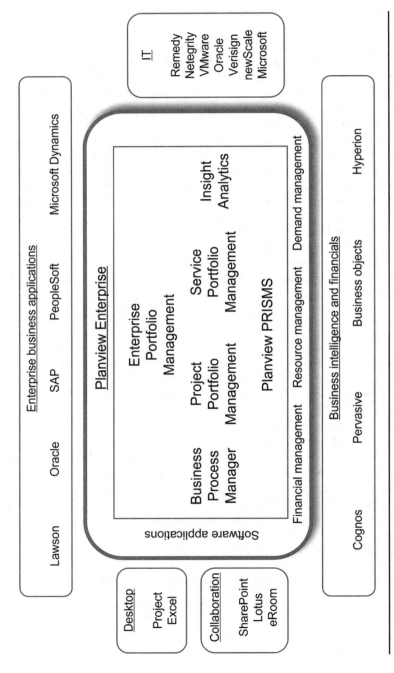

Figure 9.5 Enterprise performance management architecture

lifecycle management, productivity, and corporate resource planning and financial management. The Planview architecture approach encompasses the wide scope of functionality required, simplifies a complex and naturally heterogeneous environment, and enables a wide range of decision making and selection of the best-of-breed alternatives represented in each of the components of the overall architecture.

Summary

The *tools verses architecture* debate is one that is sure to last, and one that is sure to result in PPM risks being either mitigated or incurred by the organization. Just as organizations can benefit in numerous ways by establishing an architecture approach that provides the PPM capabilities needed to achieve scalability, economies of scale, and consistent and predictable product of the project outcomes, so too, can organizations benefit from implementing point tools from new market entrants with innovative approaches for solving their fair share of the complex problems of today. Add to the mix the collaborative nature of PPM component activities, and the end result is not a structured transactional environment that can be managed using the guiding principles of *Taylorism*, rather a complex and highly adaptive environment with more and more self-directed teams in need of structure, as well as flexibility within structure. Hence, the reason for all of the tools.

It can be a daunting task to identify, select, and implement the potpourri of things needed to achieve success with PPM and few organizations have the luxury of starting with a clean sheet of paper. With PPM as a planned management activity typically commenced in a formal manner long after the core business entities have been put in place and equipped with IT infrastructure, applications, tools, and training, there will be a great deal of past investments, some good some bad, that can hopefully be leveraged and extended more than they get in the way.

At the end of the day, point tools can only go so far. To meet immediate needs and to pass the test of time, a well thought out architecture for PPM is required. Fortunately, this is an area where leadership is in no short supply. Leading research firms such as the Gartner Group, Forrester Research, and others provide extensive research and market analysis. Their proven research methods, culture of unbiased *industry watching*, and unhesitating willingness to step in, call out, and correct oversights and mistakes periodically made within the project management community provide us all with tempered strategies, reasoned approaches, and a team of trusted advisors. Published works like the Gartner Group "Magic Quadrant for IT Project and Portfolio Management" report are annual must-reads and greatly help organizations understand PPM market trends and solution space and can be used as a key input to PPM architecture development.

In developing architecture for PPM, it would be an oversight to not take full advantage of the thought, market, and product leadership of the established PPM providers as well as that of the innovative, new market entrants. PPM is not a one-tool-does-it-all transactional proposition. The community of PPM providers have years of collective experience helping their customers implement collaborative feature sets in support of project and portfolio management while at the same time leveraging common IT infrastructure, applications, and tool components.

Lastly, for the specific purpose of demonstrating the importance, benefits, and value of establishing an architecture approach to PPM as opposed to having a one-tool-does-it-all mindset, four representative examples of PPM architecture—BOT International, Microsoft, Computer Associates, and Planview—were illustrated and discussed to provide a few different views of PPM architecture: PMO-centric, EPM-centric, integration-centric, and enterprise performance management centric. If the space in this book would have allowed it, many others would have been provided as there is significant value to the differing approaches to PPM architecture and their subtle nuances. They all seek to meet complex business problems, simplify and correctly convey a multifaceted set of needs and components that contribute to fulfilling those needs, and to avoid the risks as well as missed opportunities that a one-tool-does-it-all mindset often produces.

Questions

1. What three factors contribute to a one-tool-does-it-all mindset?
2. What factor is perceived to be the greatest contributor to the one-tool-does-it-all mindset?
3. What factor actually is the greatest contributor to the one-tool-does-it-all mindset?
4. In what ways are providers of PPM tools responsible for the one-tool-does-it-all mindset?
5. In what ways does the PPM analyst community contribute to the one-tool-does-it-all mindset?
6. In what ways are customers of PPM tools responsible for the one-tool-does-it-all mindset?
7. What purpose does architecture serve?
8. What are the four components of the PMO-centric PPM architecture?
9. How does an EPM-centric PPM architecture compare and contrast to an integration-centric PPM architecture?
10. What is the basic premise of enterprise IT management (EITM)?

References

Curran-Morton, Craig. 2010. "Baby Steps," http://www.gantthead.com.

Stang, Dan. 2010. "Magic Quadrant for IT Project and Portfolio Management." Stamford, CT: The Gartner Group.

Showcase #9:
Planview International

Extending the PPM Architecture View

Jeff Durbin and Julian Brackley, Planview International

From a vendor's perspective, there is considerable value to taking an architectural view when selecting supporting PPM technology. Taking a one-tool-does-it-all approach will probably leave the organization lacking in functionality or disconnected from corporate standards in one or more functional areas. When evaluating PPM systems, as Perry suggests in the opening of this chapter, there are three key areas that we would like to extend the PPM architecture model to include: product flexibility (ability to meet a wide variety of requirements), enterprise integration (ability to leverage existing corporate assets and standards), and deployment methods (SaaS, hosting and perpetual on-premise options).

Product Flexibility

As discussed earlier, when an evaluation is primarily based on the scoring results of a comprehensive RFP or RFI, then the vendor that is likely to be selected is the one who provides the tool with the most boxes checked. This is an increasingly common situation, which has created a challenging dilemma for most software vendors as they plan their product roadmap to keep pace with market demands. Ultimately, the size and complexity of PPM products is largely driven by the customers and the markets that the PPM vendors serve.

Leading enterprise-class vendors work to ensure that their PPM products are able to support everything from the most basic capabilities to highly sophisticated use cases, while still striving to provide a simple and intuitive user experience that can be easily adopted. Meanwhile, ever-increasing customer expectations for additional features and capabilities continue to drive additional product complexities. Ironically, only a few organizations ever progress to the point where they actually utilize many of the rich capabilities that they *required* on the RFP.

As a result, a number of basic PPM platforms have entered the market in the last decade that cater to customers who are overwhelmed by the potential cost and growth in capabilities offered by top-line tools or who are in need of a simple platform that can be quickly set up and deployed with minimal time and training. Unfortunately, these same products can quickly become outmoded as increasing organizational requirements and process maturity drives the need for additional features. However, with careful research and evaluation, it is possible to establish entry-level PPM capabilities at a reasonable cost without sacrificing anticipated future requirements for more advanced features.

Based on our experience with hundreds of organizations, the PPM implementation approach that we have found to be consistently successful is most easily described as *crawl, walk, then run*. While it may seem cliché, it aptly describes how your PPM needs will undoubtedly grow over time, rather than represent a static point solution. It also helps to convey how your PPM program will quickly mature when given a healthy, strong foundation, in much the same way that the strength and coordination of a child continues to develop.

When selecting a PPM vendor and tool set, choose a platform that can support three-to-five-year objectives, while still offering enough flexibility to quickly and easily meet current needs. Understanding your long-term business objectives and mapping the functions that the PPM tool will need to provide over its life expectancy is critical to building a PPM roadmap that is effective in terms of cost as well as features. Chapter 17 of *Taming Change with Portfolio Management* (Durbin and Doerscher, Greenleaf Book Group, 2010) provides a reference model for mapping out your PPM implementation. Overlooking the time dimension and the vendor's ability to support your growth in maturity could leave you in a situation where either a solution is resisted because it is perceived as too complex for the organization, or you quickly outgrow the capabilities of a simple product. Either outcome results in repeating the entire selection process and a costly tool replacement.

It is equally important to evaluate the capabilities that the PPM vendor provides to aid your organization with process development and tool adoption. In addition to software, a full service vendor should be able to provide your organization with one-stop shopping for supporting enablement elements, such as best practices, process maps, on-line training curriculum, and an active user community. The core PPM product provides automation for some business processes that can be extremely complex. Leveraging the experience of your vendor, as well as your peers, around best practices and organizational adoption will help ensure that you achieve the significant return you expect from your PPM investment.

Enterprise Integration

As previously described, an architectural view of a PPM application provides a cohesive picture of how all of the required functional elements of your related business processes fit, relate and work together. This picture is critical to overcoming the one-tool-fits-all mentality. When evaluating a specific functional requirement, it is important to first evaluate whether there is a competent and accepted tool in house that is already being leveraged at a corporate level.

A simple example is collaboration. Most mature PPM products on the market will offer collaboration capabilities, but from an architectural view, should you use those capabilities? Microsoft's SharePoint is the growing standard for collaboration in many large organizations. It is unlikely that collaboration functionality provided within a PPM tool will exceed SharePoint's depth of capabilities any time soon.

An additional consideration is the planned scope of your PPM deployment; if SharePoint is already being used uniformly across the enterprise, would it make sense for a particular department or business unit to convert to something different? In most cases, PPM vendors provide functionality for organizations that may not yet have an established collaboration platform in place. However, for others, it may make more sense to leverage available integration tools to give your organization the strengths of a specialized PPM product that can easily incorporate SharePoint for a richer collaboration solution.

Discussing any one individual product integration (like SharePoint) is much like discussing one *on-ramp* and one *off-ramp* on a highway. If you only want to go to one town that would be fine, but for a PPM implementation where you typically need HR data, financial data, application inventory data, and more, plus taking into account the number of commercial-off-the-shelf as well as homegrown products, a single integration is not enough. What you need is a platform that will allow your organization to quickly and easily define the business rules between systems and readily accommodate changes in these rules as maturity develops or business pressures dictate changes to processes. Similar to the implementation approach we defined in the previous section, it is important to start with a simple integration strategy.

A common mistake is to spend too much time up front trying to define and build the ultimate integration scheme. Trying to incorporate every bell and whistle that you can think of in an effort to satisfy everyone's desires will take five times longer and have a higher probability for error, compared to starting out with a minimum set of *must-have* requirements. By leveraging the experience of your PPM vendor with developing common integration points, you can typically satisfy 80 percent of your requirements with a minimum amount of time and effort. This approach also ensures that you maintain momentum for your overall PPM implementation without getting bogged down by additional technical complexities that result from needlessly sophisticated integration requirements.

An additional advantage to starting simple is that you are more likely to convince individual stakeholders to take responsibility for the quality of the data from their respective systems before adopting more sophisticated integrations. Consider carefully how you plan each phase of your integration approach. The key is to do just enough in the initial phase to deliver early value, meet critical business requirements, establish credibility and adoption, and develop a level of experience and confidence. This early success will provide the basis for lessons learned that can be incorporated into additional integrations. Although prioritization of different integration points as part of your overall PPM program strategy may be the subject of a tough discussion between stakeholders, this is effort well spent and far preferable to taking on too much and jeopardizing the overall initiative.

Deployment Methods

There are a variety of deployment methods available from PPM vendors today that can be confusing to the uninitiated, so it is useful to begin with a few definitions:

- *Perpetual on-premise*—a customer purchases the software, installs it on their hardware, and deploys the system within their own IT physical infrastructure.
- *Hosted*—the customer purchases the software (using a licensing model similar to perpetual on-premise) but pays the software vendor a monthly fee to maintain the system on the vendors IT infrastructure.
- *Software as a Service (SaaS)*—the customer pays the vendor a monthly fee, which includes software leasing, as well as the vendor maintaining the system on their IT infrastructure.

When selecting which deployment method is right for you, there are a number of things to consider: funding (capital expense versus operating expense), technology (technical architecture and the in-house skills and effort necessary for ongoing support), cost (the total cost of ownership), and vendor flexibility (ability to switch models) all rank as top considerations. So let's look at each one in more detail.

Most PPM initiatives are initially funded as a capital expense to purchase the hardware and software. It is not uncommon to find that the pre-defined PPM budget is out-of-balance between the initial cost of the hardware and software, and other costs associated with implementation, such as consulting, training, interface development, internal labor, and such. As a result, the customer may end up making compromises on a product that does not have the headroom to meet their PPM roadmap or find themselves unable to adequately fund the implementation project, which then leads to poor adoption. We recently worked with a customer in Italy where the dynamics of the initiative changed significantly once the customer looked at funding the initiative through their OPEX budget. Under one scenario, we had a situation where neither the vendor nor the customer was happy with the cost and scope parameters of the proposed PPM implementation, while the other approach resulted in a mutually agreeable scenario. In that particular situation, the customer chose to go with an SaaS solution.

Most large organizations today have a broad set of in-house IT skills, staffing, and IT infrastructure necessary to support a number of different systems and platforms, such as Oracle, Microsoft, UNIX, and Java. The more compelling consideration is determining whether it is prudent to tie up those skills supporting a PPM tool. A PPM vendor who is already supporting hundreds of customer instances in their hosted environment may be able to support your PPM platform quicker, better, and at a lower cost than you can with your in-house resources, which in turn frees them up to engage in other internal work that must be performed.

Another consideration comes into play if you are using an outsourced firm for many of your IT services. For example, we were recently approached by a customer in France who bought our software four years ago. They requested a quote for our hosting services and found that it was half of what they were currently paying a different IT global services vendor. This is a good example of the hosted model, where the customer owns the PPM software but pays the vendor a monthly fee to support and maintain the system for them.

When evaluating the three different deployment models and their costs, it is always important to help customers understand how to realistically compare them on a like-for-like basis. For example, if we compare equivalent perpetual on-premise and SaaS proposals side-by-side, the typical initial reaction is that the perpetual on-premise option is priced higher, therefore the SaaS model is the best way to go. However, if you compare the total software cost of a perpetual on-premise license that includes three years of maintenance to a three-year SaaS deal, then the SaaS deal seems more expensive. In fact, neither of these represents a fair and complete comparison. To truly compare these options, you must also add the hardware depreciation, other software (like operating systems, network monitoring, and such), and labor costs for setup and operations such as performing backups, applying patches, and the like, to the perpetual on-premise proposal. It is also important to consider the benefit that the SaaS contract provides when it comes to controlling cash outflow and better alignment of costs to when actual benefit is realized. So, when evaluating different deployment options and models, make sure you take into account all of the expenses that factor into your total cost of ownership over the expected life of the system—you might be surprised by the results that you find.

Finally, consider vendor flexibility as it relates to shifting between different commercial models. It is always beneficial to keep your options open when it relates to how you will deploy your PPM system. One or two years into your implementation, you might find that you need to switch commercial models, so it is a significant advantage to select a vendor that offers more than one option, or who does not impose a significant penalty if you decide to change. For example, consider a customer who initially deploys their basic PPM solution in a SaaS environment; a few years later, the requirement comes up to integrate financial information from SAP or Oracle. The finance

By way of background, OPM3 provides a rich process construct that takes into consideration four process management stages (standardize, measure, control, and continuously improve), five project management process groups (initiating, planning, executing, monitoring and controlling, and closing), and the three domains of formal project management (project management, program management, and portfolio management). As shown in Figure 10.1, the OPM3 process construct combines these all together and maps every best practice and the capabilities needed to achieve the best practice, hundreds of them in total, to one or more locations within the model.

When led by a capable OPM3 practitioner, organizations can use this comprehensive maturity model to focus on a measured agenda and best-fit approach for building both process capability and a culture of excellence in project management, program management, and portfolio management. In my last book, *Business Driven PMO Setup*, commenting on OPM3 is John Schlichter (2009, p. 438), "OPM3 is a foil for clarifying what the project management culture is and enabling leaders to assess the organization from a variety of perspectives in the organization, in actionable ways that predicate the creation of accountability for specific and measurable steps to build the organization's

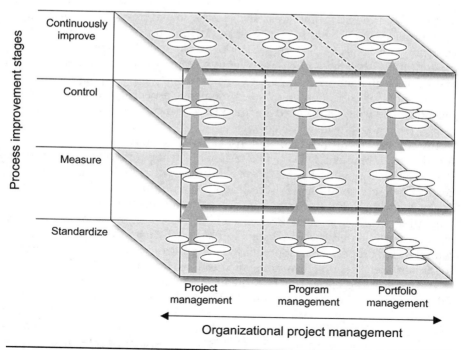

Figure 10.1   OPM3 process construct

project delivery capability." With respect to PPM maturity models such as OPM3 and their intent and the impact that they can have, this is the *good*.

Maturity models are inherently commonsense constructs. They lend themselves to a visual recognition and quick understanding. Much like the way we can envision the growth of a living organism from conception, to gestation, to birth, to childhood, to adolescence, to adulthood, so too can we envision the growth of an organizational entity within a business. However, there is a vast difference between being able to recognize what a maturity model like OPM3 is, and being able to effectively implement it. Without prior training, experience, and a deep understanding of the model, along with other requisite skills such as industry experience, deep business acumen, and organizational development skills, an attempt to informally implement a maturity model like OPM3 without the involvement and participation of a credible practitioner is likely to be doomed from the start. Nonetheless, this happens time and time again resulting in a waste of time and effort for the organization and an unnecessary and unhelpful blemish on the maturity model itself.

Take the case of a well-known Fortune 1000 firm. Their name is not important, but their story is. This firm had an IT project management office (PMO) and established an enterprise PMO for the purposes of formally advancing PPM. The first two years of operation for the enterprise PMO went fairly well, all things considered. Some areas such as the management of distinct enterprise projects and programs went well and demonstrated noted improvement over previous levels of performance prior to the establishment of the enterprise PMO. Other areas such as executive team participation, deliberation, and decision making with respect to selecting portfolio components and the management of corresponding budget elements, especially people resources, did not go as well, and a need for marked and measured improvement was clearly recognized by all involved.

In response to this need, the enterprise PMO manager presented and sold his idea to implement OPM3. The leadership team expressed concern over the time that it might take to achieve results as well as their concern over the costs of hiring a consulting firm to lead such an effort. The enterprise PMO manager responded to the noted concerns by proposing that the OPM3 implementation, in the form of assessments and action plans, would be carried out by the internal enterprise PMO staff and led by the enterprise PMO manager himself. This proposal and approach was approved. With no budget expense for an outside consulting firm to be incurred, what harm could it do?

As none of the enterprise PMO team, including the PMO manager, was OPM3 certified, they could not use the OPM3 Product Suite tool as it is only accessible by certified consultants and requires a software license to use. With that option not available, the approach taken by the enterprise PMO manager for the assessment was to use the OPM3 self-assessment tool called OPM3 Online. And as the OPM3 Online self-assessment tool provided merely a set a blind spot" or "Bill can't see the forest for the trees." These are examples of one-dimensional thinking.

For simple matters, one-dimensional thinking is all right. In fact, such one-dimensional thinking becomes more of a habit than a thought. Having an unbending and nonnegotiable mindset that your teenage daughter should be home each night no later than a specific time might be viewed as one-dimensional thinking, by the daughter that is. Most parents would view this thinking as all right. But in a business context, one-dimensional thinking can often not be all right, and it can lead to bad results. For example, applying a particular strategy or technique that has worked well in the past over and over again without much thought to changing conditions and alternative approaches could lead to an organization quickly becoming outcompeted in the marketplace and asking itself the now popularized question, "Who moved my cheese?"

For most organizations, PPM introduces new complexities, challenges, and opportunities that need to be carefully weighed in light of many changing dynamics. Though one-dimensional thinking may provide temporary efficiencies within the boundaries of a known comfort zone, it nearly always results in organizational ineffectiveness, and the comfort zone and acceptable business results are short lived. There are many dimensions to consider that can be modeled for the purposes of understanding and managing the complexities of PPM and sustaining value over time. Perhaps the two most important dimensions are how projects are viewed and how management is viewed.

How Projects Are Viewed—Myopic vs. Ubiquitous

Within the project management community, project management is typically viewed one-dimensionally. The prevailing wisdom is one that suggests that project management is a formal profession in which recognized standards are applied in the management of projects and project related work and that projects are to be managed by trained, and preferably certified, project management professionals. This way of thinking produces a myopic mindset that only recognizes formal projects and is oblivious to all other forms of project management, as well as those throughout the enterprise that have some kind of project effort to manage. As shown in Figure 10.2, like an ocean liner heading for an iceberg, the formal PMO sees only the tip of the *project iceberg* in terms of the formal IT and strategic projects and is seemingly unaware of the total depth, breadth, and ubiquitous nature of project management throughout the enterprise.

One would think that the project management community and PMOs would pay more attention to these ubiquitous projects, as they collectively represent tremendous value to an enterprise. But to the contrary, most in the

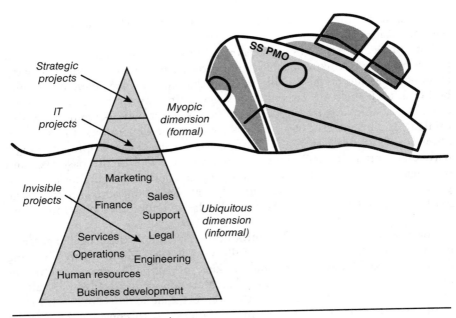

Figure 10.2   The project iceberg

project management community are quick to dismiss the idea that such informal projects are *real* projects, and they scoff at the idea that the people managing such informal projects be called "project managers"—as that is, or at least should be, a reserved title. Such attitudes toward project management as a hallowed profession are regrettable and really only serve to diminish the value of project management, not enhance or preserve it. Commenting to that effect in a spirited gantthead project management discussion forum post and exchange of replies is Anne Barks (2009, p. 1), who defends these ubiquitous informal projects and shouts out to the project management aficionados, "WAKE UP AND SMELL THE COFFEE . . . ! You can call them what you want, but we all know what they are. They're projects; get over it."

This myopic vs. ubiquitous view of project management is but one dimension that is contributing to the emergence of multi-dimensional PPM. Though it is a simple dimension to consider, it presents significant challenges and opportunities. It recognizes that projects exist throughout the enterprise in various shapes and forms. And it recognizes the value of the products of the projects outcomes. Whether or not ubiquitous projects are managed within the formal PPM system of the enterprise and whether or not they are supported by the best practices and resources of the PMO is merely a management decision, as it always has been. What's now different is that this decision

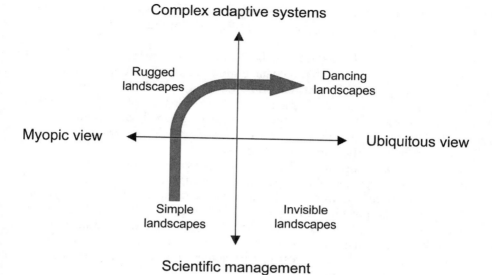

Figure 10.3   The emergence of multi-dimensional PPM

The concept of a fitness landscape is borrowed from evolutionary biology and is used as part of the CAS terminology. The ability of a system to solve its problem is its fitness. In the context of this multi-dimensional PPM model, for simplicity, consider the fitness landscape to be the equivalent of the PPM environment as determined by the nature of the project portfolio and how that portfolio is managed. The four fitness landscapes are defined and described as follows:

1. *Invisible landscapes*—These landscapes are not visible. As scientific management is the prevailing management style, only the formal projects of the organization are recognized. Though informal projects exist ubiquitously throughout the enterprise, the formal processes and methodologies of the organization are only used and applied to the formal project portfolio. As members of the formal project performing organization do not have an organizational measurement, process, or incentive for supporting informal projects, a resulting "blind-eye" for ubiquitous projects is manifested and becomes prevalent.

2. *Simple landscapes*—These landscapes represent the traditional PPM environment of today. Projects are viewed myopically, and scientific management in the form of adopted standards, defined processes, controls, measurements, and decision making is applied to the

management of the formal project portfolio. Alternative approaches to scientific management are resisted or summarily dismissed as not scalable.

3. *Rugged landscapes*—These landscapes represent the forward thinking organizations that recognize the challenges and opportunities that CAS present. Projects are still viewed myopically, but alternative approaches to scientific management are being introduced. The formal projects of the organization, previously managed with scientific management techniques, are now being performed in accordance with the principles of complex adaptive systems.

4. *Dancing landscapes*—These landscapes represent the full view of projects, formal and ubiquitous, throughout the organization and the full adoption of CAS principles. In these landscapes, organizations recognize the product of project value of all projects throughout the enterprise, and they recognize the inherent limitations and inabilities of scientific management to produce an environment from which the highest levels of success can be achieved amidst complex and ever changing dynamics.

Collectively, these fitness landscapes help to place a context to the emergence of multi-dimensional PPM.

In terms of the how-projects-are-viewed dimension, is it appropriate for the leadership team of PPM organizations to consider the ubiquitous projects of the enterprise? Over the last decade, I have posed that question to many leaders in the formal project management community. And in doing so, I cite the case of a publicly-traded high growth technology firm that, because of a ubiquitous project mishap, in this case a large sale that simply slipped from one quarter to another causing a miss in the forecasted revenue of the company, experienced a 50 percent drop in their stock price overnight. The resulting loss in market value to the firm was $1.3 billion dollars, and all parties involved agreed that, had the barest of project management rigor been applied, this ubiquitous project mishap could have been avoided. Is this not worth just a modicum of attention? Can the formal project management community be that obtuse regarding the ubiquitous dimension of project management? As evidenced by such things as standards, tools, and guidance, regrettably the answer can only be, "yes."

In terms of the how-management-is-viewed dimension, is all of what we call scientific management no longer appropriate? Is it appropriate for the leadership team of PPM organizations to think and behave in terms of CAS? For most organizations, the answer to these questions will be arrived at and found to be a unique balancing of both. First, not all project environments are complex adaptive systems. Traditional approaches, such as Taylorism, have their place. Where the environment is static, predictable, and not CAS, it may lend itself to, or even require, strict adherence to process and scientific management. Here, efficiency is valued over effectiveness.

Conversely, as PPM fitness landscapes become more complex, scientific management becomes less reliable and, in many cases, fails. Constant unexpected change and the subsequent adaption cannot be effectively addressed with top-down planning only, as plans change and require real-time adaption. In complex adaptive systems, the design of work into discrete tasks optimized individually as embodied in Taylorism, gives way to rules of thumb estimates. Detailed plans, schedules, and work breakdown structures of tasks must give way to empowered self-directed teams. Effectiveness is valued over efficiency, but this can't be just a return to the medieval guilds of the past. Accountability is still integral and required in CAS. The only difference is that the top-down processes and metrics that assumed predictability and normality and produced inaccurate measurements in the first place are replaced with best available information as determined by the self-directed team.

Summary

As is the case with most systems, a balanced approach for sustaining value involves bringing the current system under control and then seeking ways to improve. For many organizations implementing PPM, there will be a natural starting point, such as first getting their arms around the list of projects currently underway. Understanding the sheer number of projects and resources involved enables a degree of multi-project management to take place such as eliminating or consolidating duplicate projects and terminating non-essential projects and projects no longer relevant because of changing conditions. As projects become viewed with more attention to organizational priorities, capacities, and constraints, a form of enterprise project management begins to take shape. And as the organization is further enabled with strategic alignments, sophisticated tools, agreed and adhered to best practices, and dedicated resources for portfolio planning and efficient frontier analysis, a best-in-class degree of capability in PPM is enacted, enabling business strategy to better participate in, if not drive, the selection of portfolio components and realization of benefits.

This is the traditional manner in which PPM value is maintained and, for many organizations, this represents more than a full plate of work to take on now and well into the future. Beyond these common approaches and roads well travelled for establishing PPM are a number of constructs useful to consider.

PPM maturity models, such as the Project Management Institute's OPM3 and others, offer well-reasoned approaches for assessing and improving project management related capabilities. Far more than a pretty picture on a Power-Point slide, these models are comprehensive in scope and detail, yet flexible to accommodate differing implementation business use cases. With the assistance of an outside expert with deep knowledge of the model, business acumen, and years of implementation experience at complex organizations and environments, maturity models like OPM3 can provide practical guidance and actionable strategies which can be executed in phases for marked and sustained improvement in capabilities. The end result of these improved capabilities is better outcomes.

In addition to formal project management maturity models, a broader view of both projects and management systems is essential to sustain value. A broader view of projects opens up a vast set of possibilities as the once neglected ubiquitous projects of the organization are finally taken into full view and an appropriate level of consideration. The product of the project outcomes of ubiquitous projects are significant and the needs of those managing such projects have far less to do with formal project management functionality and traditional tools and far more to do with social project management functionality and new systems and features designed to provide new levels of empowerment, self-directed teamwork, and confidence.

A broader view of management systems needs to be entertained. The desire to achieve command and control oversight typical to scientific management techniques needs to be tempered with the pressing complexities, uncertainties, and realities of today. Complex adaptive systems thinking can provide an approach to acknowledge these challenges and to find ways to pursue the opportunities that they present. The combination of project management maturity models, an expanded view of projects, and an expanded view of management offers organizations a rich and diverse set of alternatives from which to sustain the value of PPM.

Questions

1. What are the four process improvement stages of the PMI OPM3?
2. What are the three domains of the PMI OPM3?
3. According to the author, in what ways are project management maturity models *good*?
4. According to the author, in what ways are project management maturity models *bad*?
5. According to the author, in what ways are project management maturity models *ugly*?
6. With respect to the how-projects-are-viewed dimension, what are myopic projects and who manages them?
7. With respect to the how-projects-are-viewed dimension, what are ubiquitous projects and who manages them?

8. What are the principles of scientific management?
9. What is Taylorism?
10. What are the principles of complex adaptive systems and in what ways are they relevant to PPM?

References

Barks, Anne. 2009. "Project Management and the Apprentice—Sound Off Here." http://www.gantthead.com.

Handler, Robert. 2010. "Harnessing Change Complexity—The New PPM Direction?" Stamford, CT: Gartner Group.

Highsmith, Jim, and Alistair Cockburn. 2001. "Agile Software Development: The Business of Innovation." http://computer.org/education/curricula2001.

Perry, Mark. 2009. *Business Driven PMO Setup: Practical Insights, Techniques, and Case Examples for Ensuring Success.* Fort Lauderdale, FL: J. Ross Publishing.

Remington, Kaye, and Julien Pollack. 2007. *Tools for Complex Projects.* Hampshire, England: Gower Publishing.

Schlichter, John. 2009. "Discussion Forum—Project Management Central" http://www.gantthead.com.

Showcase #10: AtTask

Social Project Management

Ty Kiisel, Manager of Social Outreach, At Task

Introduction

As project and portfolio management (PPM) methodologies spread departmentally throughout organizations, the greatest challenge facing executives is a lack of voluntary team member participation in the project management process. Taking a traditional top-down or command-and-control project management approach doesn't work with today's workforce. Coming to the realization that project success depends more on people and less on process or technology is a paradigm shift needed within the PPM industry.

A Better Way to Get Work Done

The search for a better way to get work done requires that we stand back and take an objective look at the PPM process with fresh eyes. Thomas Kuhn[1], who coined the phrase *paradigm shift* in 1962 said, "A paradigm is what members of a scientific community, and they alone, share." In other words, a paradigm shift can be identified as a change in the basic assumptions within the ruling theory of a scientific community.

Kuhn used the duck-rabbit illustration, as shown in Illustration 10.2, to show how a paradigm shift could cause someone to see the same information in an entirely different way.

As organizations look to project management methodologies to increase visibility, improve effectiveness, and ultimately maximize their ability to compete in a highly competitive marketplace, the need to look at traditional work management methodologies has become increasingly important. Regardless of whether you see the rabbit or the duck at first glance, as project management methodologies become more prevalent across the enterprise, we must acknowledge the need to look at the challenges faced by the PPM industry from a new perspective.

---

[1]*The Structure of Scientific Revolutions*, 1962, Thomas Kuhn

Illustration 10.2   Duck or rabbit—what do you see?

Taking a Fresh Look from a New Perspective

According to Alan Cooper[2], who is considered by many to be the father of personas, "Social scientists have long realized that human behaviors are too complex and subject to too many variables to rely solely on quantitative data to understand them. Design and usability practitioners, borrowing techniques from anthropology and other social sciences, have developed many qualitative methods for gathering useful data on user behaviors to a more pragmatic end—to help create products that better serve user needs."

In other words, human behaviors are complicated to measure. There are so many variables in how we react to different situations that quantifying our behaviors in a way that can be illustrated in a graph or spreadsheet is problematic. In my opinion, the best way (if you accept what Cooper suggests) to understand how people interact with the project management process would be to borrow from the science of anthropology—and observe. Observing how users interact with project management software is the best way to learn how to make improvements in the user experience. However, that's not the way most software, including project management software, is designed.

Typically software development follows a more iterative process that usually looks like this:

1. A need is identified.
2. Software engineers create a version (or solution) to meet the need.
3. The version is shared with a focus group (that could include both internal and external participants).
4. Feedback from the focus group is collected.

---

[2] *About Face: The Essentials of Interaction Design*, 2007, Alan Cooper, Robert Reimann, and David Cronin

5. A new iteration incorporating the feedback is created.
6. The version is shared with another focus group.
7. The process continues until the software is considered complete.

This seems like a fairly logical process, right? It might be logical, but it isn't the most effective way to create products that better serve user needs, and it *never* results in anything innovative. As opposed to an iterative process, "qualitative research helps us understand the domain, context, and constraints of a product in different, more useful ways than quantitative research does. It also helps us identify patterns of behavior among users and potential users of a product much more quickly and easily than would be possible with quantitative approaches," writes Cooper.

What Users Need vs. What Users Think They Need

Love it or hate it, the development of the Nintendo Wii is a great case in point. Genyo Takeda[3], the general manager of Nintendo's integrated research division, said the following about the possible results of allowing conventional thought to control the design of the Wii:

> *"This may sound paradoxical, but if we had followed the existing roadmaps we would have aimed to make it 'faster and flashier.' In other words, we would have tried to improve the speed at which it displays stunning graphics. But we could not help but ask ourselves, 'How big an impact would that direction really have on our customers.'"*

Takeda famously compared building a gaming console to the automobile industry. Not everyone looking to purchase a car is looking for a high-performance racecar—there is a lucrative market for automakers making fuel-efficient cars. Takeda suggested that the Wii could parallel this model. The challenge, as he saw it, was that given the choice, users would continue to ask for more and more regardless of how it really affected their gaming experience:

> *"There is no end to the desire of those who just want more. Give them one, they ask for two. Give them two, and the next time they will ask for five instead of three. Then they will want ten, thirty, a hundred, their desire growing exponentially. Giving in to this will lead us nowhere in the end. I started to feel unsure about following this path about a year into development."*

---

[3] *http://us.wii.com/iwata_asks/wii_console*, Nintendo Retrieved, 2009

The Nintendo Wii has been successful because Takeda and his team focused more on how the user interacted with the game and less on following the conventional wisdom that *faster and flashier* was better. They looked at the process with fresh eyes, unclouded by conventional thought. Could the project management industry learn from this?

Most project management software is a great example of the traditional software design process. The common paradigm for project management software today looks at the repeatable processes of the assembly lines created during the industrial age as a model for how projects should be approached. Although Henry Ford developed an effective model for building the automobile, it is not a good model for the creative problem solving that goes on within project teams by knowledge workers—which is part of the challenge associated with how today's workforce interacts with project-based work.

Consistent with the assertions made by Nintendo's Takeda, the traditional approach to project management solutions has created software that includes numerous features requested by customers or recommended by industry analysts, without any real validation as to whether or not those features add any value to the process—or are really even needed by customers. What's more, contextual inquiry, or observing how people interact with the project management process generally and project management software particularly, is the key to designing software that will meet the needs of users and fully engage them in the project management process.

Approaching the Software Development Process Like an Anthropologist

Although the software designers at AtTask might not be anthropologists, approaching software design from that perspective enabled them to learn a lot about how executives, managers, and team members interact with the project management process. Like most scientists, AtTask designers started with a hypothesis and the goal of either validating or disproving their assumptions.

Consulting stakeholders both within and outside of AtTask resulted in the theory that traditional top-down or command-and-control approaches to managing projects were not effective. From the outset, the answers to these questions were deemed critical to any effort to streamline the process and more effectively engage project teams at the grass-roots level:

1. How do you know what things you should be working on?
2. Who do you report to?
3. How do you communicate status in meetings?
4. What is the data you work with?
5. How do you prioritize work?
6. How do you get work done?

The inquiry process included a series of interview questions and observations conducted by a rotating team of three designers and engineers. To keep the learning process as objective as possible, only one member of the team participated in every inquiry. A broad cross-section of industries including, but not limited to IT, were chosen to give the research universal applicability.

Watching Project Teams and Validating Assumptions

"Basically, we just watched people interact with the project management process," said Steve Ballard, Director of UX Design for AtTask. According to Ballard:

1. We sat in status meetings.
2. We were in manufacturing areas watching people use their software.
3. We lived with these people.
4. We met with executives and project teams.
5. We sat down next to them at their desks and watched what they did and how they communicated with each other.
6. We looked at their whiteboards and Post-It notes.
7. We read the reminders they taped to their computers.
8. We looked at the documents they used to make things more productive.

"We repeated this process with as diverse an audience as we could find," said Ballard. "We observed people from a wide cross-section of industries including financial services, manufacturing, IT, and pharmaceuticals. We visited over twenty organizations from across the country, both large and small."

Casual interviews along with observation were utilized to listen and discover patterns. The goal was not to unearth the idiosyncratic needs of individual users (most users can't envision what doesn't already exist). If software design is driven strictly by user input, the software will give them no more than what they already have, it won't solve their *real* needs, and it will fail to innovate. The goal of AtTask designers was to create something truly innovative that would streamline the project management process and make any group doing project-based work more efficient.

What Did AtTask Software Designers Learn?

AtTask software designers learned that Chris (the persona they designated for individual contributors on a project team) was the lynchpin. Although Chris would not be included among any organizations' buyer personas, Chris is the key to whether or not project management software is universally accepted and adopted throughout the organization, and a critical determiner as to whether or not the information that flows upward in an organization is timely and accurate.

Ultimately, organizations utilizing traditional project management methods and software weren't seeing value from their investment because software vendors focused only on the buyer persona(s). The end user persona (Chris) wasn't even a consideration in the purchasing process. Contextual inquiry identified the failure of this approach. It allowed AtTask designers to not only observe how Chris interacts with his or her project management software, it allowed them to observe those activities that took place outside of the software to accomplish work, what things motivated Chris to perform, and what could be incorporated into project management software to help, rather than hinder, Chris—and ultimately deliver a project management solution that would provide a sustainable ROI.

Addressing Chris's Needs Improves the Project Management Process

It may seem counter-intuitive, but getting Chris involved in the project management process is critical. Anecdotally, the importance of adoption is not questioned by either users or the designers of project management software. Furthermore, those organizations that take the time to engage end users early in the process seem to be more successful at adoption and widespread usage than those that don't. Contextual inquiry confirmed that the greatest challenge facing executives today is a lack of voluntary team member participation in the project management process and that a traditional top-down or command-and-control project management approach doesn't work with today's workforce. Organizations that continue to utilize these ineffective approaches will suffer from:

1. Project information that executives don't trust
2. An overly structured management environment that people dislike
3. Frustrated project teams whose accomplishments often go unrecognized

The Three Key Drivers of Increased Project Team Participation

By observing Chris, AtTask software designers discovered that people are more willing to interact with the process and provide the accurate and timely information executives need to make decisions, if the following conditions exist:

1. *People are empowered*—People want to be empowered with ownership and flexibility regarding their deliverables and deadlines. Replacing the top-down task assignment model with a more social, team-centric model enables team members to contribute to the establishment of benchmarks and time-lines, while creating a greater sense of responsibility

among team members, because they contributed to the establishment of timelines and deadlines.

2. *Executives have confidence*—Qualitative information about projects provides deeper insight into real project status. Business leaders who leverage solutions that facilitate free-form conversations around assignments capture better information to help them keep an accurate pulse on their business and make more proactive decisions. Business leaders need to have confidence that the information they are making decisions with is not inaccurate or stale.

3. *People are recognized for their accomplishments*—People take pride in their work, and they care about what their managers and peers think of them and their accomplishments. Organizations that facilitate the recognition of individual team member accomplishments and contributions foster an environment where team members are more inclined to participate and provide the information needed by executives to make informed decisions. What's more, team members want their managers to have an understanding of what it really takes to accomplish their tasks and feel appreciation for their dedication to the work they do.

An Analyst's Perspective: Socializing the Process for Every Member of the Project Team

Executives need trustworthy and relevant information to make well-informed decisions and successfully lead their companies. In a report commissioned by AtTask and conducted by Forrester Research[4], bottom-up operational reporting was identified as three times more accurate than traditional top-down monitoring for informing decisions. What's more, missing or inaccurate information about time utilization and project progress was identified as a significant contributor to financial waste. Enabling a transparent environment, where everyone's work contributions are visible to peers and managers, provides executives a more accurate pulse of what's going on within their business. Capturing qualitative information at the source provides context, making data more understandable. When asked, "What, in your opinion, would most improve data accuracy for knowledge worker project/task time tracking?" the leading measure for improving data accuracy, according to Forrester's findings, was identified as *capturing more qualitative information.*

Managers require a voluntary, free flow of information from team members to effectively lead projects. The Forrester findings suggest that the general

---

[4]Market Credibility: Social Project Management/PPM (SPM/PPM), Tim Harmon, April Lawson, April 16, 2010

acceptance and use of social networking tools among the managers of knowledge workers, 65 percent, reinforces the case for implementing a new, more social project management process. Both managers and knowledge workers, 75 percent, view missing or inaccurate information about project progress as a significant contributor to financial waste. Forrester's findings indicate that management visibility and project status clarification are of great value to the managers of knowledge workers. Study respondents deemed giving both peers *and* management visibility into performance, and providing knowledge workers with the means to clarify project status more clearly, to be of high value. By providing a more social project management platform, organizations foster a collaborative environment that facilitates the voluntary flow of accurate and timely information—enabling managers to effectively lead project teams.

Team members are not project management experts. What's more, according to Forrester, 40 percent of managers indicate that their knowledge workers are dissatisfied with the current PPM tool. Although managers believe their teams' accomplishments are being adequately recognized, knowledge workers feel that their managers are out of touch regarding their contributions and value. Over 40 percent of knowledge workers report lack of recognition by their managers, and over 60 percent by executive management. Peer commentary was seen as highly valuable in the workplace and when the study respondents were asked, "What would make you most interested in investing in a PPM or project management software solution?" it was indicated by 50 percent that *the software makes everyone's work contributions transparent to peers and managers*. Empowering knowledge workers with input into how their work is planned, the ownership of deliverables, and allowing them to share qualitative information about their work, was identified by Forrester as the most valuable and unrealized catalyst to achieving high performance.

Implementing a Solution for Chris

Contextual inquiry and subsequent analyst research validates the importance of Chris's role in project success and is why AtTask approached a solution from Chris's perspective first. Implementing a solution for Chris started with flow-chart user stories, screen level sketches, and wireframes, along with observing the reaction from Chris as he interacted with the original framework. Designers watched Chris navigate through clickable prototypes, refined from there, and followed-up with further usability tests. The general reaction from users included:

1. "This wasn't what I expected to see."
2. "You were *really* watching us, weren't you?"
3. "You solved my hardest problems—even though they were not what I expected you to tackle."

Although the response from test subjects has been overwhelmingly positive, there have been some detractors. The overarching concern of detractors was, "This threatens my authority." The kind of paradigm shift suggested by this research is not for the weak-kneed. It implies a completely new approach from the software used to the project management style employed. This grass roots, social project approach, will necessitate the need to revisit how we manage the process and project teams from the top of the organization to the bottom. Organizations unwilling to do this may attempt to empower the workforce but frustrate the process. That being said, this new approach to project *leadership* carries with it the potential for exponential gains in project team productivity.

AtTask's Answer to the Paradigm Shift in Project Management: Stream™

Stream provides a totally new PPM approach—building on an integrated social project management platform that addresses the demands of project-based work that traditional PPM solutions can't accommodate. By recognizing a number of benefits that draw people into social networking tools, such as ease of use, the positive nature of feedback from their network, and the ability to share qualitative information about what they are doing, Stream addresses the paradigm shift required to meet the needs of end users (Chris) and streamline the project management process by:

1. Empowering the front lines by getting teams more involved in project plans, and promoting greater individual ownership over priorities and commitments.
2. Capturing the real story with a constant flow of qualitative information that delivers greater visibility and a richer representation of what's really happening within a project.
3. Recognizing accomplishments by fostering discussion, highlighting accomplishments and keeping everyone engaged (people receive recognition for accomplishments and comment on other's work and accomplishments).

Looking at the project management process from a fresh perspective made it possible to see the approaching paradigm shift regarding how individual members of project teams will interact with the project management process and how that positively impacts the quality of information executives use to make business decisions. The power of social networking within the structure of project management will deliver more relevant information and clearer visibility into business initiatives, enabling executives to more successfully lead their companies.

Epilogue

What is project portfolio management? This is a question that I often get asked. And though the text book answer is rather easy to cite, that is not the one that I give. Rather, when asked, I answer that project portfolio management is cancelling a project that is on time and on budget. This usually provokes a blank stare or a moment of silence and in that time I rhetorically ask 'when was the last time you cancelled a project that, though performing well, wasn't relevant to the needs of your business.' If the answer is that this has never happens, then that is a tell-tale sign that what you are doing is not project portfolio management.

This is in no way meant to discredit whatever management activity that is taking place regarding the project opportunities of the organization, rather it is intended to shine a bright light on just how difficult it is to view projects as inanimate objects that can be identified, categorized, evaluated, selected, prioritized, and, if need be, terminated. To the contrary, projects are not inanimate objects. Projects represent ideas, innovation, passion, inspiration, values, competitive advantages, strategic alignments, realization of some kind of potential, fulfillment of a promise, and on and on. And projects involve people, a lot of them, and it is this *people* element that is anything but inanimate.

So what exactly is project portfolio management and how do we go about it? As my good friend and trusted PPM expert, Doc Dochtermann of Microsoft, muses, "If project portfolio management is the answer, then what was the question?" And that is an excellent starting point. For most organizations the true starting point for project portfolio management will only be found after someone has answered the question, why do we want to do this?

There can be an untold list of reasons for wanting to do project portfolio management and these reasons, of course, will vary based upon organizational capabilities and nuances and can change with the wind based on industry, market, and business conditions on the ground. The issue is not so much are we doing project portfolio management technically correct, rather are we doing it for the right reasons? And what might be right for one organization may very well be wrong for another. As PPM experts such as Dochtermann and many others can attest, no amount of best practice standards and tools can truly help if the purpose and the starting point have not been properly cast.

The technical side of project portfolio management in terms of best practice standards and tools is important and challenging in their own right. Effective practices will always outcompete ineffective practices. This isn't meant to imply that effective practices need necessarily be overly detailed nor patterned after a particular approach or standard. To the contrary, effective practices are whatever approaches work best for a specific organization at a particular point in time. Like a car engine, this needs to be tuned for the particular purpose of use and must be regularly maintained.

Similarly, there are marked differences in tools for project portfolio management not to mention the provider domain knowledge and support that comes with those tools. Though often overlooked in RFIs, RFPs, and vendor selection scorecards, each tool provider has significant and often different kinds of value add to offer their customers. Hence, the time and effort required to select the best fit PPM tool for an organization should not be approached lightly or taken for granted as a routine IT procurement.

At some point in time the discussion and work effort around best practice standards and tools will come to an orderly end, and for many organizations this is when the real challenges of project portfolio management begin. Ironically, it is at this point that it is assumed that all of the heavy lifting has already been performed. Numerous issues and execution difficulties will soon take residence, and until they are addressed the efforts to manage the project portfolio will be compromised in ways both immediately noticed and undetected.

Of the top risks related to project portfolio management, this book seeks to identify and provide a mitigating remedy for them. By design, the book starts with a discussion of the importance of vision, mission, goals, and objectives that are all the bedrock of traditional scientific management. Without these things in place, a project portfolio management initiative of any kind will be at high risk. From there, attention is turned, chapter by chapter, to a number of key issues that, if not addressed, represent alarming risks that are likely to be incurred and with any one of them being capable of derailing the PPM efforts of the leadership team. And lastly, the book discusses sustaining value and, in particular, offers a caution about the various approaches that are posited in the industry. At one end within the formal project management community we have maturity models from which to draw. These maturity models are steeped in plan-driven scientific management thinking where pre-codified best practices drive capabilities that in turn result in better outcomes. At the other end within the contemporary field of the study of management systems we have complex adaptive systems that challenge and call to question the effectiveness of plan-driven scientific management approaches and in turn present a social construct of self-directed teams and agile behaviors.

The emergence of complex adaptive systems has long been accepted within the agile software development community. In fact, the Agile Manifesto, whether intended or not, is in many ways a representation of some of the characteristics and criteria that define complex adaptive systems. And, complex adaptive systems are finding their way within the traditional project management domain in various books, presentations, and whitepapers. In fact, during the writing of this book, one of the leading providers of PPM solutions, AtTask, announced a new product offering called Stream, cited to be the first ever social project management platform.

Project management as a profession and as we know it today is at a crossroads. Where the term PMO once stood for project management office and was unanimously viewed as a value add organization and one to try to get into, today it has different meanings and is viewed quite differently by others in the organization. As I am often reminded by my Agile friends, to them the term PMO stands for Pissed Me Off, and they view the PMO as only getting in the way mandating PMBOK oriented plan-driven approaches for managing projects instead of, or on top of, contemporary agile practices. And it would be a mistake to limit the downward trend of the sentiment toward the PMO and plan-driven project management in general to just the software development community. CIOs and IT executives understand the value proposition of the PMO and project management, but they are also demanding more tangible evidence of ROI as well as more flexibility to accommodate rapidly changing and uncertain business conditions before making further people, process, and tools investments.

As project portfolio management continues its course, it will be interesting to bear witness to the changes ahead. Standards organizations, tool providers, consulting companies, and training firms will no doubt weigh in and shape the coming change. However, as always, it will be the practitioners of project portfolio management in organizations of all shapes and sizes who face and deal with the seemingly unending sets of issues, execution difficulties, and risks that truly lead the way forward for all of us. In another decade of progress in project portfolio management it will be interesting to see what risks rise to the top 10.

Index